LOUIS GINZBERG

LOUIS GINZBERG
1873–1953

LOUIS GINZBERG: KEEPER OF THE LAW

BY ELI GINZBERG

THE JEWISH PUBLICATION SOCIETY

PHILADELPHIA  JERUSALEM

Copyright © 1966
The Jewish Publication Society
All rights reserved

First paperback edition 1996
ISBN 0-8276-0625-7
First Published as Keeper of the Law:
Louis Ginzberg

Library of Congress Catalog Card No. 66-11720

Designed by Sidney Feinberg

For
Abigail, Jeremy, and Rachel

Only take heed to thyself . . . lest thou forget the things which thine eyes have seen . . .

And make them known to thy children and to thy children's children.

CONTENTS

[*vii*]

ILLUSTRATIONS

Frontispiece, Louis Ginzberg: 1873-1953.

Following page 214

The Young Professor (1906) with his brothers Abraham and Asher.

Louis Ginzberg's father: Isaac Elias Ginzberg.

Louis Ginzberg's mother: Zippe Jaffe Ginzberg.

With his favorite nephew—Sol Wiener Ginsburg (1905).

Summer in Tannersville (1906) with Drs. Schechter, Marx, Magnes, Benderly and others.

With his fiancée—Adele Katzenstein, Berlin (1908).

Summer in Maine with Judge Goldberg, Harry A. Wolfson, Alexander Marx, and Louis M. Epstein (early 1930's).

With his former students: Crescent Country Club, Milton, Vermont (1927). Epstein, Solomon, Levinthal, Minkin, Goldman.

Reading on the shores of Snow Pond, Oakland, Maine (early 1930's).

A meeting at home with Baron, Morgenstern, Kohut, Husik and others (early 1930's).

With Yemenite children in Shiloah, Palestine (1933).

[ix]

LOUIS GINZBERG

CHAPTER I

MEASURE OF A MAN

Winston churchill has given us an illuminating insight about the delicate and subtle relations that can exist between father and son, especially when the son attempts to write about the father. When young Churchill asked Lord Rosebery, who had been his father's closest friend, for some details about his father's life, the Scottish Lord took the time and trouble to write at great length. But Churchill would not incorporate this material in his biography because Rosebery, the most elegant and proper of men, in recounting an episode of his friend's life at school, had used a slang term, a term that he refused upon request to delete. Churchill would not permit the slightest disrespect to be reflected on his father.

Such delicacy is very Victorian. But the episode cannot be completely explained by reference to an era which placed so high a value on decorum. In each generation, filial respect is a hallowed virtue, and even in the most tumultuous of times there is little sympathy for a man who fails to observe this propriety.

It is easier to determine the anecdotes that should be eschewed by sons who write about their fathers than to delineate the freedom and scope that remain. Each must determine these for himself. The difficulty of reaching a determination that will provide sufficient freedom to the writer and yet will place part of the subject's private and personal life out of bounds explains in part why only an occasional son will make the attempt.

My father died on Armistice Day, 1953, just over a fortnight before his eightieth birthday. During the decade and more after his death I had considered, but no more than fleetingly, whether there were sufficient materials available out of which a modest memoir could be fashioned. I knew that my father had started an informal autobiography in the years immediately preceding his death by recounting to my wife various episodes of his early youth and manhood, together with an assortment of his views about men, events, and ideas. He was a story-teller par excellence, and he reached his heights when he had a pretty girl for his audience and they could find conviviality together in the liquor which his physician had prescribed for him.

Throughout all the years of my youth and young manhood, my father had never touched a drop of liquor, on the assumption that it would further weaken an already weak digestive system. Since he had greatly enjoyed wine and beer during his student days in Germany and, in fact, had been proud of his capacity to carry liquor, his years of abstinence had been a deprivation for him. But this ban was fortunately lifted about a decade before his death. He had suffered a minor coronary episode, and his physician had insisted that he learn to drink whiskey. His last years, marred as they were by unremitting pain—the residual of an attack of *herpes zoster* (shingles)—were substantially lightened by the pleasure which he derived from this re-acquired taste.

The informal autobiographical notes came to some sixty pages of typescript. My wife transcribed the rough notes after each visit. Then there was my father's correspondence

—not the whole of it but a considerable portion, especially the letters which he wrote in his later years when he had a secretary. Always a deliberate man, he was much more deliberate when it came to the written word. There is no question that most of his letters were composed with the knowledge of the possibility, if not the expectation, that they might one day become public. His whole scholarly life had been devoted to weaving large tales from small scraps of paper; he could not fail to draw a personal analogy—his files would some day become available to those who were interested in the history of Jewish scholarship. His will was explicit: all of his papers were to be transferred to the Library of the Jewish Theological Seminary. Nothing was ordered destroyed.

The writer of a comprehensive biography would have to do much more than, as I have done, make use of my father's own files. There are scholars alive today with whom my father maintained at least an intermittent correspondence about scholarly and personal matters, and there are repositories in the United States, Europe, and Israel of the correspondence of distinguished academic, literary, and public figures where one could undoubtedly locate his handwritten letters. Such a search would be difficult, and the yield might be small. In any case, I saw no need to undertake it in preparation for this memoir.

My father taught at the Jewish Theological Seminary from the time it was reorganized in 1902, until two days before his death—more than half a century. During this period the Seminary ordained about 650 rabbis. Each one had studied with my father; a few had been quite close to him. Here was another source that might provide anecdotal material about his relationships with his students. After I decided to prepare this monograph, I requested the Rabbinical Assembly to encourage its members to write to me about interesting episodes that involved my father.

My request did not go unanswered, though the replies

were far fewer than I had hoped for or expected. Apparently such an undifferentiated appeal could at best elicit only a few responses. However, several of his students who had been closest to him—Louis M. Epstein, Solomon Goldman, Louis Finkelstein—as well as others, had written about him either while he was alive or after his death. And from these writings I was able to garner a considerable amount of material.

Again, a serious biographical effort would have to go far beyond material from his students and seek to elicit from colleagues and friends significant and relevant information about his work and life. A few men are alive today with whom my father had a close relationship for over half a century; there are others who knew him well over several decades. But I have been reluctant to tap these sources. Intimacies between friends and relationships between colleagues may be grist for the biographer's mill, but they are much more than that and only a major effort at biography would justify exploiting them. Occasionally a piece of the past was revealed to me en passant, as when Professor Scholem of the Hebrew University in Jerusalem, at the conclusion of a memorial meeting at which I spoke about my father in the tenth year after his death, recalled an interesting sidelight. Scholem had been present in Jerusalem in 1929 when my father delivered his famous address on "The Significance of the Halakhah for Jewish History." At the conclusion of his lecture, my father asked Scholem whether he had noted that there was "absolutely nothing in his presentation that evening that was in any way whatsoever inconsistent with Wellhausen's views!"

This comment is a manifestation of my father's Puck-like quality—he enjoyed disconcerting conservatives and radicals alike. He always enjoyed paradox, even if he made himself the butt.

But the Scholem story also introduces the difficulty of

placing matters in the perspective of time. Shortly before his death, I had secured my father's permission to collect and publish his major essays on law and lore, including his early article in *The Jewish Encyclopedia* on "Codification of Law." As I have already reported in the Preface to that volume—*On Jewish Law and Lore*—my father wanted to delete the first section of this article in which he accepted the theories of Wellhausen and the other higher critics of the Bible. Apparently time—and, probably, the spectacular advances in the archeology of the Holy Land—had led him to revise his views.

Ben-Gurion recently commented to me that he had changed greatly between his tenth and twentieth year, but since then the only thing that has happened to him is that time has passed. My father might have been inclined to agree with Ben-Gurion, since he was always concerned with differentiating essentials from non-essentials, and he would have accepted the view that by twenty, most men, including himself, are largely formed. But time will pass and change will occur. A scholar does change, and a conscientious scholar is likely to change a great deal. How, then, is one to consider the life of a man whose intellect was never at rest during eight decades? This could be a very difficult problem or no problem at all. I decided to attempt to avoid the problem by considering each point of my father's life as conditioned by the time and context in which it occurred, tied to the past as well as to the future, and recognizing that even in its contemporaneous guise, it might have an ambivalent rather than an unequivocal quality.

These questions and many more would concern the serious biographer seeking to understand the inner life of his subject as well as his actual performance. Even to me, in preparing this memoir, they were of some concern.

I have used the term memoir not once but several times, and I have defined it primarily by reference to what it is

not—a definitive biography. Perhaps now a more positive
definition is in order. A memoir, in my opinion, is a short-
ened and selective account of the life and particularly the
personality of one whose quality was such that it is worth
communicating to those who did not know him. The key
term is selective. For a memoir, being a selection, need not
seek to capture all the range and depth, all the colors, light
as well as dark. It can use a broad brush to reveal the essential and the significant without concern for detail. In any
case, that is the aim of this volume, nothing more, but nothing less.

In addition to the materials already identified, I want to
call attention to several other building blocks out of which
this effort has been shaped. I have placed considerable reliance on the materials contained in the biography of my
father written by David Druck, which was serialized in 1933-
34 in the *Morgen Journal-Tageblatt*. Much of Druck's account was a paraphrase of what my father told him, especially about the early years of his life. In addition, as I have
already mentioned, my father was a great story teller, and
many of the tales which he told and retold were about himself, as subject, object, or at least as bystander. Since I lived
in my father's home until I was twenty-two, and spent many
hours with him during the next twenty years, and since I
have a good memory, I have relied in substantial measure on
these stories as a clue to what my father considered significant and important in his life.

After I had grown and began to write myself, my father
and I made a truce: neither had to read the other's books!
Much of what he wrote was in one or another language
which I did not control, and most of the themes were beyond my ken. And he quickly sensed that economics was a
dull subject. But probably also, both of us were somewhat
shy and self-conscious about reading each other's works. It
was a source of some amusement and pleasure to him that he

was often cited as the author of my first monograph—"Studies in the Economics of the Bible"—an error that was only an exaggeration, since I would never have entered upon this immodest effort, and certainly I would not have completed it without his help.

Much later, as he indicated in his Preface to *A Commentary on The Palestinian Talmud*, I had an opportunity to talk out with him the shape and scope of that special introduction which he wrote in English in response to my arguments that the most important fruit of his scholarly labors should not remain totally inaccessible to those who could not read Hebrew. But these exceptions aside, there was little interaction between us with regard to our published works.

This is no longer so. In the preparation of this memoir, I read selectively but carefully through those of his published works and manuscript materials in which I had reason to believe that I would find important autobiographical clues. These, too, I have used as building blocks.

Those who have read the title pages of Volumes I and II of *The Legends of the Jews* know that they were translated by Henrietta Szold, and those who are acquainted with the authorized biography of Miss Szold know that she was a close friend of a young professor at the Seminary from 1903 to 1909. This friendship had many remarkable dimensions, personal and professional. Among my father's papers were more than fifty letters written by Miss Szold to him. And I made an effort to track down and finally succeeded in obtaining copies of his letters to her. This correspondence is illuminating in many ways, but particularly for the light which it sheds on this formative period of my father's adjustment to America.

This then will be a memoir that is highly autobiographical —his conversations with my wife; the material which he provided his biographer; the stories that I remember; and his correspondence and his writings. In addition, there are the episodes that students and colleagues recall; and the letters to and from Miss Szold that provide a mirror of his early professional life.

For several years after his death, I discouraged a considerable number of friends and admirers from venturing upon a biography of my father. I was convinced that a serious study could be undertaken only by a serious scholar and that a popular account would not have been to his liking. And while I never excluded the possibility of appending a brief biographical note to a collection of his letters, I made no move in this direction, despite occasional proddings from my mother. Then, on the tenth anniversary of my father's death, his friends and mine—Dr. Louis Finkelstein and Dr. Saul Lieberman—suggested that I speak about him in the Seminary synagogue, which had been his spiritual home for over half a century. Without their prompting and encouragement I would have remained silent. The remarks that I made were a weaving together of the stories which he told and retold about himself. And they found favor with his friends.

Some months later, the Rabbinical Assembly asked me to talk about my father, a request to which I assented somewhat more readily because of my earlier effort at the Seminary. This was a more formal presentation, since I was speaking to a mixed audience—many had been his students, but many more had not known him except through his books.

And, as I mentioned earlier, I spoke once again at the Student Center of the Jewish Theological Seminary at the Hebrew University in Jerusalem in June, 1964, when I had the honor to share the platform at a Memorial Meeting with Professor Urbach. Once again the audience was mixed, composed alike of those who had been his colleagues and students, and those who knew him only from his books.

Once I had faced up to the challenge of speaking in public about my father—not once but three times—the spell of reticence and restraint was broken, at least long enough to let me venture the attempt of committing to paper a much expanded version of these oral presentations. I had learned from the reactions of these audiences that my mother was correct in her desire that those who knew my father, and even more those who did not, should have an opportunity of reading a sketch of his life and personality.

No man can ever fully understand another, and the difficulties are trebled when a son attempts to understand his father. But he has advantages. During the last twenty years of his life, the intellectual rapport between my father and me was as close as it could be. There was much about which we did not agree, but each knew and appreciated the reasons for the disagreement. And, more often than not, there was a close parallel in views and assessments. Day after day, week after week, month after month, and year after year, we talked about important matters and trivial matters; about the past, the present, and the future; about men and women; about religion, politics, science, art. I did not know everything about my father, but I surely knew the essence of his being and his thought and it is the conservation of this knowledge that is my justification for this memoir.

Our last conversation can serve to set the measure of the man. He asked me what I thought of certain moves of the State Department to curry favor with the Arabs. I gave what I thought was a temperate reply, to the effect that the United States had indeed a difficult task in its attempt to carry water on both shoulders. And he retorted sharply, "I don't like Bible-toting Secretaries of State!" He who had witnessed the deepest depths and the greatest glory of modern Jewry had no tolerance left for those whom he suspected of still harboring ill-will. All of his life had been dedicated to strengthening the remnant whose survival would alone determine the future of Judaism.

CHAPTER II

IN THE STEPS OF HIS FATHER

IN LATE August 1939, while I was on a tour of Scotland, I found myself near Balmoral Castle and decided to spend the night at Ballater, so that I would be sure to hear the American Ambassador on the nine o'clock broadcast. As that hour approached, two Scotsmen in the hotel who were arguing about the relative virtues of Highlanders and Lowlanders were so caught up in their argument that they passed up the news, with its warning of the war that had not yet started but that might break out at any moment.

It is rare, especially for Americans, to run into people for whom family and clan have such immediacy and importance. There is some reverence for tradition in New England, and more in the states of the Old South, but these exceptions aside, Americans have little regard for family background. In the rough and tumble of American politics, for example, the man of humble origin continues to have an advantage over the scion of one of the nation's first families.

How different was the world into which Louis Ginzberg was born in Kovno, Lithuania, on November 28, 1873. Prohibited from participating actively in the cultural, social and economic life of the Russian Empire of which Lithuania was then a province, and declining to participate even when offered the opportunity, the Jewish community was a closely knit society whose ties to the Palestine of antiquity and Babylonia of the first millennium were much closer than their tenuous affiliations with their gentile neighbors.

With little material goods and even less political freedom, the Jews of Eastern Europe nevertheless developed an aristocracy. The leading families were those which could boast of a long line of scholars and saints—men who had left their mark in the fields of intellectual and ethical endeavor. Since mastery of the ancient and medieval texts required all or at least most of a man's time and energy, only those who were supported by others had an opportunity to scale the heights of scholarship.

There were a limited number of positions in the leadership structure of the community—rabbi, head of the juridical council, dean of an academy—which provided a modest living without making overwhelming inroads on a man's time and energy. Consequently, those in leadership positions attempted to secure such positions for their sons and sons-in-law. An outsider had a chance, but a young man with an important father was more likely to achieve a sinecure, if it may be so called.

There was another way for a man with intellectual aspirations but of modest circumstances to achieve success, however humble by modern standards: he could marry into a wealthy family. Although there were not many wealthy Jews in Eastern Europe, there were a considerable number who could support a son-in-law for some period of time while he sought to establish himself as a scholar.

There was one more route. Leading scholarly families sought to broaden and deepen their hegemony through carefully arranged marriages. It is interesting to speculate whether this practice of marital selection resulted in raising the genetic potential. But that it contributed to the entrenchment of a scholarly aristocracy is beyond question. My father, with his customary skepticism, was disinclined to ascribe the long generations of excellence solely to heredity. He placed a heavy weight on family tradition, superior opportunities for education, and strong motivation. But he never forgot his own lineage, and there was no influence in his own life more powerful than that of his family's tradition.

He was able to trace his paternal ancestry back to the fifteenth century, to Porto, Italy. The first to take the name *Ginzberg* was Rabbi Simon, the son of Rabbi Eliezer, the son of Rabbi Yechiel who had lived in Porto. Although the details are lost, the family moved north, over the Alps, and relocated in Bavaria. Rabbi Eliezer lived in Günzburg and it was his son, Rabbi Simon, who first took the name of the town for his surname.

This Rabbi Simon Ginzberg was not only a learned man, but he was reputed to have been the wealthiest Jew in the whole of Western Europe. It is known that he was forced to loan the Emperor Ferdinand 10,000 ducats which, as one might have suspected, were never repaid. In addition, while the Ginzberg family was still residing in Northern Italy, it owned the oldest extant manuscript of the Babylonian Talmud. The names of the successive heads of the family are written on the last page of this manuscript. This most valuable of family possessions eventually found its way into the library at Munich.

Among the interesting early members of the Ginzberg family was a female author of what today would be called "A Medical Guide for Family Use." Written in the sixteenth century in Yiddish-German, a copy of this rare volume is now in the New York Public Library.

Günzburg, which is a town high on the banks of the river Günz, is a tributary of the Danube. It lay close to the border between Württemberg and Bavaria, over which Catholics and Protestants fought for the larger part of the sixteenth century. Not many miles distant from the much larger Ulm —which in modern times became world renowned because it was the birthplace of Einstein—members of the Ginzberg family soon established close relations with the Jewish community in Ulm, and some of them began to use the surname Ginzberg-Ulm. There were many moves and many entangling alliances with well-known rabbinical families in Germany and neighboring lands, and by the seventeenth century the head of the Ginzberg family was in Friedberg near Frankfurt am Main—Rabbi Jacob Ginzberg, the head of a Talmudical Academy which had many distinguished alumni. The grandson of Rabbi Jacob, who for a time was rabbi in Worms in the Palatinate, Rabbi Isaac Ginzberg, moved to Posen and became the first of the family in Eastern Europe.

Successive generations boasted many famous men. The title "Rabbi of the Russian Community" was held by several Ginzbergs. One married into the family of a distinguished Hamburg rabbi whose lineage could be traced back to Rashi, the great Bible commentator of the eleventh century. Another took a daughter of the leading talmudic scholar— Rappaport—as his wife. The founder of the Kovno branch was Rabbi Eliezer Ginzberg; Louis Ginzberg was the fifth generation.

These ties of Louis Ginzberg to the rabbinic aristocracy were reinforced on his mother's side; she was the great granddaughter of the brother of the Vilna Gaon (1720-1797), the greatest luminary of Lithuanian Jewry. His mother's family contained not only many men of learning but also some who had succeeded in amassing considerable wealth. In Louis Finkelstein's memorial essay on my father, he summarized his background: "Through blood kinship and marriage Professor Ginzberg was related to almost every outstanding Jewish scholar in Lithuania and Poland."

But no man had a greater influence on him than his own

father, Rabbi Isaac Elias who, though he had earned the
title of rabbi, never held the office. This was true also of
others of his relatives. In consonance with the tradition that
study is not only a commandment but an act of piety, the
Ginzberg family by the nineteenth century had come to look
askance at the idea that one should be paid, as a rabbi was,
for leading the type of life that it was incumbent on all pious
Jews to lead—a life of study, prayer, and charity.

Although one of twelve children, Isaac was the only son,
and one of the only three of the twelve who survived
childhood. When he came of age to study at a *Yeshiva*, his
father wanted to send him away, for at the time Kovno did
not have a *Yeshiva* of its own. But his mother balked, insisting that she keep her sole surviving son with her since he
was highly nervous and showed other signs of poor health.
The matter went to the rabbi for decision, and he agreed
that young Isaac could stay at home since he would be able
to receive a proper talmudic training in Kovno, even if it
required somewhat make-shift arrangements. The rabbi's
judgment proved correct, for Isaac received a good talmudic education. In addition, he had the opportunity to
become a pupil of Rabbi Israel Salanter, who then was at the
height of his drive to win converts to the Moralist Movement
which he spearheaded, and in which ethical behavior rather
than study or religious devotion was the key to the good life.
Indicative of Salanter's approach was his plan to turn the
synagogue at Kovno, which also served as the house of
study, into a hospital during a cholera epidemic. Many considered this an outlandish proposition, but before his proposal lost he put his case to the full congregation and in the
process sought to undermine in every possible way the
arguments of those in opposition, including the rabbinic and
the lay leadership of the community. Isaac's father, Rabbi
Asher Ginzberg, was the head of the community, and on the
eve of the Day of Atonement, Rabbi Salanter sought him out
in his home to beg his pardon for any pain or injustice that

he might have done him and his associates by unfair argument. They became fast friends and Isaac later became Salanter's student.

When Isaac reached the age of marriage—about twenty (although the rabbis of old had stipulated many years earlier that eighteen was the preferred age), he took Zippe Jaffe of Neustadt for his wife, and thenceforth combined a life of study with the activities of a businessman and later of a community leader. His own family was well-to-do, and he broadened his connections through his marriage, for the Jaffe family were among the wealthiest Jews in Lithuania. After his marriage Isaac became a commission merchant, that is, a wholesale textile merchant, who bought and sold in distant markets, particularly in St. Petersberg and Moscow.

Louis Ginzberg was born in Kovno and lived there for the first seven years of his life. He had five older siblings and by the age of four he had three younger sisters—all of whom reached adulthood. In addition, three siblings had died in infancy or early childhood. At the time of Louis' birth, the eldest, Sarah, was about thirteen, his elder brother Abraham was ten, and Asher was not quite two.

My father was fond of relating that he had been kidnapped by his wet nurse, and that the family had had some trouble persuading her to return him. With a twinkle in his eye, he sought to leave the listener with the impression that even as an infant he had shown extraordinary qualities. In fact, he was sure, even without benefit of the authority of the Freudians, that the earliest years of life are determining for later development. He suffered all of his adult years from severe insomnia and he related with much conviction that he had manifested this trait while still in the cradle.

But the key to his character, while rooted in the first years of life, lay elsewhere. It was family tradition that a future Gaon would have blue eyes like the Gaon of Vilna, and Louis' eyes were the deepest blue. "My first memory is of when I was between three and four when I got an apple from my mother. I was a little boy, so I bit into it without saying a *Beroche*. My mother rebuked me, since the saying of the *Beroche* is taught to children at the very beginning of their Jewish education. She said: 'The Gaon would have said it.' I asked her how she knew, and she said, 'You are a silly boy. The Gaon would have said it even when he suckled.' In our family what the Gaon would have done was thrown at our heads every other minute."*

Important as the omnipresence of the Gaon's legend may have been, it does not serve as an adequate explanation of what happened to young Louis, for the same tradition left his older brothers untouched. Louis had an opinion about what happened. "As a child I was quite a prodigy. People used to say that I was the second Gaon. I was never taught how to read Hebrew. This was mainly because my brother Asher, who was a year and a half older than I, had trouble with his eyes and really couldn't see with the left one. My mother had to take him to Vilna where a prominent surgeon operated on him. This made him lose a half a year or a year in school, and since it would have been awkward to send a six-year-old boy to learn with the very beginners, he got a private tutor. . . . I was a very mischievous and restless child, so when the teacher came, I was asked to sit still. Then the teacher would tell me to be quiet, and just because of this I would put my nose in his book. Consequently, at the age of five I was able to read fairly well. When I was sent to school it was quite a miracle that I was able to read, since I had never really been taught."

That he did not use the term mischievous about himself without warrant is suggested by the following stories that my father related.

"All the things I did as a child and as a young man devel-

---

* All quotations not otherwise identified are from *Autobiographical Fragment;* see Sources and Bibliography.

oped from a sense of humor; I never did any harm. A psychiatrist might say that I was jealous of my younger sister because of what I did on one occasion when I was six and she was five. The whole family had gone on a picnic. I climbed a tree and she wanted to climb up with me, so I pushed her onto a limb from which she couldn't descend by herself and I walked away. Of course when the family discovered that she wasn't with them they were upset. I told them where she was and although they were angry, I insisted that she had only asked to be helped up to the branch. She had not asked me to help her down."

When he was seven, my father's family moved from Kovno to Klin, which is in the neighborhood of Moscow. The name Klin was repeatedly reported in the international press in 1943, since it marked the furthest advance of the German armies toward Moscow. My father recalled the severity of the winters there by telling of ravens which were often caught by a sudden drop of temperature and would fall frozen to the ground.

The relocation of the family to the heart of White Russia was prompted by my grandfather's desire to spend more time with his family. The center of his business was then Moscow and if he remained in Lithuania, he could get home only a few times during the year. But it was not easy for a Jewish family to take up residence in, or near, Moscow. This is how my father explained the situation: "There were only some parts of Russia, including Lithuania, part of White Russia and New or South Russia, where Jews were permitted to live and even there they were restricted. They couldn't live in the country because the authorities were afraid that they might cheat the farmers. And the only Jews who were permitted to live in the big cities were first-class merchants who purchased a permit, which was very expensive, and university graduates. My father could live in Moscow, since he was a merchant, but the family had to live in Klin even though Jews were not permitted there. We were able to live there only after we had 'made it right' with the police commissioner, who made his living from us and the two hundred other Jewish families. The uncle of the Emperor, Nicholas Nicholaivitch, was the Governor General of Moscow and gradually things got worse. Moscow looked into the matter of the police commissioner (of Klin), and we had to move back to the western part of Russia.

"It was possible to live under these conditions and maintain our self-respect because of our deeply religious feeling. A good Jew had enormous pride and he pitied a good *goy*. The attitude toward a bad *goy* was 'Well, what can you expect?' Culturally and morally the Jews were really much superior. In addition, although the government was anti-Jewish, the neighbors were very kind."

In Klin, young Louis started his formal education and continued his pranks. Although there were only a small number of Jewish families in Klin—an earlier estimate made by my father was 60 or 70, rather than 200—there were two ritual slaughterers who doubled as teachers. My grandfather sent Asher to one, Louis to the other. But within four months he realized that neither teacher was skillful or even competent, so, together with a few of the other well-to-do members of the community, he took steps to import a private tutor.

"Many families had private tutors. This simply meant that a group of four or five wealthy families had one teacher for their children because the classes in the community school were too large. My father was very much interested in education and spent quite a lot of money on it. He always insisted on a teacher from out of town who could thus devote all of his time and attention to us. The teacher would live with one family for one month and then move to another."

From the pupils' viewpoint, there was a drawback to a teacher who was able to concentrate on them. The first of the month was always a school holiday, but not for Louis and his fellow students, for Rabbi Gedaliah took his duties seriously and kept his pupils at their books—that is, until they acted to protect themselves by stealing the lamp and hiding it among the potatoes. The unfairness of it all continued to bother Louis, so that some years later when the family was living in Neustadt, and he was kept at work while the other boys had vacation, he resorted to an unusual stratagem. He started to spit blood. His mother rushed him to a famous lung specialist in Königsberg who, after a thorough examination which proved negative, nevertheless advised her to keep the boy away from his studies for a while so that he could enjoy the outdoors. Louis had achieved his end. He had done so by surreptitiously pricking his palate with a needle!

To return to Klin. "I remember one teacher who made a practice of pinching me, primarily to keep my attention. Since I understood the text, it was difficult for me not to let my eyes wander and be distracted; in fact, to distract the other boys. However, I hated to be touched. So one day, I filled the sleeves of my coat with straight pins so when the teacher pinched me, he got a handful of pricks. He never touched me again. Even so, he was very fond of me. Maybe he realized that I had done this in self-defense."

But Louis was not always able to get away with his pranks. "Since we were one of the wealthiest families in Klin, we always had a samovar ready to serve any visitor. One day the *shammash*, a man named Hirshel, came to call. He was a dirty old man with a big long beard, and I couldn't stand him. He used to take snuff, and it was always all over his beard. He used to sit in our house and yawn, and I was tremendously repelled. One day, I gathered a handful of flies, and as he yawned I threw them into his mouth. This was the first time my father beat me. He was furious with me—not because I had been naughty but because I had made Hirshel transgress six laws. Flies belong to the lowest family and there are six prohibitions in the Bible against eating them."

There was at least one other occasion when young Louis' pranks brought him into conflict with his father because of a transgression of a law. It was said that every Jewish community in Russia had three characters: a rabbi, a crazy man, and a wild goat. The laws of sacrifice were suspended after the destruction of the Temple; they did not apply to the Diaspora. Nevertheless, Orthodox Jews would make no use of a first-born goat, and it was permitted to run wild so that it would develop a blemish that would make it unsuitable for sacrifice.

Louis and his friends managed to catch such a wild goat, and Louis mounted him and rode him for a bit. He was caught by his father and severely reprimanded because, as his father reminded him, no one was supposed to derive any use—or pleasure—from a first-born goat.

One of the ways in which prominent families found it easy to protect and enhance their good name and fortune was to encourage marriages between near relatives. This included the marriage of an uncle and his niece, although a nephew was not permitted to marry his aunt. Louis' uncle, Hermann Jaffe, married Louis' oldest sister, Sarah. This uncle-brother-in-law early developed a marked liking for young Louis. "He was very fond of me, but he was a big tease. When I started to study Talmud, he said he would give me ten kopeks if I would repeat by heart the first page that I had studied. I did this, but when I finished, he said he wouldn't pay me because I had made three mistakes. Whether I did make any mistakes or not I don't know, but I felt that he owed me the money. He was to leave for Moscow the next day and when my sister was packing for him, I grabbed a shirt out of his suitcase and ran off with it. Since he really needed it, he was forced to pay me ten kopeks.

"The way we were brought up, there were only two ways by which one could judge the capacity of a young boy. The first was a good memory, which I evidenced at a very early age. The second was a quick understanding of intellectual problems. At the age of six, when I started Talmud, I was able to grasp the argumentative problems which were beyond the comprehension of an ordinary child.

"As a matter of fact, memory is not an indication of intellectual ability. Memory is useful, but in modern times it is not nearly as important as it used to be. In my *Legends*, I have 36,000 references, all of which I kept in my head. I did not gain very much by this, since I might easily have written them down, but if one has a good memory he hates to bother, and secondly, my handwriting is so bad that I wouldn't have been able to read it.

"In modern days, one has only to remember one word of a reference and he can find it in any source book, but in those days there were no reference books, and memorizing was considered almost the most important ability. Today memory is valuable only if one has a constructive mind; you are thus able to acquire material with which to elaborate a concept or subject. It is also important in enabling you to coordinate all that you have known or studied."

We have come to learn in the Western world the sad fact that even good schools and good teachers will not insure that young people become good students. There is the all-important element of motivation. The child must want to learn, and whether he develops an interest and drive will depend primarily on whether he has a model to imitate and whether the process of learning leads to rewards. In the Jewish communities of Eastern Europe, as we have seen, the scholar was at the top of the hierarchy and the educational system was so organized and operated as to reinforce the interest and proclivities of young children who showed intellectual aptitude.

"My teachers must have noticed my mathematical gifts at an early age. There are many mathematical problems in the Talmud, many of which were too difficult for the rabbi, who would have liked to have skipped them, but I insisted that they all be covered thoroughly. In spite of this and in spite of the fact that some of my teachers must have realized that I knew more than they, they were very fond of me. In those days, learning and intellectual ability were everything. A child could do anything mischievous or naughty as long as he studied and understood."

Rabbi Isaac did not leave young Louis' education to chance. He stipulated that Louis' formal instruction begin with the study of the Bible. Only after one had become well acquainted not only with the Pentateuch but with the Prophets and the Historical Books as well, was he ready to begin the study of the Talmud, which was after all the second stage in the development of Jewish literature and law. This had been the pedagogical theory of the Gaon of Vilna, but it had not won general favor. It has been said that the Jews learned their Bible from the Talmud and the Talmud from the later Commentaries which were studied intensively in the *Yeshivoth.*

But theory aside, there were some practical problems to be met. When young Louis was ready to begin his study of the Talmud, there were no readily available texts. His father had a complete set of the Talmud, but he did not want to risk making one of the volumes available for the instruction of Louis and his friends for fear that they would mutilate it. Finally, he found that he had a duplicate of one tractate— "On the Laws of Tabernacles"—and this determined where the youngster would begin his talmudic studies.

Concerned as they were about education, the development of intellect and the nurturing of scholarship, the pedagogical leadership apparently never gave much attention to what we would call the sequencing of the curriculum. One started a youngster off by throwing him into the "Sea of the Talmud." This was as good a way as any to teach him to swim.

But there were other problems which were not so easy to solve. It was difficult for many pupils to get to and from the *Cheder*, where they passed most of their day in study. My father used to tell the story of a young fellow who was repeatedly frightened by a vicious dog on his way to and from school. The lad told his friends one day how he had solved the problem: he had developed a Cabalistic formula which included such phrases as, "I am Jacob and you are Esau." This would protect him. The next day, his classmates asked him how the formula had worked. He reported that the formula was fine, but regrettably the dog didn't understand Hebrew!

After the family had been in Klin for about two years, the authorities made it increasingly difficult for Jews to continue to reside there. This fact, combined with my grandfather's concern about the small size of the Jewish community and its comparatively low level of intellectuality, led him to move his family back to western Russia, this time to Neustadt on the Lithuanian-German border. Neustadt had a much more substantial Jewish community; it boasted about 1,500 souls. Moreover, Louis' maternal grandfather had been born there and many relatives were still living there. Louis was nine when the family relocated.

For the next two years, young Louis was educated in Neustadt, primarily by private tutors imported from other communities, on my grandfather's theory that only a man without blood ties to his charges would be able to deal fairly and effectively with their education. But by the time he was eleven, it was clear that the resources of Neustadt, even if supplemented from elsewhere, could not provide adequate intellectual stimulation for young Louis, who continued to demonstrate great aptitude for his studies. His father decided to enroll him in the newly founded *Yeshiva* of Telsh at which a cousin, Rabbi Shlomo Zalman Abel, was one of the key members of the newly organized faculty.

The trip to Telsh was an odyssey. Father and son left Neustadt on a Sunday morning and arrived in Telsh on the following Friday. The distance they covered was thirteen Russian miles or a little less than eighty U. S. miles. It was autumn, after the Feast of Tabernacles and, as all students of Russian history know so well, the countryside was one big sea of mud—the very same mud that trapped Napoleon and many other generals. One travelled by carriage which conveyed both men and merchandise. Passengers had to accommodate themselves to the needs of the merchants who organized the transportation.

The mud insured that travel would be slow. The necessity to change horses and drivers added further delays. But the snail's pace of this particular trip was further retarded by the attitude and behavior of Louis' father, Rabbi Isaac. Since the age of thirteen, Rabbi Isaac had made it a practice to say his morning and evening prayers as a part of a *minyan* (a group of ten male Jews above the age of thirteen who, according to Jewish law, comprise a congregation), and he had no intention of breaking a life-long practice on this trip. Therefore the schedule for departing and arriving had to be so arranged that Rabbi Isaac would find himself at an inn or in a community where he would be able to corral the additional number of adult Jewish males required for prayers. This was a logistical enterprise requiring no mean talents, since there was not a large number of Jewish communities along the route. At one inn, Rabbi Isaac was able to assemble only nine; there was a tenth Jew in the neighborhood who ran another inn. But the two innkeepers were mortal enemies and had not spoken to each other for many years. Yet Rabbi Isaac was so intent that he finally prevailed on the keeper of the inn where he had stopped to go after his competitor and to bring him to the service.

Mud and prayer were not the only challenges. Food was likewise a problem. Rabbi Isaac and his son arrived late one night in a small town. They had not eaten for many hours and Rabbi Isaac refused to eat the bread at the inn in case it had been made from new grain sown after Passover. According to biblical law, that grain could be eaten only after the second day of the following Passover. While most of the rabbinical authorities held that this law was applicable only to Palestine and not to the Diaspora, a small minority who were extremely observant considered that it was also binding on them even if they lived outside of Palestine. When Rabbi Isaac discovered that the rabbi in this small community had been a classmate of his, he decided to seek him out. Young Louis tagged along since he was more hungry than tired.

The visitors found a light on in the rabbi's house, suggesting that he was still studying, and they did not hesitate to knock and seek entrance. But for a long time their knocking went unanswered. It took a considerable time for the rabbi to decide that he should take some action; then he had to wake his wife, and she in turn had to wake the maid, who then had to get dressed. No rabbi could awaken the maid! The former classmates found much pleasure in their reunion, and they were soon engrossed in a heated discussion about the passage in Maimonides that the rabbi had been studying when his unexpected visitors arrived. Young Louis helped himself to the bread, jam and tea that the lady of the house provided, but his father was too involved in the argument to take time off to eat. The argument continued until after sunrise. And then Rabbi Isaac still could not eat. He first had to say his morning prayers.

Telsh was a large Jewish community with six hundred families, and the recent organization of the *Yeshiva* by Louis' cousin, Rabbi Abel, and his slightly senior colleague, Rabbi Atlas, had been stimulated by the determination of the conservatives to counter the steady drift toward enlightenment which carried with it the threat of assimilation. Telsh had been the home of the modern Jewish poet Judah Leib Gordon, whose life and works were anathema to the believers. And Gordon was impressing many young people.

With great organizational skill, Atlas and Abel were able within remarkably few years to obtain the financial resources, the faculty, and the student body to establish what quickly became a major institution for talmudic studies. They were able to attract Rabbi Eliezer Gordon, a well-known talmudic scholar, to head the Academy, and Gordon brought with him his son-in-law, Rabbi Joseph Leib Bloch. These four men were soon able to attract over five hundred students. Atlas and Abel had arranged for Rabbi Gordon to receive his salary from the community, and this assured him a great amount of freedom in running the Academy. They, in turn, being men of means, did not take a salary; therefore the funds that were subscribed could be used almost exclusively for the support of the students.

When Rabbi Abel examined young Louis to determine into which of the three classes to place him, he was amazed by the brilliance of Louis' answers. He put Louis into the second class, which he himself taught together with Rabbi Atlas.

The Ginzbergs had other relatives in Telsh. Another cousin was the head of the ritual slaughterers, and it was with this cousin that Louis was put to board. His father settled on the price of one ruble per week, for which Louis was fed chicken soup, chicken, and cakes. During the course of the week he was also to have the remainder of the wine used for sacramental purposes on the Sabbath. It was arranged that on the Sabbath, Louis would be with his teacher, Rabbi Abel.

In later years, my father, reflecting on his studies at Telsh, emphasized that despite widespread belief to the contrary, there was no distinctive Telsh approach to talmudic studies.

Each member of the faculty had a style of his own. Rabbi Gordon was a master dialectician. He had the ability to tie together the most discrete phenomena. Abel, on the other hand, was less given to pyrotechnics. His concern was to delve to the heart of the issue and to rely on common sense to help the student find his way through difficult passages. He contended that there was no need to resort to esoteric formulation; every talmudic problem had a simple solution. The challenge to the student was to find the key.

However, even if the faculty was not cut from the same cloth, the program of studies at Telsh had certain distinctive characteristics. The students ignored the classic commentary on the Talmud (*Rabbenu Hananel*) that was published along with the text. In place of this, they relied upon three other more recent commentaries.

Good teachers are not the same as a good system, and my father, in his mature years, felt that the *Yeshiva* at Telsh had been deficient in not developing a system for the study of the Talmud. The Gaon of Vilna had, after all, shown the way. The dialectical brilliance of Rabbi Gordon was impressive, but brilliance was not an adequate substitute for system.

Louis did well at Telsh, but he stubbed his toe. This is how he told about it: "When I was about eleven, I was in the *Yeshiva*. Until then, I had read only the Talmud. One day, one of the boys, all of whom were much older than I, about twenty-two or twenty-three, gave me some modern Hebrew poetry which was anti-Talmud. This was the first time I had ever seen anything modern. In order to read it, I had to hide it inside the big folio of the Talmud. It was a little thing, so it was quite easy. But I got caught. And at the end of the term when I was going home, the teacher told me that he was going to send a letter to my father. He told me to read it first.

"It was a perfectly truthful letter. He said that I was a

bright student, a diligent student, and then came the *but*. But, he said, some one had given me some literature to read that really should be burned. When I brought it home to my father, he was very upset. He knew that I was a bright student, he knew that I was a diligent student; but he was horrified at the *but*. He wanted to know who had given me the banned poem but of course I wouldn't tell him."

Young Louis studied at Telsh for two years, until shortly after his Bar Mitzvah. Ten rabbis attended the ceremonies which marked his attaining maturity and during which he delivered a learned address. This performance elicited the admiration of the distinguished visitors, and it remained a conversation piece at Telsh for many years to come.

By the middle 1880's, the Moralist Movement was receiving the enthusiastic support of many among the student body at Telsh. Many young people were attracted to the regimen, which prescribed that they devote much time and effort to introspection and to exercising strenuous self-discipline as well as to participating actively in the performance of good deeds. Of course, time thus spent had to be taken from study, and young Louis' father became sufficiently concerned about this matter that he decided to transfer him to another Academy. Rabbi Isaac, himself, had been a student of Salanter, and he did not want to make too sharp a break. He therefore decided to enroll his son at Slobodka, the famous *Yeshiva* on the outskirts of Kovno which, in fact, was the center of the Moralist Movement. One cannot ignore the likelihood that, matters of doctrine aside, Rabbi Isaac had reached the conclusion that it was time to put his son in a new intellectual environment with new teachers and new points of view.

Slobodka differed from Telsh in several regards. First, the students made use of the classic commentary which was printed along with the text of the Talmud, the commentary which, we recall, had been ignored at Telsh. Moreover,

Slobodka also brought within its purview the famous commentaries written in medieval times—which Telsh also ignored—which brought the student a long step closer to the original texts.

The Moralist Movement at Slobodka at that time required that each student spend a minimum of a quarter of an hour prior to his four-hour stint of studying in the morning and another quarter of an hour prior to the four-hour afternoon period in devotional activities. This was the minimum requirement. Many students went much further, especially under the encouragement of one of the heads of the *Yeshiva*, Rabbi Finkel, who had acquired the nickname of "The Old One." Salanter's successor, Rabbi Itzile Peterburger, would withdraw in the month prior to the High Holidays with his favorite pupils to what in modern language might be called a retreat. Young Louis was one of the initiated.

Shortly before his fourteenth birthday, young Louis, primarily to test himself, entered upon a period of forty days of silence. During this period his mother, in accordance with the tradition that one should periodically visit the graves of one's parents, came by steamer from near Neustadt to Kovno. Young Louis met her, and when she inquired about his health and work he refused to answer, explaining to her through a written note that he was observing a period of silence.

His mother was deeply disturbed by his behavior and complained about it to her uncle, one of the leaders of the Kovno community, with whom she was stopping. This cousin reprimanded Louis for disrespect to his mother, but Louis said in writing that obligations to the Lord took precedence over those owed one's parents. At this point, Rabbi Haskell Jaffe went to the Chief Rabbi of Kovno, who had so far assiduously avoided aligning himself either with the heads of the *Yeshiva*, who provided the major support of the Moralists, or with the rest of the rabbinical community who

were for the most part strongly opposed to the Moralists.
Jaffe insisted that piety went too far when young people no
longer recognized their filial duty.

As far as young Louis was concerned, it was not difficult
for his relatives to come to a quick decision. Clearly, he
could not remain any longer at Slobodka. The best alternative was to send him to Volozhin, where the head of the
Yeshiva was a brother-in-law of Jaffe. Here, once again,
Louis could study under a distinguished scholar who was
also a relative. But before sending him off to Volozhin, it
seemed desirable to let him spend a short time with his aunt
and uncle in Vilna. Rabbi Raskis, who had married Rabbi
Isaac's sister, was a great talmudist. What was to have been
a short visit was prolonged because of young Louis' health.
Long hours of study and the turmoil of early adolescence
had taken their toll. It was therefore agreed that his aunt
would build him up before he set off for the strenuous years
of study at Volozhin that lay ahead.

As young Louis lived with his aunt, he developed the
deepest admiration and affection for Rabbi Raskis. Among
his contributions to the education of the young scholar,
Rabbi Raskis introduced him to the Palestinian Talmud,
which so far was unknown to him. The fact that the Gaon
had devoted much of his brilliance to illuminating the
Palestinian Talmud was not sufficient to establish it as a
proper field of study in the *Yeshivoth*. In fact, the Gaon, for
all of his greatness, had had little direct influence on the
development of the academies, primarily because his un-
conventional methods and extremely critical views had
proved too disturbing to the tradition-oriented rabbis. My
father's close friend, colleague and successor, Dr. Saul
Lieberman, told me that he first became acquainted with
the Palestinian Talmud when he came to the Hebrew University as a mature man, after many years of Hebraic studies.

During the course of Louis' sojourn in Vilna, a distinguished rabbi died, and his uncle took young Louis along on a condolence call to the family. There Louis was introduced to another of the leading scholars, who inquired why Louis had not called on him, especially because they were distantly related. With the sharp tongue that he early developed and the knowledge of his own ability which he already had, but also with a sense of humor that made the other traits less abrasive, Louis announced that he thought it was a tradition in Vilna not to call on learned men, since no one had called on him!

A close friend of his family who was living at the time in Vilna, Rabbi Jacob Joseph, made it a habit to call weekly at the Raskis' home to see how young Louis was getting on, and then he would send a report on to his parents in Amsterdam. They had recently moved there because business conditions in Russia had taken a turn for the worse, at least as far as Rabbi Isaac was concerned. Since Rabbi Isaac had some contracts with Jewish diamond merchants in Holland, and since friends and relatives had emigrated earlier to South Africa where they became involved in the diamond trade, prospects for Rabbi Isaac looked a little better in Holland than in Russia.

In one of his weekly reports, Rabbi Joseph suggested that young Louis go to Holland to visit his parents, since he was still below par both physically and emotionally. And before long, Louis was on his way to Amsterdam, never to return to Lithuania except for a short visit when he was twenty-one.

He reported on this most important episode of his life:

"My father took the family to Amsterdam when conditions became so difficult in Russia. I stayed because my father said it would be silly for me to move to where there was no opportunity for study. I went to stay with an uncle, a rabbi in Schnippshok at the other side of Vilna when I was fourteen and in rather delicate health. Rabbi Jacob Joseph, who lived in Vilna proper, who was close to the family, never missed a Friday to drop in at my uncle's to see how I was getting along. Once he found me in poor health. He wrote to my father that I needed the care of a mother. My aunt had her own children. My father had to translate that letter, which was in Hebrew, for my mother. My mother wanted to know exactly what Rabbi Joseph had written. When she heard that I was in poor health, she cried, and it was then and there decided that I should go to my parents in Amsterdam. . . . Joseph was responsible for my leaving Russia. Otherwise I would probably have been a big rabbi in Russia."

But in one of his last letters, Louis Ginzberg indicated that he saw more clearly what would have happened: he would have become a victim of Hitler!

CHAPTER III

GERMAN SCHOLARSHIP
AT ITS BEST

ALTHOUGH HE had learned to read by the age of four or five, although he knew most of the Bible by heart by the time he was seven, and although he had mastered much of the rabbinic literature by the time he was fourteen, young Louis arrived in his parents' home in Amsterdam with only a single exposure to modern writing—the banned poem.The gap between what he knew and what he didn't know was truly immense.

While he was still in Kovno attending the Slobodka *Yeshiva,* his old teacher, Rabbi Eliezer Gordon, the head of the Telsh *Yeshiva,* came to town for the auctioning of the right to collect the tax on kosher meat and to decide with the leadership of the Jewish community how the proceeds therefrom were to be distributed among competing communal activities. Young Louis came to pay his respects to his old teacher and master, who was attended by a large coterie of admirers. During their conversation, Louis asked whether he might propound a talmudic question to his teacher. Rabbi Gordon assented. Knowing that his teacher was not completely familiar with that section of the Talmud which dealt with the laws of sacrifice and purity which were not part of the conventional curriculum, Louis formulated a query involving these materials. The old rabbi was not able to answer immediately. He indicated that he needed to refer to Maimonides' Code, but did not have a copy at hand. With the audience enjoying every minute of the duel between young and old, Louis said he knew where he could find a copy of the Code, and he soon returned with it.

The next day, when Rabbi Gordon called on Louis' maternal great uncle, Mr. Haskell Jaffe, one of the heads of the Kovno community, he talked about Louis' genius but he was quick to add that he was more than that—he was an insufferable brat! The matching of wits was an integral part of the educational process. But respect for elders and a modest restraint were also important values. Young Louis' explanation of his behavior this time and on similar occasions was that he was motivated by his sense of humor.

The young man who arrived in Amsterdam was fourteen and a half, a repository of a great amount of talmudic knowledge, with a sense of humor and a penchant for mischief-making, but with not even a smattering of the basic knowledge to which all children in the West were routinely exposed. He was in delicate health and his family wanted first to attend to this. Other matters could wait.

"They took me to a lung specialist, Professor Hirtz, who said that my lungs were affected. He said I should take it easy, and that I should not study. He prescribed good cognac and oranges, including the skin, because of its vitamin content. He charged 10 *gulden* ($4) per visit. A year later I was dismissed as cured. What then? My father said that the rabbis in Amsterdam were not for me, and my mother cried again. My father said, if you remain here, there will be no opportunity. Perhaps you should go to Hungary, where you can get both talmudic teaching plus a modern education. But my father knew something about Hungarian rabbis, and he didn't like their superficial way of teaching."

Rabbi Rabbinovich, who was distantly related to the Ginzberg family and who was travelling through Western Europe to study the different manuscripts of the Talmud in connection with his monumental edition of variant manuscript readings, called on Louis' father in Amsterdam and apparently played a major part in scotching the preliminary plans to send Louis to Hungary. The fact that Hungary was a land of milk and honey, at least in comparison to the stark poverty of Lithuania, must have added to its attractiveness for a time as a possible locale in which Louis could continue his studies. In Hungary, Louis could at least look forward to being well fed. But Rabbi Rabbinovich's critical appraisal of the state of Jewish learning in Hungary proved determining.

"I couldn't go to Russia; I didn't want to go to Hungary; and Holland was useless. Only one place remained which was sufficiently Orthodox and where I could still get a modern education—Germany. Up to that time I couldn't read or write anything but Hebrew [of course he knew Yiddish]. I needed a teacher for German. Half a year later, the teacher said that I knew more than he—he couldn't teach me any more."

The decision was finally made. Louis would be sent to Frankfurt am Main, where he could pursue his Jewish studies and at the same time acquire the fundamentals of a Western education in an environment that would support and reinforce his Orthodox upbringing.

"I was sent to Frankfurt alone. I got a room and prepared for matriculation, the entrance examination for the university. The gymnasium was an eight-year course. I was a special student; however, I was permitted to take the final examinations.

"I learned enough Latin, Greek, German in two years to pass the final exams. I also learned enough mathematics and natural science. As far as Greek was concerned, I learned enough in fourteen weeks, during which time I learned the 280 irregular verbs, to write an essay in Greek for the final exams. And my Greek studies earned me ten cents. Last year, I was at Idlewild Airport meeting my cousin, Dr. Henny Posen, who was arriving from Israel. It was a terribly hot day, so I bought some ice cream. The vendor was obviously Greek, so I conversed with him in his language. He was overcome, and he wouldn't let me pay the ten cents.

"The only thing I didn't learn so well at the gymnasium was natural science. At that time, the examiners were appointed by the government. The examiner with whom I came into contact was a real Prussian; he had a fine long beard and was a true Nordic type. My mathematics teacher, who was also head of the natural science department, was very fond of me. He told the examiner not to bother me, that I was really very good in mathematics and that I could never learn science.

"During the examination, he asked me a question in analytic geometry. I gave him the proof and said that that was the proof in the book, but that I had a better one. This sort of astounded him. Then he asked me a question in botany. He asked me to describe the *bulbus domesticus*. Well I didn't know what that was, but being a smart Jew, I didn't want to admit that I didn't know, so I told him that I had been brought up in a country which was very poor in plants. He asked me where I lived and I told him Lithuania, near Kovno. He smiled at me benignly and said, 'I never knew that they had no potatoes in Lithuania.' He gave me an A anyhow.

"While I was at school, I became very friendly with the son of the Lord Mayor of Frankfurt, Von Nickel, later a financial wizard in Prussia. My friend was really a clever fellow, but he spent a lot of time with girls, and in reality he became a bum. One night at 2 a.m. he almost broke my door down. He wanted me to write an essay for him which was due the next day. I usually wrote most of his stuff, but I was mad that he had waited until the last minute. Anyhow, I got up. He wrote as I dictated an essay on 'The Importance of the Discovery of Printing.' The essay was delivered at 9 a.m. Two weeks later the professor returned the essay with the remark, 'The voice is the voice of Jacob, but the hand is the hand of Esau.' "

Frankfurt proved to be a good choice. It provided enough continuity with young Ginzberg's past so that he was able to find his way into the culture of the West without losing all contact and relationship with the wisdom of the East. Among the friends he made in Frankfurt was Isadore Wechsler, who later moved to Berlin. It was at his house in Berlin that Louis Ginzberg met his future bride, herself a native of Frankfurt. But that was many years later. My mother would remind my father on occasion that she was only a child of three when he was a student at the gymnasium! Louis and Isadore tutored each other; Louis helped Isadore with his Hebrew studies while Isadore gave Louis lessons in German.

Young Ginzberg's reactions to his years in Frankfurt were never fully described either in writing or in conversation. However, they can be pieced together both from what he said and left unsaid. Basically, he had a highly critical view of Frankfurt Jewry. Neither Samson Raphael Hirsch, the founder of the ultra-Orthodox community, nor his successor Rabbi Breuer, contributed significantly to the development of Jewish thought. My father appreciated that Hirsch was a man of deep conviction and that he was able to help stem the rapid advances of the Reform Movement, but the rigid formalism which became the hallmark of the ultra-Orthodox left him bemused and critical. He knew that this group did not fully understand the intricacies of the law and that they appreciated its essence even less; consequently, they were its prisoners.

But the ultra-Orthodox, while a significant and noisy group, were not the whole of Frankfurt Jewry. Frankfurt boasted a laity that was devoted to the furtherance of Jewish life and values, business and professional men who made room in their active lives for systematic study. This impressed the young student. Here was a first concrete example of an integration, however imperfect, between the tradition in which he had been reared and the ways of the West to which he was now exposed.

An insight into my father's Frankfurt years was communicated to me by Rabbi Steven Schwarzchild, who while still an undergraduate was taken to visit my father, then a mature man. "He took me into his book-lined study. I expected to spend the next hour discussing profound philosophical and talmudic subjects, whereupon your father said, 'Schwarzchild, that sounds like a Frankfurt name.' When I told him that it was indeed a Frankfurt family, he introduced me to your mother as another Frankfurter, told me of his years in Frankfurt, and asked me whether I knew who Stoltze was [a Frankfurt dialect poet whose importance was only slightly less than that of his Indiana equivalent, James Whitcomb Riley]. After I told him that I remembered my grandmother reciting Stoltze to me, he spent the rest of the afternoon with me reciting Stoltze's 'poetry' in reams."

When my father wanted to tease my mother, he would say that there were only two good things about Frankfurt —Goethe and herself; and when he sought to annoy her on occasion he would limit it to one—Goethe.

But whatever his feelings about Frankfurt, and they were doubtless ambivalent, there came a time when he had to make another major decision. When he passed the matriculation examinations, the question was where to continue his studies.

He finally decided to go to Berlin and enter the Orthodox Rabbinical Seminary (Hildesheimer) and simultaneously to pursue his studies at the University of Berlin. He arrived one afternoon for an interview with Dr. Hildesheimer. Dr. Hildesheimer interrupted a short exploratory conversation with an apology that it was time for afternoon prayers, and left in search of ten men. He succeeded in finding only seven. My father then asked him whether he did not know that, according to a rabbinic source, seven men sufficed. Hildesheimer was at a loss; he could not identify the source nor did he know what to make of the suggestion.

My father quickly concluded that this was no place for him to pursue his studies. He had more control over the texts than did the head of the institution; moreover, Hildesheimer did not even know how to parry the challenge that seven men sufficed for congregational prayers. There is support in one of the minor tractates of the Talmud for this position, but it had never been accepted. The smart boy from Lithuania had merely used the gambit to test the *Herr Doktor Rabbiner* and had found him wanting.

And so he decided that he might just as well, in fact, that it would be preferable for him to continue his Jewish studies on his own. He entered the University of Berlin and made an initial selection of courses primarily in mathematics and physics. He knew that he not only loved mathematics, but that he had an aptitude for it. If I were not inhibited by the knowledge of my father's distaste for psychoanalytical methods of historical interpretation, I would state that here was one more piece of evidence of his identification with the Vilna Gaon, who had written a mathematical treatise.

At the end of his first year at Berlin, my father returned to Frankfurt on a visit and encountered on the street one of his former teachers, Dr. Heinemann, who asked him what he was studying. When my father replied that he had selected mathematics, Dr. Heinemann asked him how he hoped eventually to support himself. Heinemann pointed out that it was hopeless for a Russian Jew to expect ever to be appointed at a German University. Thus forced to confront reality, Louis returned to Berlin and shifted his field of concentration to Orientalia, thereby laying the groundwork for tying together what he already knew and what he would now have an opportunity to learn.

This shift from mathematics to Orientalia was radical, but it did not prevent young Louis from exploring the highways and the byways of all of Western knowledge. His intellectual curiosity was now fully aroused; he wanted to absorb all that he had missed and all that was available to the university student of his day. And the faculty at Berlin, as well as the faculties of Strassburg and Heidelberg, where he later studied, were studded with truly great scholars and teachers. Louis exposed himself to many of them; he even went further and immersed himself in the cultural, political, and even artistic currents of his day.

Five years earlier, the German language had been unknown to him. Now he was able to supplement the funds which he received from his family in Amsterdam and his brother-in-law in South Africa by writing dramatic criticism and other pieces for the *Frankfurter Zeitung*. He tried his hand at lyric poetry: the first item in his bibliography is *Gedichte*, Basle, 1894. Many years later, his good friend Dr. Freidus, who for many years was in charge of the Jewish collection at the New York Public Library, used to clip poems from the Yiddish press by one Louis Ginsberg and send them on to my father. I suspect that Freidus had stumbled across the bibliographic reference.

"My decision to give up mathematics was probably the most difficult one I ever made. . . . I knew I had a mathematical mind, but I certainly do not know today whether I would have been a great mathematician. I have used the mathematical approach even in my philological work. For instance, I have distinguished between a theory which can be proved and a theory that must be proved."

Dr. David Aronson, one of my father's pupils, relates the following incident. "When my older son Raphael first joined me in one of my visits with my revered teacher, it was about half a century after Dr. Ginzberg had given up the idea of majoring in mathematics. Raphael was fresh out of Harvard, where he had majored in theoretical physics. The man who was world-renowned for his contributions to an understanding of rabbinic law and lore, and whose doctoral thesis was 'Die Haggada bei den Kirchenvätern,' dealing with the legends of the Jews in the Church Fathers, and the young alert student who wrote his thesis on 'Proton Isobars and High-Energy Proton-Proton Scattering,' were soon absorbed in a discussion of mathematical theories, where I found myself completely lost. On the way home, Raphael said with a note of wonder and deep respect in his voice: 'Daddy, that man knows his math. He is familiar with the latest scientific work.' "

My father was not able to cut himself off entirely from his early interest in the subject, even if he could not keep abreast of the latest developments, as young Aronson thought he did. One of the strengths of a German university education was that a good student would remember the core of what he had been taught, and it is true that my father was able to coach his favorite nephew, Sol, in calculus, when Sol was a student at Columbia University, about thirty years after my father had studied the subject.

It is likely that throughout his student days he remained friendly with students and professors of mathematics, and he was fond of telling how once he confounded them. He challenged them to find the formula which would explain how he could rattle off a long series of numbers at great speed and then repeat them, even in reverse order. He repeated the challenge over several evenings, while the mathematicians sought the answer. Actually, it was nothing more or less than an elaborate version of the trick that New York youngsters play based on the subway stops. The Hebrew alphabet has numerical values. My father knew whole sections of the Bible and Talmud and other Jewish literature by heart. He could find a piece that would match the opening number, and then with great speed could rattle off numbers almost without end, and his photographic memory enabled him to recall them in reverse order.

But his years in Berlin were not confined to his love affair with mathematics and his renunciation of it. The Berlin faculty boasted a great many luminaries, some of whom played a prominent role not only in science and scholarship but also in politics. Virchow, the great physiologist, was a prominent liberal. Treitschke was an overt anti-Semite. There was the great Roman historian Mommsen, whose quaint behavior is illustrated by his announcement in the local newspapers: "I am pleased to report the annual confinement of my wife." Mommsen had a great many children; a story made the rounds to the effect that one day he passed a lad on the darkened stairs. He stopped him and asked him his name. The young boy answered in amazement, "Papa, don't you know me?"

Louis was growing up fast and becoming a western sophisticate, but he still enjoyed practical jokes. In later years he recalled two.

"When I was a student in Berlin, I complained to my landlady, and with good cause, that there were mice in my room. She insisted that I was wrong. So one night I constructed a trap of four heavy dictionaries tied with a string. Inside of them I placed a piece of cheese. I darkened the room and sat quietly for a few minutes, until I heard the mouse go after my bait. I quickly pulled the string, which let the heavy book fall on the mouse. This stunned it but did not kill it. I put the mouse in my pocket and went into the dining room where my landlady and her niece were sitting. I said to her, 'There are mice in my room.' She said, 'Oh no, you are mistaken. That is impossible.' So I pulled the mouse out of my pocket and swung it in front of her face shouting, 'Violà, c'est ici!' Both ladies were horrified, although to this day I cannot understand why. They jumped on the table and screamed for many minutes after I had disposed of the mouse. . . ."

"One day a friend and I were sitting in the Tiergarten. Two girls were sitting on a neighboring bench speaking Italian. My friend and I started talking vociferously in Hebrew. The girls were curious and, probably because we paid no attention to them, their curiosity finally made them ask us what we were speaking. I said that we were speaking Italian. One girl remarked, 'My friend and I just came from our Italian lesson and we have been practicing Italian.' She said that she had not been able to follow our conversation. I told her that people speak different dialects and that probably her teacher was from the south. I said we were speaking the pure language as spoken in Florence. They were impressed and asked us to help them do their lessons. So we did their translations in a mixture of Italian and Hebrew, and laughed at the prospect of their confronting their teacher with nonsense syllables."

Having decided to study Oriental languages and literature, Louis decided to leave Berlin at the end of his second year and to transfer to Strassburg where Theodore Noeldeke, the greatest Orientalist of his day and, in my father's considered opinion, the greatest Orientalist of all times, lived and taught. When Alsace-Lorraine, at the end of World War I, reverted to France, Noeldeke, who was already long in retirement, was offered an opportunity to remain. The French government indicated that it would be honored to assume responsibility for his pension. But Noeldeke, whatever doubts he may have had about German militarism and other even less attractive German characteristics, did not accept the generous French offer; instead, he moved to Karlsruhe, where members of his family were living.

Louis was twenty-one when he decided to move from Ber-

lin to Strassburg. But on the prompting of his father, he
decided that before moving he would return to Russia to
attend to various matters, primarily to his formal and official
release from liability for military service. It was Rabbi
Isaac's opinion that no man should ever make it impossible
to return to his homeland. Who knows—Rabbi Isaac may
still have entertained the hope that at the end of his studies
in Germany, my father might decide to return to Lithuania
to devote his life to talmudic scholarship. In any case, set-
tling the matter of his military service was the first and
major reason for his trip. He had left Lithuania seven years
earlier, and it was a very different young man who returned.

It turned out that Louis did not have much difficulty with
the military authorities. The fact that he had a small build,
that he was underweight, and that he could prove that he
had been under the care of a lung specialist led the military
authorities to reject him.

My grandfather also advised my father to arrange to
secure *Semikhah* [rabbinical ordination] during the course
of his visit. With this he could always obtain a position as rabbi; without it, he would automatically cut himself
off from such a career. In accordance with the custom of the
times, he took the examinations from three rabbis. Professor
Lieberman informed me that twenty-one was a typical age
for a young man in Lithuania or Poland to obtain *Semikhah*,
while in Hungary, where the study of Codes was the central
part of the curriculum, students acquired it at a much
younger age—at around sixteen or so. In Lithuania, where
the weight of rabbinic study was on the basic texts, not on
rules and regulations governing religious observance, a student would not normally master the field of Codes without
a special effort. He did so only when he wanted to acquire
professional standing. There was little in Codes to attract
the serious student.

Another reason for his trip, the first and only visit that he
was to make to the land of his birth, was that his favorite

grandmother, his mother's mother, who had survived the death of nine of her twelve children, had recently returned to Lithuania after spending some years with her son-in-law in Amsterdam. She was in her high eighties or early nineties when she decided to go back home. Remarkable in the breadth of her knowledge and intellectual acumen, she was also extremely observant, and she never was completely reconciled to the conditions that she found in Amsterdam. She did not doubt her son-in-law, but she questioned the communal supervision of ritual slaughter, the preparation of bread and other food. She decided that she would be better off at home, in Lithuania, even if she had to live without those closest and dearest to her.

But in fact, my grandfather was extremely observant. My father told of the difficulties that his father experienced, not once but several times, in finding a poor Jew to bring home for the Sabbath meal. My grandfather, in accordance with hallowed custom, would not sit down to eat his Sabbath meal unless he were able to share his bread with a stranger in need. In Lithuania there were poor Jews aplenty, but not in Amsterdam in the late 1880's and early 1890's.

Much later, when he was travelling with his wife from Bad Homburg, near Frankfurt, my grandfather, then close to seventy, stood for the whole of the eight-hour trip. His wife was in poor health and therefore they were travelling second class, where the carriages had upholstered seats. On the outside chance that if he sat down he might violate the biblical injunction against making use of a mixture of wool and flax, he preferred to stand the entire time.

And this was the man whose house his mother-in-law decided to forsake for fear that she might accidently transgress one or another law or regulation. The three months that Louis spent in Lithuania gave him the opportunity for an extended visit with his grandmother, who, he found, had made an excellent readjustment.

With all this behind him, Louis was ready to get down to

serious studying at Strassburg. As did every student, he had
a considerable number of professors in fields in, close to, and
distant from his major. But the four years that he spent at
Strassburg were first and foremost years of study with Noeldeke. In several courses he was the only student, and since
Professor Noeldeke rose early, my father's instruction began
at seven a.m. at the professor's home. A great compliment
assuredly, but not without its drawbacks. He had to be fresh
and clear. One morning, toward the end of his years at
Strassburg, he arrived at Noeldeke's house directly from the
Bierstube where he had spent the entire night celebrating
the successful completion of a friend's doctoral examination.
He slipped on one word, and a few minutes later on a second. At that point Noeldeke closed the book and told him to
go home and sleep it off!

Although he appreciated his good fortune in receiving
private instruction from Noeldeke, he did not always take
advantage of opportunities for such intensive instruction. He
signed up one semester for an esoteric course, assuming that
it would attract at least a handful of students. However, at
the first session, as the time drew near for the professor to
arrive, he saw that he was alone in the room. Since the eti-
quette was that an only student could never cut a class, my
father ducked behind the desk as he heard the professor's
footsteps approaching. He remained hidden while the old
man said to himself: *"Es scheint als ob Niemand hier ist"*
[It seems that nobody is here].

My father's admiration for Noeldeke knew no bounds. It
was admiration not only for a scholar of outstanding
knowledge of the entire domain of Semitic languages and
literature, but for a man of character, sensitivity, and integrity. Noeldeke taught him how to use philology as a primary
tool of research into the ancient texts. He had great knowledge of Mandaic, which is also called Eastern Aramaic, the
language of the Talmud. He also knew his way through all

of the Semitic languages and literature, not simply as a craftsman, but as an historian, philosopher and artist. He knew how to probe into the souls of these people from the scattered texts that survived. Interestingly enough, although he devoted his life to a deeper understanding of the civilizations of the Fertile Crescent, this was not the culture he admired most. For Noeldeke, the people of Semitic tongue and culture were too absolutistic, too rigid, too ideological. He preferred the culture of ancient Athens. The Hellenes more nearly measured up to his concept of the ideal. Unlike the Near Easterners, who were more likely than not to seek out and commit themselves to an extreme position, the Greeks were always looking for the golden mean.

Noeldeke was not the only one among the great German scholars of his day to see the Greeks as the epitome of the highest development of world culture. My father was exposed to others who shared this view, particularly his teacher of philosophy at Strassburg, Windelband, who, next to Noeldeke, he said, had the greatest influence on him during his student days. It was probably Windelband's approach that led my father in his later years to consider Plato as the greatest mind the world had produced.

To return to Noeldeke, the man. Many Christian scholars not only knew the Hebrew Bible, but were also students of the Talmud. While they were able to master the Bible and take part in deepening understanding of its sources and codification, they were never able to master adequately the "Great Sea" of the Talmud. Many studied it too late; others made too limited an investment; and none of them had the constant reinforcement supplied by the life and experience of every Orthodox Jew who devoted himself to the study of rabbinic texts. But with arrogance typical of many German professors and reinforced by a substantial dose of anti-Semitism, most of these Christian scholars had no awareness of their own limitations. Each considered himself an expert. Not so Noeldeke. He believed that with respect to the Talmud, Christian scholars could be no more than cobblers; only a Jew could be a master craftsman.

This realistic and modest view of his own command and that of others over the Talmud was appreciated by my father, who with many other Jewish students from Russia was disturbed by the arrogance and effrontery of some of the leading German scholars who concerned themselves with Hebraica. The fact that even the least gifted of these professors frequently had competence in philology, history, and comparative religion far beyond their own only made their dilemma more acute. They knew, as only a bright student would know, that many of these Christian scholars often did not understand the rabbinic sources which they used. But at the same time, the Christian scholars were able to bring to bear on the problems which they were exploring broad general knowledge and powerful research techniques.

Noeldeke not only knew where his knowledge of Hebraic literature stopped, but he was free of the latent and overt anti-Semitism which was characteristic of the German academic community of that day. He was anti-Church, and therefore he was free of the religious virus which, in my father's opinion, has always played a major role in anti-Semitism. Noeldeke even had a particular fondness for his Jewish students, at least the best of them, who had spent so much of their youth at study and who were so eager and quick to absorb what he had to offer them.

At one point, the State Minister of Education asked Noeldeke to propose three candidates for a chair in Semitics that had become vacant at the University of Halle. The Minister indicated that he would select one of the three, and was quick to add that it was his clear preference that no Jews be on the list. Noeldeke informed the Minister that in that event he had better seek the counsel of a pastor!

Noeldeke had another quality which my father admired.

He did not strive, as did most professors, for the honors and awards that the officialdom bestowed from time to time on those engaged in academic work. His refusal to curry favor with those in power must have recalled some of the great teachers of Lithuania, who were not only men of great learning but men of high ethical principles.

One of the interesting paradoxes of German academic life was that it was hospitable to men of genius, and yet at the same time encouraged a great amount of pedantry. Possibly the paradox can be explained by the fact that although Germany's greatest scholars—men such as Wilamowitz Moellendorff, Eduard Meyer, Max Weber—had been thoroughly trained in the ways of research, they were separated from the pedants by their unique ability, which went so far beyond their training. They had a spark that enabled them to make the materials come to life.

Noeldeke's freedom from pedantry is encapsulated in the tale that my father was particularly fond of relating about the morning he arrived at the professor's home and was asked to help in packaging a dissertation which Noeldeke had just read and which he felt constrained to return to the student because it was unsatisfactory. Just as the last page was being put into place, my father's eye was attracted by a footnote. He called the Professor's attention to it and Noeldeke, agreeing that it contained a suggestive point, decided to unwrap the dissertation and accept it. I myself have participated in doctoral examinations for over thirty years, and I find merit in Noeldeke's criterion—one good point per dissertation. How many have been accepted that have not met this test!

Attractive as Strassburg was as a place for Ginzberg the student, it was a dreary place for Ginzberg the man to live. The Jewish community was made up primarily of people with neither Hebraic nor Germanic learning. In general they had a narrow background and a narrow outlook. The community had neither a rabbinical nor a lay leadership. In comparison to Strassburg, Frankfurt had been a great cultural metropolis. Young Ginzberg's relationships with the community were limited to attending synagogue services and eating a daily meal at the kosher restaurant.

Reference to the kosher restaurant recalls a story that my father told about a young St. Bernard which belonged to the owner. Always fond of dogs, he had played with and fed the young dog over a period of many months. Four or five years later, when he was walking down a main street in Basle, Switzerland, he heard a loud commotion behind him and as he turned to see what it was about, a huge beast jumped over him. Blocks back, a man was shouting to passers-by to stop the runaway dog. The St. Bernard had broken his leash when he picked up my father's scent!

There were a handful of Jews on the faculty of the University, but almost without exception they kept themselves aloof both from the Jewish community and from their Jewish students. They wanted to get ahead, and they saw no point in calling attention to their ethnic origins. In fact, most of them had been officially converted. The religious and marital confusions that arose in one instance were a source of sly satisfaction to my father. A distinguished Jewish professor had to be converted to Christianity in order to marry the daughter of another Jewish professor who had brought his children up as Christians. And one of the offspring of this marriage, who in turn became a distinguished academic, had to be officially converted back to Judaism because he fell in love with a young lady whose parents would not contemplate her marrying any but a Jew.

Times change slowly and not always for the best. When I was a student at Heidelberg in 1928-29, I was invited to the home of one of my professors, a member of the Faculty of Law. It did not require a competent anthropologist to observe that I was the only Jew among the twenty or so students who were there. And of course I could be, and was, classified as an American. My host's grandfather had been one of the greatest Jewish preachers in the old Austrian-Hungarian Empire, and although the professor sought to escape the stigma of Judaism, he still had hanging on the wall a small miniature of this grandfather.

It is foolish to seek rational explanations for irrational actions. Hitler's determination to eliminate all Jewish blood from Germany and later from Europe was irrational, whatever else it may have been. But I cannot suppress the feeling that the significant minority of rich, educated, and cultured Jews who had earlier become converted to Christianity made it easier for all anti-Semites, including Hitler, to look with disdain and scorn upon all Jews. What was the value of heritage that was denied by its own people?

The Germans had made a special effort after 1870-71 to turn Strassburg into a major seat of learning. They even sought to follow a somewhat liberal approach in order to convince the Francophile population that Germany was in fact a modern and progressive country. But as happens so often where Germans are concerned, they did not find it possible to act like reasonable people. My father recalled the excitement of the day when the police roped off an area in the heart of the city so that firemen on high ladders could remove an *accent aigu* from the name of a store's owner. Apparently this vestige of identification with the past was more than the German authorities were able or willing to tolerate.

Recollections of events such as these, even after sixty years, help to explain the following comment which my father made in the face of the post-World War II political rapprochement between France and Western Germany. "I know only two nations that really hate—the French and the Germans. I believe the French hate the Germans much more than the reverse, except that the Germans are still only half civilized, and their hatred is not restrained."

In 1922 my father visited his old teacher, Theodore Noeldeke, who was then living with his son in Karlsruhe. In taking leave, my father said that he looked forward to the pleasure of seeing him on his next trip to Europe, to which Noeldeke replied—"Please do not wish this; I am so old [he was over ninety], I want to die." Some time later my father received the following letter from Noeldeke, which reveals as much about the times as it does about the man:

My dear Colleague,

That was indeed a surprise! Accept my warmest thanks! I hardly trusted my eyes when the note was brought me—"12 bottles of white wine to Professor Th. Noeldeke, Ettlingerstr. 53 at the request of Professor Louis Ginzberg in Frankfurt a/Main" and when I learned at the same time that the note served merely as an accompaniment to the gift which had already arrived. Since I do not have your Frankfurt address I have, as you see, asked my excellent friend and colleague Horovitz to see that you receive this brief note of thanks.

As far as any of us could be said to take pleasure from anything in this terrible time, we do. This is all the more unusual since nothing else of a really quieting nature has reached me from America which "plunged us into misery in the first place." At the moment it is unclear whether England offers no opposition to the frightful outrages of the French only because she is hampered by Ireland, the difficulties in the Orient, as well as by the military superiority of France or whether as the apparent instigator of war herself she views the complete destruction of Germany with approval for reasons of commercial jealousy and out of fear of increasing German naval power. You will pardon these words but what good German could keep silence now over all these continually disturbing matters. How much more could be said about our problems!

Once more the most cordial thanks for your kindness to an ancient feeble colleague in bestowing upon me the noblest product of the Rhine.

My father's American friend, Harry H. Mayer, about whom more will be said later, was enrolled with him in Karl

Budde's seminar on the Bible and in Noeldeke's courses. He wrote about conditions at Strassburg: "Anti-Semitism at Strassburg during our time as students there was less evident than elsewhere in the German Empire, where obscene placards and shouts reviling the Jews were to be encountered always and everywhere. While I saw and heard many insulting signs of hatred against the 'Prussian swine,' signs bidding them 'get back to their land of arrogant, shouting, square-headed, land-grabbing fellow gangsters,' I seldom encountered displays of vulgar feeling against the Jews, probably because the popular spitefulness towards the Germans was so bitter and so all-absorbing that no room remained in the Alsatian mentality for other political, economic and religious sentiments."

My father also recalled the substantial absence of anti-Semitism in Strassburg in his tale of mountain-climbing. One summer he was one of a group of four who walked from Basle over the Alps down to Milan. He was the only Jew; one of the company was a Catholic chaplain in the German army. It was agreed from the outset that they would rest on Saturdays. Whenever they arrived at a new town, his friends would scatter to see whether they could find a Jewish family, so that my father might have a kosher meal.

Strassburg also furnished my father with a local walking companion. One of the great chemists of modern times, Van't Hoff, a Dutchman, who contributed so much to the foundations of physical chemistry, was on the faculty at Strassburg. My father got to know him and they shared many a nocturnal walk, since both were erratic sleepers.

By 1897, after four years at Strassburg, young Ginzberg was ready to take his examinations, write his dissertation, and earn his doctorate. He was preparing for these final steps when one of his examiners, the Professor of Assyriology, took a leave from Strassburg to go to Marburg. He was supposed to return at the end of a year, and my father origi-

nally decided to delay his examination. But Noeldeke coun-
selled otherwise. He pointed out that the Professor might
not return, that not one but two or three years might pass
before his chair was filled. He advised Ginzberg to go to
Heidelberg, where Bezold held the chair in Assyriology,
and to take his degree there.

The fields on which he had to stand examination included
his major, Semitics, and two minors: Assyriology and Philosophy. We know that he was examined by Kuno Fischer in
Philosophy. Heidelberg had recently celebrated its five hundredth anniversary, which made it the oldest university in
Germany, and the second oldest German university, second
only to Prague. It had a renowned faculty, and Kuno Fischer
was one of its brightest stars. It was Fischer who had had
the honor of delivering the formal commemorative address
at St. Peter's Church, to an audience which included the
Crown Prince, later Wilhelm II. Fischer, knowing that the
Crown Prince was an impatient man, determined to do
honor to the occasion and ordered the church doors locked
while he held forth for a period of more than two hours!

Fischer, although he had little true originality, was nevertheless a perceptive synthesizer of philosophical thought
and a man of considerable literary style. As frequently happens, his fame was greater among the educated public than
among his colleagues, and the Kaiser had conferred on him
the title of "Excellency," which was granted to very few.
However one might appraise his scholarly worth, on one
point there was no doubt. Fischer was an exceedingly vain
man. Some time after he had been given the title, Excellency, he received a bill from his shoemaker, addressed to
Herr Gerheimrat Hofrat Professor Doktor Kuno Fischer. Although he had lived in the same house for several decades,
he sent it back with the notation, *Unbekannt* (unknown);
the envelope had to be readdressed properly so as to include
his new title, Excellency.

All of this is a prelude to reporting on my father's examination with Fischer. As an opening gambit, Fischer inquired where my father had spent the vacation that had just come to an end, and when my father told him that he had visited his parents in Amsterdam, Fischer said, "Good, we will talk about Spinoza." He asked my father to trace the principal elements in Spinoza's system. My father replied at length, concluding with the comment, "as you recently outlined the issues in your two-volume work on Spinoza." Professor Fischer, catching the nuance, inquired whether my father had some other ideas on the subject. My father said yes, he did, and for the next three-quarters of an hour launched into an analysis of Spinoza's system of thought in relation to medieval Jewish philosophy and to the Cabbala, about which Fischer knew very little and about which he had written even less.

Many years later, a senior professor at Heidelberg, who had been a young *dozent* (instructor) present at the examination called on my father in New York, and regaled him with stories about the forecasts that each of those present had made about the likely outcome. Almost without exception, they had expected the old man to explode with anger and to take it out on the impertinent youngster who had shown him up before his colleagues. But the professor had fooled them. He had swallowed his pride, invited my father to tea, and voted to grant him his degree *"cum laude superate,"* a distinction that had been awarded to only a handful of students during the preceding century.

My father's dissertation showed how far he had come during the decade since he had left Lithuania. *Die Haggada bei den Kirchenvätern* was an ambitious start of a search through the whole of the patristic literature for old biblical legends. He knew that many of these legends could be found only in the works of the Church Fathers, who had resorted repeatedly to them for exegetical purposes. The very fact that Christianity had appropriated the legendary materials had led the Jews to neglect and disregard them; they did not want to keep alive stories of their Bible heros that had been used to foretell the coming of Jesus and otherwise support the doctrines of Christianity.

The collateral descendent of the Gaon of Vilna had truly escaped from the confines of rabbinic literature. He was treading on ground that few if any Orthodox Jews had ever before explored. But he did so with a discipline and self-control that would have been worthy of the Gaon. When his dissertation was reviewed in a leading Jesuit publication, the writer observed that "it was indeed encouraging to see that young Catholic theologians are again taking up the study of rabbinics!"

CHAPTER IV

THE NEW WORLD

LOUIS GINZBERG arrived in New York in August, 1899. As he came off the boat, his brother Abraham handed him a letter. He glanced at it and put it into his pocket. When his brother asked whether it was important, he shook his head. In point of fact, the letter was from the Secretary of the Hebrew Union College to the effect that the Board of Governors had not confirmed the recommendation of President Wise that he be appointed to the faculty.

The major outlines of the story can be pieced together without too much difficulty, although some of the links remain missing to this day. Louis Ginzberg had continued a correspondence with his American friend, Harry Mayer, after he had transferred to Heidelberg and Mayer had returned home. In fact, it was a relationship that endured for almost sixty years. Writing five years after my father's death, Mayer recalled their early friendship:

"Still fresh in my memory are the hours on end that passed as, side by side, we sauntered along, engrossed in far-reaching discussions of life and literature and all the lovely high hope of youth. Ginzberg was delighted to discover that his friend could relate, on excellent authority, a number of unpublished anecdotes about one of Ginzberg's favorite characters, Seligmann Baer Bamberger, under whom my father had studied at the great rabbinical academy at Würzburg." It is likely that Mayer was the one man to whom my father ever bared his soul. The Hebrew acrostic which my father wrote in later years on the flyleaf of a Hebrew book which he had succeeded in locating for his friend suggests the depth of their relationship: "This book I am sending you as a gift; a token of our mutual love; may it bring to mind bygone days of such sweetness that words cannot do them justice."

After passing his examinations in Heidelberg, my father returned to Amsterdam and during 1898-99 pursued his studies at the University of Amsterdam. But this was a holding operation. Mayer reported: "From his letters during the summer of 1898, I learned that Ginzberg had become unhappy over conditions in a Europe which denied him any immediate prospect of a place on the teaching staff of one or another of the leading universities to which he aspired. I broached to Ginzberg the idea of his becoming a United States citizen in view of the priceless boon of equal liberty and justice for all before the law, and went on to ask whether Ginzberg could be induced to accept a call from the Hebrew Union College. With Ginzberg's permission, I told him, I would do what I could. I was confident that Ginzberg's name needed only to be suggested and his credentials presented for all to want him. Ginzberg replied that a call from the Cincinnati school to become a member of its faculty would be an honor, and that he would be receptive to such an offer. I then got in touch with Rabbi David Philipson, at the time a member of the Hebrew Union College's Board of Governors. Philipson agreed to sponsor the election of Ginzberg, whose appointment as 'preceptor' in biblical exegesis at the College followed in due course. Yet while the brilliant young scholar whom I had come to know so well in Europe was en route from his home in Amsterdam to take up his position in Cincinnati, he was notified by order of the College Board that his election had been invalidated."

I have a vague recollection, nothing more, that at this point Noeldeke was striving to obtain some fellowship funds to enable my father to spend some time at Oxford, but since we know that Noeldeke was asked by Cincinnati for a reference, it is likely that he counseled my father to accept the American offer, underscoring thereby his own pessimistic appraisal of the possibility that a suitable academic position would open up for him in Germany.

On the basis of Mayer's study of the Board's records, this is what transpired during those meetings of the Executive Committee in May, June and July of 1899. At the first meeting, President Wise reported that he had "corresponded with some Doctors of Philosophy in the Shemetic [sic] Department with the intention of adding a competent man to our honorable and distinguished corps of teachers" and that he had "succeeded in finding one, whose precedents are quite promising . . .

"Dr. Ginzberg is a young man. He made his doctorate at Heidelberg but was a favored and prominent student at the University of Strassburg. He came to the University with considerable talmudical learning from Kovno. It seems to me that Dr. Ginzberg would, after some practice, do good work in the Department of Exegesis in the College." But Wise went on to say that he was "not in a position to vouch for him with any degree of certainty" and therefore proposed Ginzberg's name to the Board for "a probationary election as a teacher for the next scholastic year . . . at a salary not to exceed $1,000. After one year's service," said Wise, "we will be able to judge whether Dr. Ginzberg is the man we want." For his part, Wise declared he "had a good deal of confidence in the University of Strassburg and in the reputation of Dr. Ginzberg."

The records of the June meeting state:

Agreeable to the suggestion of the President of the College, he [Wise] was instructed to issue a call to Dr. Ginzberg to temporarily fill the position of preceptor of the College from September 1898 to June 1900 as a probationary term at a salary of $1,000 payable in monthly installments of $100 commencing on October 1st.

The records for the July 25 executive session contain the following statement by Wise:

. . . in respect to the appointment of Dr. Ginzberg of Amsterdam, I received July 9th the enclosed letter of your secretary . . . in which I was informed that I may *issue a call* to the said gentleman, not that you elected him for such time with such salary. . . . Understanding that the candidate was not elected, I issued no call and hereby propose to your honorable body as assistant professor for one year at a salary of one thousand dollars, Dr. Heinrich Malter of Berlin, Germany. . . .

It was not the Board but President Wise who had reneged. The question that we must still explore and explain is—why? This is Louis Ginzberg's version, more than a half a century after the event: "I got a letter from the old president, Wise, saying, 'I understand that you have a brother in America. I would advise you to study English and come to America and accept the position. The Board meets in September, but this would be a purely formal matter. You can consider yourself appointed.' I wrote my brother and asked his advice and he replied that my coming to America was a good idea."

After receiving the letter at the dock which cancelled the arrangement, my father wrote to Wise, "I deeply regret that your influence with the Board of Governors wasn't strong enough to have them confirm your recommendation. The future historians of the College will have one thing to record about the Board—that they didn't confirm my appointment." Hardly a modest comment, and yet one that history justified.

"What actually happened," he said, "was that no one knew

me personally. Someone told Deutsch (a professor at the Hebrew Union College), who made a practice of collecting gossip, that I was very independent and a great radical when it came to the Higher Criticism of the Bible. Further, that I would try to influence the students to lead an Orthodox life. I was a radical, as far as they were concerned, and this was the bone of the contention."

On the face of it, the two objections to his appointment appear to be contradictory—he was too liberal in his thought and at the same time too conservative in his behavior. But each objection was valid and each made President Wise look for a way out of his commitment. Louis Ginzberg was apparently a man of strong opinions and strong will. He was not likely to accept the domination of a president who, whatever his skills as an organizer, had no scholarly competence, and whose conception of Judaism, despite his fundamentalist stand with respect to the interpretation of the Bible, was as a religion of accommodation. The university-trained son of Rabbi Isaac would never have remained at Cincinnati. As one of Ginzberg's new American friends, Rabbi Marcus Jastrow of Philadelphia remarked to him, "Wise's breaking the contract simply saved you the return fare from Cincinnati."

Despite Wise's enthusiastic comments about Dr. Malter, whose name he submitted in place of Louis Ginzberg, that appointment likewise proved unsuccessful. Malter left after a few years. The environment, with its virulent anti-Zionism and its lack of respect for serious scholarly investigations, was uncongenial. In later years, when Malter became professor at the Dropsie College in Philadelphia, he and my father established a close friendship.

Aside from whatever miscalculations and errors were made in Cincinnati, it is clear, at least in retrospect, that Louis Ginzberg was innocent when he accepted the call in the first place. Undoubtedly he relied on the judgment of his university friend, Harry Mayer, whose enthusiasm apparently got the upper hand over his judgment. But the fact that my father asked his brother for advice is indicative of how little he knew about conditions in the New World. His brother was a modest textile merchant, who had had little Hebrew and less general education and who was in no position to judge the situation himself, nor could he obtain reliable counsel. In economic theory, the movement of people is considered either as the result of "push factors" or of "pull factors." It is quite clear that it was the "push factors" that played the major role in Louis Ginzberg's coming to the United States.

Shortly after his arrival in New York, where he moved in with his brother and his family of three youngsters with a fourth on the way, he had to have an infected wisdom tooth removed. This required surgery and he was admitted to the old German Hospital, later renamed Lenox Hill Hospital. After a day or so, he became ambulatory and he visited the wards. In one, he found a pious Jew wearing a skull cap reading a Hebrew book. My father asked him why, considering his piety, he was not in a Jewish hospital. The old man explained that if he were forced to violate tradition, including the prohibition against eating non-kosher food, he preferred to do so in a non-Jewish environment. This was my father's first hint of the anarchy that prevailed in American Jewish life, where Jewish hospitals violated Jewish law and tradition.

His hospital stay was memorable for another reason. While his head and cheek were still bandaged, he recalled that a very big man, whom he had never seen before, bent over him, and, after ascertaining that he was Louis Ginzberg, asked him his interpretation of an obscure verse in Isaiah. The impetuous interrogator as Arnold Ehrlich, a three-hundred-pound man who became one of my father's most intimate friends, a constant visitor to our home, and who designated my father as his literary executor. Ehrlich was married to a hard-working woman, who had little education, and who supported herself and her husband by her ability with the needle. After his death, aware that she had been married to a man of international repute and renown, his wife was convinced that there were riches in the manuscripts that he left behind. Since he had not supported her in life, she was determined to be well paid before she released his papers after his death. My father had nothing but trouble from his literary trusteeship. It is my recollection that he never succeeded in salvaging very much of Ehrlich's literary remains.

I have a very clear picture of my father's considered opinion of Ehrlich, because he advised me to use Ehrlich's *Randglossen zur Hebräischen Bibel* when I was attempting to understand the development of the Sabbatical and Jubilee laws. In his opinion, Ehrlich was second to none in understanding the Bible and in shedding light on its more obscure passages.

Although Cincinnati was many hundreds of miles away from New York, the Wise-Ginzberg episode did not remain hidden for long. Most scholars, including Jewish scholars, enjoy gossip, particularly if, as in this instance, religious and theological issues are involved. In a move aimed apparently at justifying what was at best questionable behavior on legal and surely on ethical grounds, my father's views were attacked in the *American Israelite*, the principal organ of the Reform Movement. The young scholar from Europe was without a job, but he early acquired a reputation as a man that Wise was unwilling to tangle with.

But he did not remain out of work for long. He was soon writing articles for *The Jewish Encyclopedia*. "The head of the encyclopedia was Isidore Singer, a second-rate journalist who was a native of Austria and had lived for many years in Paris. Actually, he came to the United States as an adventurer. His idea was to incorporate in his encyclopedia the biographies of Jewish prize fighters and big businessmen. He thought that if businessmen were approached and the proposal put to them that if they contributed five hundred dollars they would have half a page in the encyclopedia, and if they contributed one thousand dollars they would have a full page, the result would be a small fortune for himself. Singer had acquired his training and background through the 'revolver journalism' of Paris where prominent men, each of whom undoubtedly had some skeleton or other in his closet, would pay sums of money to keep the gossip out of the paper. The other way the journals and journalists amassed money was to promise the nouveaux riches that their soirées, etc., would be fully reported—for certain considerations. Funk and Wagnalls was the publisher of the encyclopedia. Dr. Funk was a very shrewd man; he recognized the possibility of getting very large funds from the Jews and proceeded to do so."

So much for the background of the undertaking. How did Louis Ginzberg come into contact with the promoters? "I started to work with the encyclopedia purely by accident. Their building was on Lafayette Street, which was then right next to the Public Library. I had met Singer and others who suggested that I drop into the encyclopedia office. When I did, I apparently impressed the editors when I picked up a piece of paper on which was written a list of proposed names and subjects. The compilers had copied from French and German and other sources, which made for a duplication of titles. On one page, I found 25 repetitions. Kohler suggested that I write some articles for them and we were off."

Rabbi Marcus Jastrow, who was the head of a large congregation in Philadelphia and who, in addition to his career as minister, pursued scholarly investigations, was in charge of the Rabbinical Department of the *Encyclopedia*. The articles prepared by young Ginzberg, who was at first paid by the piece, so impressed Jastrow that he recommended to the Board of Editors that primary responsibility be transferred from himself to Ginzberg, who clearly had the greater knowledge. This generous act by an older man smoothed Ginzberg's way. He was soon on the regular payroll, writing on a wide range of subjects and receiving a salary of $25 per week, approximately the same that he would have earned at the Hebrew Union College.

Singer may have had many weaknesses, but he was clearly able to excite the enthusiasm of outstanding people and to elicit their cooperation. The editorial board of the *Encyclopedia* was composed of most of the Jewish scholars in the United States, many of whom, like Kaufmann Kohler and Marcus Jastrow, were also busy rabbis. It was a lively and hard-working group, and it is difficult to think of a better environment for a newly arrived young scholar to get his American land legs.

My father must have found the environment very congenial, for his output was prodigious. In the two years that he was with them, his initials were signed to 234 articles under the letter "A," with almost another 100 under the letter "B"; altogether he prepared a total of 406 articles. While many were brief biographies, several were of monograph length and three stood the test of time sufficiently to be reprinted in a volume of his collected essays, *On Jewish Law and Lore*, more than a half century later: "Allegorical Interpretation of Scripture"; "The Cabbala: History and System"; and "Codification of Jewish Law."

It is generally acknowledged that *The Jewish Encyclopedia* that Singer promoted and to which my father contributed so much had no predecessor, and to this day has had no true successor. There have been many Jewish encyclopedias in the intervening decades, but even the best of them have borrowed indiscriminately from *The Jewish Encyclopedia* of the early 1900's, the product of an unsuccessful promoter, a shrewd publisher, generous laymen, and an intrepid band of scholars and writers, among whom Louis Ginzberg came to play a key role.

By the time the first volume was completed and published, in 1900, Funk and Wagnalls had invested at least $50,000 in the venture. My father recalled that "the general press as well as the Jewish press, of course, received the first volume enthusiastically, and it was after all a very respectable achievement. The company gave a dinner for the editors and the first volume was launched with enthusiasm and acclaim. But Dr. Funk said that his company could no longer afford to continue the undertaking. He said that he would rather lose all of the money already invested than to pour more money into a bad venture. By this time, wealthy and influential Jews were becoming interested, and immediately offers of assistance poured in. Mr. Schiff promised to buy a large number of sets. But work on the *Encyclopedia* prematurely stopped." Louis Ginzberg was earning $60 a week by this time, a very nice salary indeed, but he was restive about what the future held in store. He was afraid that Kohler might try to retrench in a manner that would inevitably jeopardize the scholarly standards that the first volume had set.

Jewish life in the United States held many surprises for young Ginzberg. He had some business to transact with Kohler, and went down to the *Encyclopedia* office one Sunday morning in search of him. There he was informed that Kohler was conducting services. Ginzberg went to the Temple. After services, Kohler remarked that he was surprised to find Ginzberg in a Reform temple, and quoted a rabbinic phrase about the Prophet Elijah being found in a cemetery, although as a member of a priestly family he was forbidden to come into contact with the dead. My father was quick to retort that there was no violation of the laws of purity in either situation—Elijah had not been in a Jewish cemetery, and he had not been in a Jewish house of worship!

Kohler was by no means the most estranged member of the rabbinate with whom my father came in contact in those early days. He told the story, but it was clearly distasteful to him and therefore not part of his repertoire, of a dinner he had one Friday evening shortly after his arrival in this country at the home of one of New York's leading rabbis. He did not know the names of all of the forbidden dishes which were placed before him, but he recognized the main course, lobster, and knew that he could eat nothing other than the dessert, which was ice-cream. The leaders of Reform Judaism in those days were not satisfied with breaking the laws and disregarding the customs and traditions. They were belligerent in their attitudes and behavior. They were determined to prove their emancipation by going out of their way to break the law.

My father continued to write pieces for the *Frankfurter Zeitung*, and in one he told about his visit to a house of worship in the new land. He remarked that the architecture, external and internal, was not distinctive, and that he was unable to determine the religion of the worshippers. After inspecting the prayer book, he was not much wiser because, while it consisted primarily of selections from the Old Testament, these were part of the religious tradition of Catholicism, Protestantism, and even Mohammedism, as well as of Judaism. Nor was there any clue in the appearance of the minister. He had on clerical robes and wore no hat, and his attire was not distinctive. He was clean shaven, but that also was not revealing. But when the minister began to preach about Jesus, my father wrote, he realized that he was in a synagogue, for Jesus was no longer a fashionable subject in church.

In a similar vein was his story about Rabbi Emil Hirsch of Chicago, perhaps the outstanding rabbi in the country, and

an orator of great renown with whom my father early became friendly as a result of his work on the *Encyclopedia.*
"One day Hirsch said, 'Let's have lunch.' I said, 'You
can have lunch with me but I cannot have lunch with
you.' So we went to Felix, a restaurant run by an Alsatian
Jew on Mercer Street. When we reached it, Hirsch said,
'There's a man on the other side of the street who is one of
the trustees of my synagogue and when he gets back to Chicago he'll say, "Hirsch has nothing better to do than eat in
kosher restaurants."' I said, 'Don't worry; I don't believe that
it's really kosher!'"

One summer my father traveled to Europe with Hirsch
and found that he was the proud owner of two hundred
risqué French novels. Different lands, different standards.
But my father had a soft spot for Hirsch, and contributed
the following appreciation of him on his seventieth birthday.

"More than twenty years have passed since I first met Dr.
Hirsch. The impression, however, that his marked personality made upon me is still very vivid in my memory. I was
then a new arrival, grappling with the difficult problem of
adjusting myself to a new environment. Having spent my
youth at Lithuanian *Yeshivot* and my early manhood at
German universities, I had before me the task of accustom-
ing myself to the conditions of a country where Jewish learning is ignored by lay and clergy alike. . . . As joint editors of
The Jewish Encyclopedia, we often discussed many a subject of Jewish history and literature. The display of his fine
understanding, his good judgment and wise counsel was no
less admirable than that of his absolute impartiality and respect for true learning.

"A famous scientist once defined man as the animal with
the ability to laugh. It often occurred to me that Jewish
humor is the real criterion for pulsating Jewish life and
thought. Whatever the rabbis of old were or were not, they
certainly were entirely free of sanctimoniousness and cant—

their strong sense of humor guarded them against these vices. Dr. Hirsch's healthy and refreshing humor stamps him as a worthy successor to the rabbis of old. As an admiring pupil of these rabbis, I hope many, many more years will be granted to Dr. Hirsch to continue his work against cant and sanctimoniousness in any form or garb."

One more story out of this early period, this one about Felix Adler, who had had the opportunity to succeed his father as rabbi of Temple Emanu-El but who had instead decided to found the Ethical Culture Movement. He had heard of the bright young Semitics scholar recently arrived from Strassburg, and he invited him to lunch. As dessert was being cleared away, Adler said, "Now tell me, what are the latest academic findings with respect to Mohammed and Mohammedism?" My father replied that he had little interest in the subject and knew little about this area of research, since he didn't have much taste for people who went around founding new religions. Adler took this as a personal affront, got up, paid the check, and left. Although my father insisted that his remark about the founding of new religions was innocent and not *ad hominem,* I suspect that he was back to his old probing tricks and was testing to see whether Adler really took himself seriously. It puts too much strain on the imagination to believe that my father would have gone to lunch with Dr. Adler without having first familiarized himself at least broadly with his past and present work.

Not all of his early experiences in this country led to shock, amazement, or disconcertment. He early made the acquaintance of two of America's foremost Semitics scholars, George Foote Moore of Harvard and Charles Torrey of Yale. During the Easter vacation of 1900, the Oriental Society of America met in Philadelphia and Moore and Torrey said "that it would be a good idea for me to come to Philadelphia to get acquainted with some of these people. After all, *The Jewish Encyclopedia* job might not last forever. Judge

Mayer Sulzberger learned about my being in town and came to pay me a visit. (He was lucky to find me. I had registered at a hotel near the station and had gone off to another where the meetings were being held. That night found me wandering in and out of a series of hotels looking at the registers for a friend whose name I was ostensibly seeking, while in fact I searched for my own signature.) Later, I spent a whole day with Sulzberger, from 11 a.m. to 11 p.m. at his home. When I left, he said, 'People tell me that you are a great Oriental scholar, that you are a great talmudist. Of this I am no judge, but I know that you are certainly a fine judge of cigars.' His brother was a manufacturer of cigars, and Sulzberger always had three boxes on his desk. I had taken one from each of the three and had then smoked those in the second box. Sulzberger said that no other man had ever noticed the difference among them, but that I had settled on the very best that he had."

My father had the highest regard for Sulzberger and his regard was based on matters more substantial than cigars! "In a certain sense, Sulzberger was the most genuine American Jew I ever met. He was a bachelor; he was a collector; he had an extraordinary fine literary style—he could be a professor of English at any university; he was a leading jurist of the day, probably he was the best-known citizen of Philadelphia. He was Judge of Common Pleas and a man of great integrity among men of little integrity. He was an unique personality. He had a Jewish background in life and thought. He knew Jewish life by living it, not by reading about it. He was a man of action and a man of vision. Take, for instance, his idea that we should have a fine Jewish library in America. He came to this conclusion before any institution of Jewish learning had such an idea. He helped build the nucleus of the library which is now the library of the Jewish Theological Seminary (the greatest collection of Jewish books in the world). Three years after my arrival in this country, one of the richest private libraries in the world was sold in Amsterdam. Sulzberger cabled orders directly to my father, and he continued to buy manuscripts and rare books."

The advice given by Moore and Torrey proved to be sensible. The *Encyclopedia* job did not last forever. My father found himself employed on a week to week basis, an unsatisfactory arrangement. He gave serious consideration to returning to Europe. He talked about this to Sulzberger, who said, "You would be the first man of ability to go back. If America can't do anything, Europe certainly can't. Something will turn up." To help bridge the gap until the *Encyclopedia* would again go full throttle ahead or an academic post could be found for him, Sulzberger suggested that my father write a small popular volume of Jewish legends which the Jewish Publication Society could publish. Since he had worked with legendary materials both in connection with his doctoral dissertation and in connection with his many assignments for the *Encyclopedia*, this suggestion to do a popular volume was attractive.

The terms of the agreement have been preserved in a letter from Henrietta Szold, the Secretary of the Society, to my father, dated November 6, 1901:

Your letter of September 18 submitting (your) plan for the proposed work on "Jewish Legends Relating to Biblical Matters" was put before the Publication Committee by the Chairman early in October and by it approved and recommended for adoption to the Board of Trustees. The latter has now had its meeting, and I am instructed to write you that your proposition has been accepted, together with the terms you suggest. The understanding is that you will write, in German, a book on the lines laid down in your proposition, to contain approximately one hundred thousand words and to be available for use of the Society in the year 1903, all rights in the book to be ceded to the Jewish Publication Society of America for an honorarium of $1,000.

The Committee suggests that as the manuscript must be handled by a translator, it be written in ink, and only on one side of the paper.

Agreements are usually entered in good faith, but here is proof, if proof be needed, of how fate and time can alter the plans of men—and women. No volume was made available for the use of the Society in 1903, nor in the next year, or the year following. The first volume of what eventually came to be a seven-volume work entitled *The Legends of the Jews* appeared in 1909. It was not until 1913 that the fourth volume of text appeared. And it was more than a decade later, in 1925, that the first volume of the notes was published, followed three years later by the second volume of the notes. And still many more years passed before the appearance of the Index Volume, because those guiding the Society were apprehensive about the expense, and failed to realize that it would soon more than pay for itself, since it would unlock the treasures that were contained in the six volumes that had been published earlier, particularly the volumes containing the notes.

We cannot help wondering in light of what happened whether Miss Szold was prescient in recommending to the author to write in ink and on only one side of the paper in order to lighten the task of the translator; she herself translated the first two volumes.

There were other matters which could not have been foreseen. No one could know that the man who translated Volume III, Paul Radin, who later became one of America's most distinguished anthropologists, would bear the author a lifelong grudge for preventing him from translating the fourth volume—a decision over which the author had no control.

Nor could anybody have foreseen the problem that the title would pose. The work, despite its broad scope, is limited to legends about the heroes—and the villains—of the

Bible. It does not cover the considerable folkloristic material that is rooted in the experiences of the Jews in post-biblical times. Whatever the exaggeration of the original title—and each of the volumes had a subtitle which specified its scope —the efforts to improve it were not successful. It was my father's conviction throughout his later years that the sale of *The Legends of the Jews* would have been much greater had the title stressed the Bible rather than the Jews. Therefore, after his death in 1953, when Simon and Schuster decided to bring out in a single volume the entire text less the variants of the same legend—approximately eighty percent of the original first four volumes—we resorted to a new title: *The Legends of the Bible.* It is never safe to speculate why a book sells well or poorly, and the problem is compounded in the case of a classic which had already had a substantial sale over the years. But there was considerable indirect evidence that the new title was a distinct liability. Fundamentalists and Catholics were disconcerted at seeing the words legend and Bible in juxtaposition. What had legend to do with the Holy Writ? And so Simon and Schuster returned to the original title for the next printing of both the hard cover and paperback editions.

The 1901 letter from the Secretary of the Society to Louis Ginzberg about a volume of legends referred to action by the Publication Committee and subsequent action by the Board of Directors. More than a half century later it fell to me as a member of the Publication Committee and at the request of the Board to devise an improved method for securing and appraising manuscripts. This too could not have been easily foreseen!

Sulzberger's gambit was successful beyond his wildest dreams. Although the Jewish Publication Society had to wait a long time for the volume that had been promised for 1903, it eventually had the distinction of publishing one of the most important studies ever written on the folkloristic materials of the Bible. The gambit was also successful in its primary aim: it helped to keep Louis Ginzberg in America.

At the end of about three-quarters of a year of shrewd negotiations between Dr. Funk and the leadership of the American Jewish community, the money was in hand to proceed with the original plan and to bring out a comprehensive encyclopedia which would be distinguished for its authoritative treatment of every significant aspect of Jewish life and letters in ancient, medieval and modern times.

Work resumed and Louis Ginzberg returned to his editorial duties. The volume of legends to which he had recently committed himself had to be put aside. It is interesting to record my father's picture of Dr. Funk, who played such a determining role in this most ambitious publishing undertaking. "Funk was a Lutheran minister who was very active in the temperance movement. He was at one time the Prohibition Party's candidate for vice president. One day he invited me to lunch at the Astor, then the swankiest hotel in town. I knew he was a temperance man. Our waiter—all of the waiters were German—asked me what I would drink. I said that I would start with some beer, then have some Rhine wine; after that a glass of Bordeaux and end with a cognac. Funk just sat there trembling; he couldn't say a word. Finally, I said I *would* drink that, but my doctor says that I shouldn't, so I will just have water.

"I had an office in a building which was next to the Public Library on 8th Street. I rarely worked in the office. I preferred to work in the library. Funk asked me what I was doing spending so much time in the library. I told him that I was just disarranging books.

"A European scholar by the name of Ratner wrote to Funk and indicated his desire to write for the *Encyclopedia*. His letter began, 'My dear gentleman.' Funk asked me what kind of a person would write that? I said that Ratner, living in Russia, was a little backward: he still thought that an editor might be a gentleman!" Clearly, Louis Ginzberg had not yet lost his pleasure in repartee, nor had he learned to respect the wealthy and the powerful.

Some time later my father was introduced to the mightiest of them all—Jacob H. Schiff—perhaps the wealthiest Jew in the United States and the self-appointed as well as generally acknowledged head of American Jewry. Without much general or Jewish learning, Schiff nevertheless had been brought up in a sufficiently Jewish world in Frankfurt am Main that he sought to discharge his responsibilities both with regard to supporting his brethen in need and to building and supporting Jewish institutions that would contribute to their religious and cultural life. He was a philanthropist on the grand scale. There is a story, and it is probably true considering the nature of Frankfurt Orthodoxy and Schiff's wealth, that when his sister visited him in the United States, she had a new stove put aboard the trans-Atlantic liner on which she travelled so that she would be certain that her food was prepared strictly in accordance with the prescribed ritual.

When my father met him, Mr. Schiff inquired whether he was related to his good friend, Baron Günzburg of St. Petersburg. This was my father's reply: "The Ginzberg family for many hundreds of years devoted itself almost exclusively to scholarship. Then, at the beginning of the nineteenth century, a split occurred. One branch continued to be scholars and rabbis; the second decided to make money. Baron Günzburg belongs to the other branch!"

My father early acquired and never lost his highly critical attitude toward men of wealth in the United States. As far as I was able to analyze what for lack of a better term might be called a blind spot, it derived from the differences in attitude toward men of means which he found between the United States and Europe. He knew some and heard about other wealthy Jews in Russia, Germany, Holland, and France. Moreover, he understood that the making of money probably called for certain traits that are not noble. But this was not the source of his coldness. What he could not tolerate about the wealthy was their sense of self-importance and their presumption that, because they had made a lot of money, they were entitled to an opinion on every subject and, even worse, expected others to respect it. He really was more critical of the culture that placed men of wealth on pedestals than of the arrogance and lack of humility of the individual millionaire. He could never understand a country in which a successful automobile manufacturer during the course of court testimony could state under oath that "history is bunk," and have his statement taken seriously by press and public. He always had a soft spot for Julius Rosenwald, whom he met many years later, who repeated to him that his "fortune was ninety-five percent luck and five percent brains."

With two of his three sons and one daughter in the United States, Rabbi Isaac, who had not experienced any pronounced improvement in his business affairs after his removal to Amsterdam, considered emigrating to America. But much as Louis would have been pleased to have his parents close to him, he discouraged his father from going through with his plan. He explained that the United States simply did not provide a congenial environment for a religious Jew, to whom study and good works were the center of life.

Louis Ginzberg had seen money corrupt and defile; he had seen it eat into the vitals of the Orthodox community, most of whom were poor. The control of the slaughtering and butchering trades, though ostensibly in the hands of the rabbinate, was in fact infiltrated by gangsters. The man who had sprung young Louis out of Lithuania, Rabbi Jacob Joseph, had been brought to New York to be Chief Rabbi. A man of character, he set about to strengthen the system of rabbinical supervision to insure that the law was complied with in all respects, and thereby came into head-on conflict with nefarious interests. First they tried small bribes and then larger ones. When Rabbi Joseph proved adamant, they increased the pressure by threatening him with bodily harm and even death. He did not die at the hands of an assassin, but he died a victim of their harassment and persecution. A country that was responsible for the death of Rabbi Joseph was no place for Rabbi Isaac. Yet Rabbi Isaac's son was willing to see what the future would bring. For the time being, it was bearable: he had a job, a good income; he was doing useful work; he had made a large number of friends. There was much about the United States that was attractive. This was the situation at the beginning of 1902.

CHAPTER V

THE YOUNG PROFESSOR

IN 1902 there occurred an event that could, as they say, happen "only in America." A group of wealthy German Jews who belonged to the leading Reform temple in the United States, Temple Emanu-El, decided to support the reorganization of the Jewish Theological Seminary for the purpose of training rabbis grounded in talmudic law who could eventually cater to the religious needs of the masses of newly arrived immigrants from Eastern Europe.

To accomplish their purpose, they invited Solomon Schechter, Reader in Rabbinics at Cambridge, England, to become President of the reorganized institution. Strange as these actions might appear today, they were neither impetuous nor romantic, but deliberate and imaginative.

The gap between the established Jewish community and the new immigrants was immense, and nowhere was the distance greater than between the religious orientation and practices of the old and those of the new. For the most part, the older immigrants had become Americanized. They had even modified their religious tradition to a point where it had become almost identical with that of the most liberal of the Protestant sects. Reform Judaism stressed the moral and ethical teachings of the prophets; it denied the authority of the Talmud; it ignored most customs and traditions; it even established Sunday as a day for prayer; it recognized Jesus as a great religious leader; it adopted a hostile attitude towards Zionism.

My father argued with considerable persuasiveness, at least it carried conviction for me, that the progress of Unitarianism, which had made major gains early in the century, was aborted when the Christian community saw that there was no longer any clear difference between the Unitarian orientation and that of Reform Judaism. Many Christians were willing to lighten the theological baggage which they were carrying, but not at the price of blurring the lines between themselves and the Jews.

Despite the fact that the Reform movement stood closer to liberal Protestantism than to authentic Jewish tradition, the lay leaders of New York Jewry threw their support back of the efforts to revitalize what had been an old but moribund institution for educating rabbis along traditional lines.

Moreover, they knew exactly what they were doing and why they were doing it. They sought to bring order and discipline into the fragmented and disorganized immigrant groups, something which would be possible only if religious leaders were available to cater to this large immigrant population and particularly to their children. They realized that, unable to make any compromises or adjustments, the Orthodox rabbis would soon become estranged from the children of the newcomers. What was needed was an indigenous rabbinate which could help to bridge the gap and in the process speed the assimilation of these hordes of Yiddish-speaking, tradition-bound Jews.

Schechter's first task was to build a faculty, and before the reorganized Seminary opened for the academic year 1902-03, he had found its first member, Louis Ginzberg, whom he appointed Professor of Talmud. At the age of twenty-nine, without any prior teaching experience, Louis Ginzberg was appointed full professor in a post-graduate institution with "the understanding that he was to have charge of the entire Rabbinical Department excepting the Codes." The faculty that first year consisted of Schechter and Ginzberg, with two hold-overs with the rank of instructor, Bernard Drachman and Joshua Joffé. The Circular of Information for 1903-1904 contained a listing of the faculty which included the following: Professor of Talmud, Louis Ginzberg, Ph.D. (Heidelberg); Professor of History, Chair temporarily filled by Doctor Ginzberg. In later years my father said that at one time or another he had taught every course in the Seminary with the one exception of Homiletics.

We do not know who first called young Ginzberg's name to Schechter's attention, but we do know that Schechter wrote to Rabbi Marcus Jastrow to inquire what school Ginzberg belonged to. Jastrow sent Schechter's question on and was told to report back to Schechter that "Ginzberg belonged to his own school."

There were many stories, most of them now lost, about how a man rejected as being too radical for the faculty at the Hebrew Union College could be found acceptable for appointment to the faculty of the Jewish Theological Seminary. One, probably apocryphal, is that at Cincinnati, they inquired of young Ginzberg whether he was observant and he replied affirmatively; they next asked whether he "believed" and the reply was in the negative. At the Seminary they asked only the first question. But like most apocrypha, there is some basis in reality. The Preliminary Announcement of the reorganized Seminary carried the following paragraph: "Every student candidate for a degree is expected to observe the Jewish Sabbath and to conform to the Jewish dietary laws." Louis Ginzberg could meet these criteria without difficulty.

The listing of the courses in the Preliminary Announcement for 1902-1903 included: "Dr. Kaufmann Kohler will deliver a course of six lectures on the Apocryphal and Apocalyptic Literature of the Jews in the spring of 1903." A Seminary that could sponsor a course of lectures by Kohler would have no difficulty in making its peace with the theological views of Ginzberg.

At the time the Seminary offer was made to him, and it appears that Schechter committed himself by letter without a personal interview, my father was working full time for the *Encyclopedia* for a very substantial salary; he was earning $5,000 per annum. The proffered teaching post carried a salary of $3,000, but he had no hesitancy in accepting a cut of forty percent in salary. He was a bachelor and he could live very nicely on the lower amount. What he wanted and needed was time for serious work. He had nothing to gain from writing additional articles under pressure. He was filled, almost to the point of overflowing, with what he had learned. And he had a great many ideas, original and insightful, that he wanted to work out and publish. But for that he needed, above all else, freedom and time. And this is just what the Seminary offer implied. He was quick to accept it.

According to my research on the shaping of a career, a successful occupational choice requires that a man know how to distinguish between what he wants and what he must have. Everybody wants more money; the only question is whether a man is willing to pay the price that almost always attaches to earning a higher salary. My father ran no danger of making the wrong decision. He never had any question about the relative importance of money versus the other good things in life. I suspect, in fact I am reasonably sure, that his adamant refusal to barter any part of his freedom for money or power was an important reminder to me the few times that I was tempted: at the beginning of my career, I was offered a position in the Federal Government in the early hectic days of the New Deal, when helping to serve one's country especially at a good salary had great attraction for a young economist. And again, at the end of World War II, when I received a tentative offer of a senior research position in industry that carried a salary roughly six times what Columbia would pay me on my return to the classroom. I am indebted to my father on a great many different grounds, but never did he teach me a more important lesson than to assess the costs of earning money as well as the pleasure of spending it.

The *Encyclopedia* did not release him so readily. When the editors realized that he was determined to accept the Seminary appointment, they explored the possibility of making an arrangement with him that would be less than full time. This too would have been very lucrative. But my father wanted no part of it. He had come to a turning point in his life. His years of preparation, of holding operations, had come to an end. He felt that it would be best to make a clean break. And so he did.

He worked hard that first year at the Seminary. He lectured for five hours a week on Talmud; he gave a history lecture, and two hours of Judeo-Aramaic grammar. By the next academic year his schedule had been reduced to six hours, and by the third year he was down to four hours of lectures.

The major reason for the reduction in his teaching load was the success that Schechter had had in recruiting additional faculty. At the end of the first academic year, Schechter and my father set off for Europe. Schechter found Alexander Marx, who became Professor of History and who built up the Seminary library to its position of pre-eminence, and my father found Israel Friedlaender, who became Professor of Biblical Literature and Exegesis. In Schechter's report to the Board of Directors dated November 1, 1903, he had the following to say about the two men who became my father's most intimate colleagues: "Dr. Israel Friedlaender was *Privat-Dozent* at the University of Strassburg, has his academic degree, is an excellent Hebrew scholar, and knows Arabic, Syriac, and Cuneiform. . . . He was born in Russia. . . . He has recommendations from Professors Noeldeke, Landau, Barth. . . . I may add that Doctor Friedlaender is strictly conservative in his life. For the Chair of History I have secured the services of Doctor Alexander Marx, a native of Elberfield and a graduate of the Gymnasium and the University of Königsberg. He attended the Universities of Königsberg and Berlin. . . . pursued his rabbinic studies at Halberstadt . . . and (at) the Rabbinic Seminary at Berlin, . . . has worked in the Libraries of London, Oxford, and Cambridge. . . . I made an arrangement with Doctor Marx for the Professorship of Jewish History and Literature . . . and further, that he should act as Chief Librarian, giving five hours a day to the Library." Since according to the terms worked out by Dr. Schechter, Dr. Marx was also committed to lecture on "Jewish Hellenistic Literature (and the Philosophy of the Spanish-Arabic period)," it was clear that here was one faculty member who would not have much free time. I am reminded of the story that my teacher, John Maurice Clark, told me about the work schedule of his father, John Bates Clark, when he was a young member of the faculty at Carleton College, Minnesota. John Bates was in delicate health and to lighten his chores he was required to teach only twenty-five hours a week and to serve as librarian!

The Reverend Joseph Asher, who held an active pulpit in New York and who had a Master of Arts degree from the University of Manchester, had been appointed Professor of Homiletics during the first year after the reorganization. In the academic year 1906-07, Israel Davidson (Ph.D., Columbia) became a member of the faculty with the rank of Instructor in Hebrew and Rabbinics. My father had become acquainted with Dr. Davidson some time earlier when he was serving as Chaplain at Sing Sing and had sponsored his appointment. On one occasion my father visited Davidson at the prison. It was shortly after the High Holidays. Davidson took him through a block of cells so that he could talk with the prisoners. One complained bitterly to my father about Dr. Davidson's having omitted certain prayers during services on the Day of Atonement. My father reported this conversation to Davidson, who told him that this particular prisoner had been committed to life imprisonment for the brutal murder of his wife.

To return to the Seminary: it had a small but gifted faculty very much dominated by its President, who was a man of great ability and equally great charm. When Schechter died in 1915, the students devoted their third *Annual* to a *Schechter Memorial.* Included in it is a piece written by my father on "Dr. Schechter as Scholar" which was later included in his book entitled, *Students, Scholars and Saints.* In my father's copy of the *Annual,* he has the numbers 1 to 13 written in pencil beside the paragraphs in which he noted Schechter's important contributions. Among the points which he made were his discovery of the original of Ecclesiasticus; the discovery of the Sectarian Document; the discovery of the lost Tannaitic commentaries; his contributions to deepening understanding of the Geonic periods; his biographical essays on leading Jewish scholars and saints; and his work on Jewish theology. In a more personal vein he wrote: "Dr. Schechter combined with great intellectual prowess a disdain for conventionality, a temper imperious and resolute, along with a most touching gentleness, sweetness, singleness of heart and purpose."

Solomon Goldman, writing about my father in *The Portrait of A Teacher,* recalled: "I shall never forget the morning of October 23, 1916. It was the first hour of the first day of school after the summer sessions and eleven months since the death of Dr. Schechter. We expected to find Professor

Ginzberg well rested and bodily fit. Instead he was ashen pale, his eyes sad, his forehead puckered, his lips compressed. I thought I had seen the muscles of his face twitch once or twice. He was slow getting started, and when he did begin he was speaking under a great strain, his voice was thinner than usual, his words barely audible. 'This is the first time,' he was saying, 'that we are opening our academic year at the Seminary without Dr. Sch. . . .' He never finished the word or sentence. He was unable to choke down his tears. He rose, walked off the platform, and left the room. The class disbanded. Nobody broke the silence; nobody made any comment. We filed out mourning the dead and loving the living. We had had our lesson for the day, a lesson in the reverence and affection we owed the scholars and sages of our people."

The relations between an older and a younger man working in the same institution, in the same field, and even on occasion on the same documents, can fit into only one of two patterns: that of master and disciple or that of colleagues. By the time Louis Ginzberg came to the Seminary he could no longer be any man's disciple. He could respect and admire others, but he had to deal with them as equals—at least in all matters of scholarship. The love and affection that my father revealed for Schechter many months after his death reflected the deep personal loss that he had sustained. Not only had Schechter given him his start, but he had the deepest admiration and affection for him. As early as 1903, Schechter wrote letters of introduction for his young colleague to his friends in England soliciting their assistance and informing them that Dr. Ginzberg was one of the "world's leading authorities of rabbinic literature." A generous comment from a senior man about a junior.

No one who is acquainted with Schechter's work and life, including his "big Jewish soul," his lack of conventionality, his passions, and his style, and who is also acquainted with the deeper springs of my father's being can question that the young Ginzberg found much to emulate in the older Schechter.

I have no personal recollections of Schechter, although I saw him often when I was young, particularly in the Seminary synagogue on Saturday mornings. But I have a very clear recollection of rushing to meet my father on his return from his lectures to ask for the chocolate that Dr. Schechter never failed to send along for me. And I recall the sad day when he was buried. My parents were having a heated discussion: my mother told my father that as an honorary pallbearer he would have to wear gloves but my father balked, saying that he never wore them and had no intention of starting then.

It was years later, in the late 1920's and early 1930's, when I became intimate with his only son, Frank I. Schechter, who was also a close friend of my father, that I had an opportunity to appreciate the man that Schechter was. It could be said of him, as Napoleon said of Goethe—*Voilà un homme!*

Time confuses and alters a man's views. During the last years of his life, my father spoke to my wife about Schechter. "Schechter had been ill for many years before he died. During this period he had often asked me to deliver a lecture for him. This even happened the day he died. I was sitting in the library when he came in and said, 'Do me a favor, Ginzberg. I'm supposed to give a lecture on Saadia at ten o'clock and I don't feel well.' Saadia was an early Jewish philosopher of great importance. I didn't know where he was in his lecture but I gave a resume of his different activities. Schechter went home and was dead by two o'clock. Even though he had been in bad health, he had not taken care of himself. He was very fond of highly spiced Jewish food. He used to smoke a lot, and in general was quite careless. The

year before, he had had an appendectomy, so this all contributed to his death at about sixty-nine or seventy.

"Schechter was a Rumanian who had never had a proper
modern education. He did pass some kind of college examinations in English but spoke it poorly. Nevertheless, he
wrote English beautifully. In fact, I considered him a master
of the English language. I once described him as a Chasidic
rabbi for Fifth Avenue Jews. Externally he was very impressive; he had beautiful eyes and a beautiful beard. . . . He had
great convictions and great courage, but he didn't have the
patience necessary for a scholar. He had intuition but not
the essential knowledge. If one has a great range of knowledge without intuition, the knowledge becomes dead matter.
At one time intuition was sufficient for scholars. A century
ago knowledge was very limited, but in our times one must
have both. To be an historian, one must also be a philologist
as well; one must have a sense of economics, of archeology,
etc.

"Schechter had a deep soul. He knew the living power of
the Jews—by which I mean: for the past two thousand years
the Jews have suffered. During the time of Hitler they had
to suffer, but in the Middle Ages, one only had to be converted to avoid suffering. The 'living power of the Jews' explains why all the Jews were not converted.

"When Schechter was a lecturer or reader at Cambridge,
some friends gave him the money to go to Egypt. It was in
Cairo that he 'found' the Genizah, which he didn't really find
at all. The word 'Genizah' at one time meant treasury. Then
it meant preserving things, and finally, hiding things which
were not used. The Jews have always had a great respect for
books because their books usually repeated the name of
God, and when their books—Bibles, prayer books, or
Talmud—were worn out, they would put them in safekeep-
ing. In Eastern Europe the custom was to bury books in the
cemetery. When a great man died, he was honored by hav-

ing his books buried next to him. In Egypt, the climate was so dry that it wasn't necessary to bury them and consequently they were simply stacked in a room in back of the synagogue.

"In connection with this keeping of books, there are certain lamentations which are chanted on the ninth day of Ab, which are called the *Kinah*. My father used to read these chants (it would take from early morning to noon), and would cry like a child. He would never take the books home because he always assumed that the Messiah would come during the next year. This fastday was the commemoration of the destruction of the Temple, so the books were just left there and we boys used to collect them and if they were in good condition, we would keep them for the next year.

"To get back to Egypt. The sexton of the synagogue had early discovered that Europeans were crazy people, that if one gave them a bunch of these tattered papers, they would give you a *baksheesh*. Many people had seen some fragments of the Cairo Genizah before Schechter, but Schechter was methodical. He got acquainted with the Chief Rabbi, and got permission to clear the whole room. He transferred the entire Genizah to the University Library at Cambridge, and then he started to study it. He published a number of things of importance. For instance, he wrote about a hitherto unknown sect. I believe that he was wrong about this, and the fragments recently found in Jerusalem corroborate my views and even my emendations to Schechter's work. I myself published more than Schechter or anyone else about the Genizah. However, the 'discovery' was very important, especially for the history of Jews in Palestine after 400 A. D. Very little had been known about them during this period because conditions under the Church had been so intolerable that many had emigrated. There was one fragment which proved that there had been contact between Babylonian Jews and the great Jewish culture in Kairvan, North

Africa. There were two great academies in Babylonia—one at Sura and one at Pumbedita—and scholars at these two academies corresponded with Jews all over the world. I was the first to discover a fragment proving that there had been correspondence between a rabbi in Lucca, Italy, and Iraq about 1,000 A. D. This was tremendously important because the old families in Italy later moved to Germany, thus transmitting both Italian and Iraqi culture to Germany."

The names of the men who contributed to the endowment of the reorganized Seminary according to the size of their gift in descending order follow: Jacob H. Schiff, Felix M. Warburg, James Loeb, Louis Marshall, Simon Guggenheim, Daniel Guggenheim, Ph. S. King, L. Strauss & Sons, Emanuel Lehman, L. A. Heinsheimer, Solomon Loeb, Jas. Seligman, Henry Morgenthau, Sigd. Neustadt, William Guggenheim, Ferdinand Sulzberger, Benjamin Guggenheim—and there were other heads of leading German Jewish families of the day who contributed.

These were generous men, but they did not make life easy for Dr. Schechter. His son Frank told me about the hours of humiliation that Dr. Schechter had to experience in order to wheedle a few additional tons of coal from the Directors to heat the Seminary building. Frank's memory is corroborated by a note found in my father's files to the effect that the superintendent of the Seminary building must have assumed that my father derived great warmth from studying the Talmud, since he did not provide any heat. The uncertainty of the Seminary's future at that time is indicated by the story told to me by Dr. Joseph Breuer about his father, the Seminary's superintendent, who took a degree in pharmacy on the side to protect himself against the eventuality that the Seminary might be forced to close for lack of financial support. Then there is the joint letter addressed by the senior professors, Ginzberg, Friedlaender, Marx, dated 1912, requesting Dr. Schechter's help in getting the Board of

Directors to raise their salaries, which were still at $3,500 per annum, the amount they had been paid in 1905. Clearly, Schechter's life was not easy.

His difficulties were not limited to such mundane matters as money. There were other conflicts. The incongruity of the Seminary's being endowed and supported by rich Jews whose affiliations were with the Reform movement became manifest over the issue of Zionism. The first decade of the century saw steady gains in the growth of Theodor Herzl's followers who believed that, instead of waiting for the Messiah, the Jews could work actively to rebuild the Holy Land. The road of the Zionists within as well as outside of the Jewish community was not easy. The extreme Orthodox balked at cooperating in any undertaking that would substitute human for divine effort. More significant, the most wealthy sector of Jewry in Western Europe and the United States was identified with the Reform movement that wanted no part of a Jewish nationalism that could suggest a conflict because of dual loyalty—to the countries of which Jews were citizens and to Palestine. While there were exceptions, the rabbis and lay leaders of the Reform movement in the United States were overwhelmingly opposed to the spread of the Zionist movement. As the head of the Seminary, Schechter found himself in the middle. His principal backers, including the important Jacob H. Schiff, were not only unfriendly, but overtly hostile to Zionism, while everything that the Seminary taught and stood for that was subsumed under such rubrics as "the historical school," "conservatism," "Catholic Israel," demanded unequivocal support for the redemption of Zion. A Jew to whom Judaism was real had to be a Zionist. And Schechter, to the chagrin of his Board, came out in favor of Zionism.

He disappointed his Board in still other respects. He failed to bring the order and decorum into the religious and communal life of the large immigrant masses for which his sponsors had brought him from England to the United States. Since Schechter did not meet the aspirations and goals of his sponsors, surely not their more extreme desires, their continued support of the Seminary was less than spectacular. They supplemented the endowment income and covered the deficit every year, although the deficit was very modest. How modest is revealed by the following letter that my father felt constrained to write Schechter in 1909:

As I have already told you in conversation, my volume of *Genizah Studies* is now completely printed off, and the question of its disposition is a matter on which I should much like your advice.

You are aware of the conditions through which it has come into existence. There being no medium for the publication of such contributions to Jewish scholarship in this country, either in a special journal or in the transactions of any Jewish learned body, I found myself obliged to publish them piecemeal in the *Jewish Quarterly Review* (in England) in which some 165 pages of it appeared during the last five years. I had, however, collected very much more material on which my labor would have been entirely lost if this had not been printed, and on the cessation of the *Review*, I had no alternative but to print the remainder, which brings the volume up to about 450 pages. The expense of this has proved very high, reaching to nearly $600, and I am in great embarrassment as to the means of paying so large a sum purely in the interests of Jewish learning.

If the subject had been Arabic or Sanscrit, I feel sure I should have had no difficulty in having it published without cost to myself, by some learned society either in this country or in Europe, and would even have had the heavy expenses reimbursed which I have incurred in travelling to England for the purpose of studying the MSS, obtaining photographs and copies of them, and in many other ways.

I scarcely think it is creditable to the position of Jewish scholarship in America that I should be placed in this position. I feel convinced that if I had been connected with any of the Jewish Seminaries in Europe, however small its means, there would be no difficulty in publishing the volume as part of the ordinary expenses of a learned institution. Even as it is, if I had written my accompanying comments in German, I should have had no difficulty in obtaining a subvention from either the Zunz Stiftung or the Verein für Förderung der Wissenschaft des Judenthums, either of which, I feel confident, would have been willing to publish this work. But having cast in my lot with American Jewry, I felt myself bound to write in the language of the land of my adoption, and trust I shall not suffer in regarding myself as an American Jew.

The Trustees of the Seminary have recognized their obligations to encourage scientific Jewish scholarship by agreeing to publish that part of my *Genizah Studies* which relates to the Talmud Jerushalmi, which is now entirely printed off, and ready for publication, the expenses of which—$350—have already been paid by the Seminary. But you will doubtless agree with me that an average expenditure of $50 per annum for the past seven years is scarcely an adequate amount of encouragement to Jewish scholarship, or to the research work of the scholars connected with the Seminary.

During the course of my researches on the Genizah Fragments, I was led into an examination of the whole Halakhic literature of the Geonic period with surprisingly important and novel results. I have accordingly written an English introduction to my Genizah studies, which has grown into a separate volume entitled *Contributions to the Post-Talmudic Halakhah*, which is also printed off to the amount of 200 pages, and for the means of publication of which I am in the same difficulty as with regards the Genizah Studies themselves.

I shall feel greatly obliged to you if you could suggest any steps that could be taken by which I might be relieved of the heavy financial responsibility which I have incurred in the interests of Jewish scholarship.

In a letter written to my father some four months previously while he was still in Europe, Henrietta Szold reported on a visit with the head of the Seminary: "Dr. Schechter has come to the same conclusion as Zunz. Although he is full of praise for the character of the people he was thrown together with this summer, he nevertheless has returned more pessimistic than ever regarding the future of American Judaism in general and the Seminary in particular. I was not able to console him. From day to day my feeling grows that we are defending a forlorn hope. What I wanted to tell you, however, was that after an outburst against things in general by which he prognosticated the break-up of the Seminary after he was gone, he said that seeing the futility of it all he had made up his mind henceforth to husband his time and put as much of it as possible into the writing of books. I am afraid, however, that he will find it hard to undo the effects of his earlier policy. He has been drawn into too many practical schemes and affairs to be the master of his time, or even of himself, since he has engendered in himself the sort of appetite that grows with what it feeds upon."

Schechter suffered from other episodes of despondency. In 1914, the year before his death, he wrote to my father. After reporting at length on his several examinations by leading physicians and the regimens they prescribed for him, he added: "I wish to take here the opportunity of expressing to you my heartfelt thanks for the kindnesses and the many thoughtful attentions you have shown to me during my absence. These were very trying days, but your presence did a great deal to soothe pains and to rouse my despondent spirits."

Aside from the single episode over my father's analysis of the Sectarian Document which Schechter had dealt with initially and which had led to hurt feelings on both sides, the thirteen-year relationship between *"der Alte,"* as Mrs. Schechter referred to her husband, and the "little Doctor," as she called my father, was mutually warm and supportive. There is no reason to question the story that the Schechters would have looked with favor on young Ginzberg's marrying their older daughter Ruth. But Schechter could not have escaped moments of disquietude when he realized that my father's singlehanded devotion to scholarship was propelling him into a position of international renown, and that the other members of the faculty knew that in matters of scholarship he was the first among them, including their revered president. Despite his imperious personality and leadership position, Schechter did not hesitate to recognize the intellectual pre-eminence of his younger colleague. Dr. A. A. Neuman remembers Dr. Schechter's advising him to accept a pulpit in Cleveland; Schechter remarked in passing that it paid a salary twice that received by Professor Ginzberg, "the greatest Jewish scholar of our times." It is to Schechter's lasting credit that it was a happy and not a contentious faculty and that, despite his periodic misgivings, the Seminary which he built, even if it did not accomplish all that the Board had hoped for, grew and prospered and became the leading center of Jewish learning in the New World.

The years between 1902 and 1908, when my father became engaged to be married, were very busy years for him. He taught his courses at the Seminary; he delivered occasional public lectures; he wrote popular as well as scholarly articles; he participated in a limited amount of community activities, and above all he pushed ahead on his major research investigations into the Jerusalem Talmud, Geonica, and the much expanded and deepened study of the Legends. Each summer, except in 1906, he left for Europe to visit his family in Amsterdam and to travel, sometimes for pleasure but usually for work in the great libraries of England and the Continent. It was a full life and on occasion even an exciting one. It is a characteristic of academic life that the principals, whenever they find things too dull, can arrange to create excitement by attacking the administration, each other, or by publishing material that brings them into conflict with guardians of the public weal.

In 1906, Louis Ginzberg wrote a long review of a book entitled *Jewish Biblical Commentators* by William Rosenau, a rabbi in Baltimore, which was composed of a series of lectures which the author had earlier delivered at Johns Hopkins University. The review article which appeared in *The American Hebrew* was entitled "A Specimen of Jewish Learning at American Universities." In the concluding paragraphs of the sixteen-page review, my father stated that he "was reluctant to review the book and was persuaded only by the consideration that silence is a sin where the honor of Jewish learning is concerned." The paragraph went on: "In the whole domain of science, no book containing such amusing and at the same time saddening mistakes, mistakes calculated to lower one's respect for science, has been issued from out of a University of the standing of Johns Hopkins." The preceding fifteen pages detailed the errors, amusing and saddening. The following excerpt provides one sample of the hostility which permeates the review: "Our author is particularly keen about this Teutonism. . . . There is nothing so nauseating to me as 'provincial Judaism'. . . . Truth requires the admission that achievements of the German Jew of modern times are peculiarly insignificant in the field of biblical science. The nineteenth century produced three great Jewish exegetes: Luzzatto in Italy and Malbim and Erhlich in Poland. . . ." Early in the essay my father pointed in passing to the critical manner with which the talmudists dealt with the Bible; they suspected that Isaiah was not the sole author of the book ascribed to him; similarly with the book of Jeremiah; Ezra was called a psalmist; "even the integrity of the Pentateuch is not accepted without reservations: two sections are traced to Joshua instead of Moses. . . ."

Never again did he let himself go with all of his guns firing. He had a similar review article under way when he became engaged, and as a token of respect for his fiancée he tore it up, never to write in such a vein again.

The winters meant hard work, but the summers in Europe provided diversion and stimulation. My father told my wife of one of those summer excursions. "I got into trouble another year on this same fastday (The Fast of Ab). In 1908, my good friend Chajes (who later became Chief Rabbi of Vienna) and I made arrangements to meet in Oslo a few days before the international conference of Orientalists in Copenhagen. This was the first time in my life that I had linguistic difficulties. I spoke no Norwegian. I was looking for a substantial meal, especially since in Norway, night doesn't begin until 11:30 and twilight begins at 8:00—so there would have been twenty-seven hours of fast. I walked through the streets of Oslo and saw a store with a sign announcing that the proprietor was named Abramsen. I didn't know then that the 'sen' is a typically Nordic suffix, but I went in. I asked the storekeeper if there were a synagogue around. He looked blank. At that moment his son walked in. He was about sixteen and was obviously coming home from school. He threw his books on the table, and I noticed that one of them was a Latin book. I addressed him in Latin, and he indicated that I should write it down. He got out a dictionary and I wrote down, 'Are you a Jew?' He said, 'No.' I asked, 'Is there a synagogue in town?' He said, 'Yes.' I asked him, 'Where?' He said he didn't know exactly and asked his father. He then wrote down that his father had a friend who was Jewish and who would surely know. His father told him to take me to his friend. We found the synagogue but it was locked, so I wrote down that there must be some indication at the synagogue of where the sexton lives. The boy looked and found it and we found the sexton was a Landsman from Vilna. He was very surprised that a student should be as particular as I, but when I told him that I was a descendant of the Gaon, he was very enthusiastic and did what he could. I had a very good meal with him and the following day, I went to synagogue. Chajes came a day later. We spent a few good days together and then went to Copenhagen."

He recalled another summer for the benefit of his biographer, David Druck. The father of his colleague, Alexander Marx, was not only a leading banker in Königsberg, but also a patron of Jewish learning. He kept open house for the learned rabbis of Lithuania and Poland, many of whom spent their summer vacations at Kranz, a spa close to Königsberg, where he had a large estate. My father called on the senior Marx one day when he was entertaining two rabbis, one of whom was the renowned Rabbi Eliezar Gordon of Telsh. Marx, in good German fashion, introduced my father as Professor and identified him as coming from New York. Rabbi Gordon was unimpressed and proceeded with his discussions with Marx, ignoring the newcomer who took himself off to the corner where he began to read. At one point the conversation between the rabbis and Marx faltered when Marx couldn't follow the rabbis' Yiddish, and they in turn had trouble with Marx's German. The discussion was concerned with an intricate matter involving supervision of the slaughtering trade. At this point my father offered his services as interpreter. Rabbi Gordon was amazed that a Professor from New York knew Yiddish so well and, in addition, appreciated the subtleties of the problem. When my father told him that he was his former pupil, Levi, the son of Rabbi Isaac from Neustadt, there was much rejoicing. Rabbi Gordon had not known that his gifted pupil had continued to pursue Hebrew studies.

On one summer trip, a missed train had pleasant consequences.

"In 1905, I was travelling from Strassburg to Munich. The train stopped at Ulm, which is famous primarily for its cathedral. At that time I was very fond of beer, so during the stopover, I went into the station and had a glass, and I had a second glass, and maybe a third. In any case, I didn't notice that my train had left. It wasn't very serious; it just involved telling the station master about my luggage. However, I had to spend the whole day in Ulm. It is a cathedral town of about forty thousand people with only one main street. The only thing to see was the cathedral which I had seen two or three times before, but I went again. I still had the whole day in front of me, so I went for a walk. When I passed a bookstore, I went in and asked the storekeeper whether he had any old books. He showed me several. One of them, a Latin textbook, struck my fancy. He asked eight marks for it, but after talking it over, he gave it to me for five. This is the rarest book I own. It is so rare that a professor at Oxford, finding four pages of manuscript, published them as a great discovery. These four pages were from my book. The book was published in 1518. It had been translated from the Greek, and originally had been translated from Hebrew. Apparently, all the Greek and Hebrew texts have been lost. The text was ascribed to Philo, but I think that is spurious. A professor from Yale who published a complete bibliography of Philo included this work, but said that there was no copy in the United States."

Truth demands that a sequel be added. At the end of the week of mourning following my father's death in 1953, we discovered that the book had disappeared. It is probable that someone who knew him well, and who knew the value of this book, walked off with it.

On one of these visits to England my father was a house-guest of a wealthy professor who had the reputation of being stingy. When my father came down to breakfast one day, his host asked him whether he would have one or two eggs. Without batting an eye, my father replied that he would have three.

Humor was his staff of life. "Once, before my marriage, I was on a boat; my deck chair bore my name, Dr. Louis Ginzberg. A couple who knew a mutual friend thought I was a physician. They asked me all kinds of questions, such as how to prevent sunburn. Many people on board knew me, and one day the woman who had asked all the questions

THE YOUNG PROFESSOR [101]

came over to me very excitedly. 'You're not a physician,' she
said. 'Of course not,' I said. 'Do you think I would have
given you all that advice for nothing if I were a physician?' "
    All that was humorous or exciting did not occur during
my father's travelling abroad. There was the episode at the
Jersey shore. "Sulzberger, the father of the prominent *New
York Times* publisher, was a great friend of mine. He invited
me to his home. But his youngsters made too much noise. So,
he said, 'I will take you to a hotel on Friday night.' At the
hotel, he registered me as Dr. Louis Ginzberg. At about 2:00
a. m. there was a knock on the door. I went to see what was
going on. The hotel clerk was there. He said, 'A young lady
has been taken ill with a stomach ache. Do you have any
objections to taking a look at her?' I said, 'By no means, I
have no objection. But the young lady might, since I am not
a physician.' "
    Many decades later, I ran into similar problems, except
that the range for misinterpretation was much greater. In
World War II, I served as logistical adviser to the Surgeon
General of the Army. I was the only one called "doctor"
among several hundred physicians, all of whom were in uniform. In the apartment house where I lived in Washington, I
was known as Dr. Ginzberg from the Surgeon General's
Office. When a young lady broke her leg one evening and
the telephone operator sought my help, it was very difficult
for me to clarify the fact that although I was called "doctor"
and although I worked in the Surgeon General's Office, I
could not help her.
    During his early years in the United States, my father had
occasion to make frequent trips to Philadelphia—as a result
of which he became a life-long Democrat. He used to remark
that if he had to choose between the Republicans, who
abused their power by permitting the rich Pennsylvania railroad to run through the streets of Philadelphia, and Tam-
many Hall, which took part of its spoils and distributed

them in the form of Christmas baskets to the poor, he saw a clear advantage in supporting the latter.

Actually, he was truly critical of the Republicans. But as usual, he could jest. He was fond of telling about a visit of a close relative of the Kaiser. The Prince was on a round-the-world tour when he found himself in Harrisburg, Pennsylvania. Since he had seen many of the wonders of the world, it was not easy for the Governor of Pennsylvania to interest him in the sights that the Capitol had to offer. But the Governor finally caught his attention when he stopped the carriage before a new state building and, calling the Prince's attention to a nondescript building, said, "More money was stolen in the erection of that building than of any other building in the world!"

But teaching, lecturing, and trips to Europe, even to Pennsylvania, were peripheral to my father's major efforts, which were to break new ground in the field of Jewish scholarship. This is what his long years of training had been directed towards; this is why the work on the *Encyclopedia* was a diversion; this is why he jumped at the Seminary offer with its promise of enabling him to conserve most of his time and energies for his scholarly investigations.

He had been at the Seminary only a year when he informed the Jewish Publication Society of his revised plans for the *Legends*. He announced that he was recasting his approach so that it could yield a larger catch, and asked therefore for a modification of the original terms, but without success. A letter dated October 20, 1903, from Miss Szold, Secretary of the Society, stated:

> . . . The Committee could not see its way clear to granting your request for a readjustment of terms. The Committee realizes the position in which you are placed and appreciates the fact that your labor will be greater than you had anticipated, and perhaps, under the circumstances, could have anticipated. On the other hand, the Society will be put to much greater expense in provid-

ing for the translation and publication of your book than it had planned.

Furthermore, the Committee wishes me to say that it hopes the completion of the book will not be too long delayed.

Four years later, Miss Szold wrote again, this time about a book of essays which my father had earlier discussed with Dr. Schechter.

The Committee is prepared to recommend the publication of this book to the Board of Trustees as soon as financial terms can be agreed upon, and I am authorized to offer you an honorarium of three hundred dollars ($300). Also, the Committee would be pleased to know when, approximately, the book will be ready for press.

And then, apparently, negotiations on the volume of essays ran into a snag. The author refused to have his manuscript reviewed. There is a glimpse of the conflict in a personal letter from Miss Szold, sent to my father when he was abroad in 1907:

"And after the meeting [of the Society], one of the gentlemen to whom your proposed book had been assigned—was it a year ago—? stopped to ask me how it had been that it had never reached him. He had been absent from the meeting at which the explanation had been forced from me that you refused to submit manuscripts to examination. When he was told the reason, he exclaimed with some vigor of manner and expression that your stand was entirely correct—you were not the man to subject yourself to such tests as were devised for the general."

For reasons that are not altogether clear, there was a delay of twenty-one years in the publication of the volume. Of the eleven essays that finally comprised the collection, only five were available in 1907. We know from that same letter of Miss Szold's that Dr. Schechter had reported that my father had planned to write "the Voloshin article" and add it to his book of essays and lectures. It was never written. I suspect the volume was delayed because other more important work pre-empted my father's time and energies.

In the seventh year of my father's connection with the Jewish Theological Seminary, he published four major works. This is how they are noted in the *Bibliography of the Writings of Professor Louis Ginzberg* by Boaz Cohen:

Geonica
> Vol. I. *The Geonim and the Halakhic Writings*
> Vol. II. *Genizah Studies*

Yerushalmi Fragments from the Genizah
> Vol. I. *Text with Various Readings for the Editio Princeps*

The Legends of the Jews
> Vol. I. *Bible Times and Characters from the Creation to Jacob.* Translated from the German Manuscript by Henrietta Szold.

The year 1909 was a turning point in still other ways. It was the year in which my father married.

CHAPTER VI

AN EXCEPTIONAL FRIENDSHIP

As I have reported, the first contact between my father and Henrietta Szold was in 1901 in a letter from Miss Szold which presented the terms under which the Jewish Publication Society would publish a volume dealing with Jewish legends. They met for the first time in 1903 in New York City, and for the last time in 1934 in Jerusalem. But their "exceptional friendship," as my father once called it, came to an end in the early fall of 1908, when on his return from Europe, my father stopped off at Miss Szold's home to tell her that he had become engaged.

Those who are interested in the details of what was clearly an exceptional friendship can look to the hundred and more pages which Miss Szold's recent biographer devotes to this subject. Relying on Miss Szold's notebooks, he describes the heights and depths of an unrequited love. It is a sad tale composed of strange elements: of the displacement of a daughter's love for a revered father long dead to a scholar in the same field with youth and genius; of the relations between a master of many ancient and modern tongues and his instructress in English; of a professor at a rabbinical school whose most devoted pupil is a woman; of a prolific author bursting with ideas being helped in a hundred little ways to prepare his manuscripts for press by a woman who finds her greatest joy in assisting him.

They met in the classroom; they met in the library; they met at Miss Szold's home where they shared many meals with her mother; they met frequently at friends' homes; they took long walks together on Riverside Drive; they wrote at length to each other when they were separated. An exceptional friendship indeed, since in 1903 the young professor was thirty and Miss Szold was forty-three. In the year of the dénouement, their ages were thirty-five and forty-eight.

As I have noted, one of the less pleasant manifestations of academic life is that many of the men and even more of their wives derive a great deal of pleasure from gossip, some idle and much malicious. When my father announced his engagement in 1908, the Seminary community and groups on its periphery had a *cause célèbre* on their hands. A remarkable woman had been jilted by a remarkable man. What juicier morsel could gossipy and jealous academicians ask for?

I have an unpleasant recollection of early in my own academic career when, because of incompatibility, I found it necessary to release from my research staff the wife of a colleague. I was the target of much malicious gossip which lasted for almost a year, until it spent itself against a wall of silence, which I had early recognized was the only possible defense.

My father was reticent about two episodes in his life; they were never discussed at home. The first was the fiasco with the Hebrew Union College; the second, his relationship with Miss Szold. I suspect that in the first case, he felt self-conscious about ever having accepted a call to an institution that was so clearly at variance with his beliefs and outlook. As far as Miss Szold was concerned, he indicated that she had broken off the relationship, and that under these circumstances a gentleman was under obligation to keep his lips sealed.

Unlike Miss Szold's biographer, who was concerned with the purely personal aspects of the relationship and with whether "he had done her wrong," my concern is more with extracting from this correspondence between a highly gifted woman in public life and a brilliant young scholar, new perspectives about their roles and reactions to the turbulent developments on the American Jewish scene during the first decade of this century.

But it would be coy for me to refuse to set forth my understanding of what transpired, especially since the existing picture based primarily on Miss Szold's diary is as unclear as it is poignant. The present account is able to draw on the extended correspondence that passed between them.

This is how the matter now appears to me. Miss Szold early fell in love with my father but, realizing the discrepancy in their ages, she was careful to keep tight rein on her emotions and aspirations. As the years of friendship lengthened and the ties of intimacy deepened, she found it increasingly difficult to control her emotions, but she succeeded nevertheless. From 1903 to 1907, the relationship remained in reasonable balance: it was a close working friendship as far as my father was concerned, and Miss Szold did not permit herself to admit more than that.

But in the spring of 1907 my father left to be at his father's side during his terminal illness. These were very hard weeks that stretched into months. In his anguish, he needed solace and broke through his own reserve. The letters between him and Miss Szold take on a deeper hue. No longer are they limited solely to manuscripts and galleys, current events, and pleasantries. They become introspective, personal, emotional.

My father begins to question everything that he is, that he stands for, that he aspires to. He suspects that his father is saddened and disappointed in him: he is a bachelor; he has absorbed the ways of the West; he has broken with tradition both in scholarship and in his personal life. He bares all this and more in his letters to Miss Szold and she does her best to steady and reassure him. And slowly, he regains his composure and his equilibrium. But at what a price for her. Her defenses are now down, and if my cousin with whom my father lived recollected correctly, so were his. My cousin recalls that there were family discussions in Amsterdam not only about whether my father should marry, but also about the implications of his marrying a woman much older than he. In later years, one of the few remarks that my father ever made on the subject was to the effect that he could never have contemplated marrying Miss Szold, for the simple reason that his pride would never have permitted him to marry a woman so much his senior; and that one reason for his ever marrying was his desire for children, a desire that could not have been fulfilled by Miss Szold.

The pieces begin to fall into place. Up to 1907, the relationship was controlled by both. In that fateful summer, my father's defenses broke and in turn Miss Szold's were demolished. When he returned to the United States, the relationship was re-established, but at a different level. It is likely that he felt mounting pressures to move one way or another in this relationship, and he came to understand, at least unconsciously, that time was running out. He would have to move or propinquity would force a decision.

This is how he explained what happened in reminiscing with his daughter-in-law. He began with some general observations about his bachelor friends:

"The best marriageable age for a man is between twenty-five and thirty-five. As he nears forty, he becomes one-sided and afraid. The longer he remains a bachelor, the more difficult the adjustment, and at forty a difference in ages becomes a real difficulty. When N. was twenty-five or thirty, he was not in a position to marry. He had a small income and many family responsibilities. When he did finally establish himself, he was close to fifty—and whom could he then marry? Not anyone near his age, and certainly not a youngster of twenty-five. This, more or less, also applies to L., who for a long time had to support his parents.

"There is also the question of associations. N. would have had to find someone who would fall in with his friends. For instance, I had a very queer collection of friends. A friend of mine, a Romanist who later committed suicide, insisted that his tea be made with two drops of tea and the rest water. Another friend insisted that rice be cooked a certain way. However, Adele [L. G.'s wife], who is very proud of her culinary prowess, took all of this very good-naturedly."

And then he moved from the general to the specific:

"In 1908, I went to Berlin in the summer, exactly one month before Rosh Hashanah. I stayed with an old friend [Wechsler] from Frankfurt, whose wife was a good friend of Adele. I used to go every year to Berlin, usually stopping with these people, but of course this was during everybody's vacation, and I never met Adele until 1908. Wechsler's wife must have talked to Adele about me—about the professor from New York. In the synagogue, of course, the women were sitting in the gallery and we were sitting below. Wechsler's wife pointed me out to Adele and I, of course, always had good eyesight. That afternoon, she came for a visit. Later all of us went to a garden café—the Wechslers, Adele and I, and an old admirer of Adele, Elbogen, who was then a professor at the Hochschule. I took her home from the café.

"The next day, Sunday, Adele came to the Wechslers. They suggested that she go buy cold-cuts and I accompanied her. Sunday night I told her that I would write to her, and the next day I left Berlin. I went to Amsterdam to visit my mother and stayed with her over Rosh Hashanah.

During this time I began writing to Adele. She couldn't read my handwriting so she showed my first two letters to an uncle. From then on, however, she had to decipher them herself.

"After I had been away from her about two weeks, I asked her to marry me and she accepted. The day after Rosh Hashanah I returned to Berlin to meet her family. In the meantime, she had written to an uncle in Paris to find out about my family. It so happened that the brother-in-law of this uncle was an intimate friend of my father and he apparently gave a good report.

"When I returned to Berlin, even though we were engaged, her family didn't let her meet me at the train alone; so her brother came with her. Nevertheless, I kissed her for the first time at the station. I stayed for a week, met her parents, and then came home to New York. From here, I wrote her every day until we were married.

"As soon as I left Berlin, Adele and her stepmother went to a small place called Flinsberg. There are two such places in Germany—one in Bavaria and one in Silesia, but I didn't identify the right one and she did not get my first few letters. Of course, they believed they had seen the last of me.

"One reason that I was able to make such a quick decision was that Adele was very fond of children. She acted very motherly with the two children of the Wechslers. I had always been very fond of children. Even when I was a student, many young children liked me. Once this almost got me into trouble. In Strassburg, I was sitting in the park when a little girl about six or seven, named Gretchen, saw me, ran to me, hugged me and sat down. We talked for a while, and then along came a very enraged man. Apparently she had run off from her father. . . .

"However, it's difficult to tell why a man at a certain age makes a certain decision. It very likely was gland trouble."

In these reminiscences which he related to his daughter-in-law, my father included a few additional observations.

"At important moments in my life, I have always decided quickly. One reason for my quick marriage might have been my awareness that my mother was very unhappy that I wasn't married. My father had died the year before, and he had been very anxious for me to marry.

"Partly, it was a question of vanity. I felt that I was a great judge of people, and actually I have hardly ever been deceived after meeting a person once or twice. I don't believe that I have ever changed my mind.

"After I had made this decision based on emotion, I rationalized it. Had it been a purely intellectual decision, there were many reasons against it. I could have worried about Adele's adjustment to a strange country whose language she didn't know; I could have concerned myself with the fact that she came from a strictly Orthodox family and would be unhappy with my liberalism. However, this was not an intellectual matter. Up until then, marriage had been intellectualized for me. There had always been reasons for not marrying—one girl, I felt, was so attractive that she wouldn't be able to understand my work; another girl was not attractive enough, etc."

My mother was a striking beauty—and she was young, just twenty-two. Only an immature student of psychology or a great novelist should seek to explain why a man chooses the girl he marries. But I cannot shake off the impression that my father left the United States in 1908 in a highly receptive mood. His relations with Miss Szold had reached a point where he was under increasing pressures to act.

My father's later reticence about the relationship to Miss Szold was undoubtedly reinforced by the treatment meted out to my mother upon her arrival in New York after their marriage in London in May, 1909. These were painful months for a young bride in a strange country. My mother recalls that if perchance, she should call on a mutual friend when Miss Szold was present, she was usually whisked away into a side room. And fifty-five years after the event she can recall the discomfort that she felt at a Seminary dinner on the occasion of Dr. Schechter's departure for a sabbatical year abroad, when the Ginzbergs were inadvertently seated near Miss Szold. The young bride had further reasons for remembering that dinner. Mr. Schiff let it be known that he was interested in meeting Professor Ginzberg's most attractive young wife. And Professor Ginzberg let it be known that if Mr. Schiff wanted to meet her, all he had to do was to come over and be introduced!

To end this part of the tale, no communication other than a few formal letters from the Secretary of the Jewish Publication Society to an author passed between Henrietta Szold and Louis Ginzberg after she broke off the relationship early in 1909.

But at a reception at the home of the High Commissioner in Jerusalem in 1933 in honor of the Hebrew University Survey Committee, of which my father was one of three members, my mother saw Miss Szold, with whom she had become acquainted, and half dragged my father across the room insisting that he greet her.

A decade later, I brought to my parents' home for the Passover *seder* a young lady whom I introduced to my father as Ruth Szold. He said, "Oh yes, I once knew a Szold, a very nice man from Peoria, Illinois; as I recall, he was something of a scholar."

When the young Miss Szold's parents and family friends became aware that her acquaintanceship with a young man by the name of Ginzberg was more than superficial, they were quick to tell her about the sad history of her illustrious cousin, and warned her to be on guard. But all the humor is not on the Ginzberg's side. Ruth insists that she married me to right the record. No longer would it be correct to say that a Szold had been jilted by a Ginzberg.

Regrettably, Miss Henrietta died some twelve months before our marriage. She may have heard rumors of the prospective event, but probably she did not. Nevertheless, the
record is now formally closed; our only son is named Jeremy
Szold Ginzberg.

To return to the heart of our story. It is uncertain how
many letters passed between the principals, but it was believed in my home that after the rift in the friendship, my
father disposed of all of Miss Szold's letters. However, we
now know that he didn't. We found in New York and
Jerusalem most if not all of the correspondence between the
principals of this exceptional friendship from its beginnings
in 1903 to its abrupt ending in 1908. There is a great deal
in these letters that gives us some insights into the personalities of Henrietta Szold and Louis Ginzberg; they also
contain their critical appraisals of men and events on the
Jewish scene in the United States and abroad.

The mood of the early correspondence is reflected in the
following letter written by my father in July 1905: "My dear
Miss Szold: - You will undoubtedly be very much surprised
to receive my first letter from Paris. But you know the saying: 'bad company spoils good manners,' and having had for
ten days exclusively the company of women—the men did
nothing but gamble all the time—I acquired some weaknesses of the fair sex, among others the custom of changing
the mind. When we were near Cherbourg it suddenly occurred to me that it would not be a bad idea to visit Paris,
and so I am again in '*la ville lumière*.'

"The weather and the sea were splendid all the time of my
voyage. I spent all my time in sleeping, walking and dreaming. I believe that I might have entered in a sleeping match
with Miss Adele [Miss Szold's sister] without great risk of
losing it. As to my dreams in the state of waking, they were
not of a very pleasant mind. The grandeur and monotony of

the sea has always a melancholy-producing effect on me, and it is very good for me to be in the gay city of Paris again. I have met here Mrs. Friedenwald and her children who asked to be remembered to you.

"With kind regards to you, Mrs. Szold and Miss Adele, I am - Your - Louis Ginzberg."

A month later in a much longer letter from Amsterdam, my father animadverted to news contained in one of Miss Szold's notes to him:

"If I were rude I would have said what a pity that Dropsie did not die a few years earlier, but as I am too gentle to make such remarks, I will deplore only the fact that his will was not known four years ago. We would have had a Jewish Academy instead of a Theological Seminary. But *'das geschehene lässt sich nicht mehr ungesteben machen.'* Let us hope that the Seminary will benefit by it not only pecuniarily, but also spiritually." Apparently his restiveness about an institution dedicated to theological training was of long standing! At the end of this long letter, Louis Ginzberg writes in a more personal vein: "My mother sends her regards to you *'unbekanntweise'* and my father also said that if it were not against the talmudic law . . . he would like to send his regards to you. As for myself, I only hope that you will punish me for my long letter by writing a much longer one to your Louis Ginzberg."

A month later my father, commenting on a play that Miss Szold had recommended he read, remarked: "I believe that a woman can't master more than one strong feeling at once. When in love, nothing but the object of her love exists for her, while the man is strong enough to love a woman and have other passions at the same time." In this same letter he tells Miss Szold that he has a surprise for her. He has been reading Labriola, Kautsky, and Bernstein: "I consider it needless to say that I am still opposed to the socialistic interpretation of history. I am still the old aristocrat who can't and will not believe that Caesar, Alexander the Great, Napoleon, etc., did not make history, but that it was the headless, heartless, mindless vulgus who produced civilization."

The following summer, 1906, was an exception: Louis Ginzberg did not go abroad but vacationed in Tannersville, New York, in the company of many friends, including Drs. Schechter, Marx, Benderly, Magnes, and Malter. In August, my father writes to Miss Szold: "For the last week I tried to become a pupil of the Hindus, i.e., to worship 'the great nothing' . . . and I succeeded. . . . But when I happen to look at the well-fed and well-dressed Jewesses strutting on the porch, I cannot help asking with the prophet Ezekiel . . . Is there any hope for Israel if its representative elements are so degenerated?" And in a more personal vein: "And how are you? Do you take your daily walk on Riverside Drive? Many a time I thought of our walks which I would prefer to those in the mountains."

Letters follow at about weekly intervals. In one my father thanks Miss Szold for her comments about a letter of his about ritual slaughtering which appeared in *The Nation*, and gallantly explains that it was well received not because of "what *I* said . . . but the form in which *you* expressed it." Apparently the Yiddish press entered the fray by reprinting the correspondence that appeared in *The Nation*, a journalistic effort that "disgusted" him. But he is more deeply concerned with a visitor recently arrived from St. Petersburg: "This concrete illustration of the misery of the Jews in Russia made me so miserable that for days I could not think about any other thing than the Jewish situation in Russia." More than a half century and a revolution later, the same depression would follow upon hearing a recital of the woes of the Jews of Russia!

In April of 1907, we find a curt note from L. G. to H. S. which is difficult to interpret. One possible explanation is that L. G., deeply disturbed by his knowledge that his father was gravely ill, could not cope with any additional pressure.

"Dear Miss Szold: - Your desire to get the third volume done can not be greater than mine, yet I regret to say that I hardly believe I will succeed in getting it finished. For reasons which I do not care to explain to you, I must leave for Europe not later than May twelfth and I do not see how I shall manage to complete the work in such a short time. Of course, I am willing to read the proof and pass on it during my stay in Europe. My address will be 24 Swammerdam Street, Amsterdam. If you would ask my advice, I would advise you to stop working on my book *immediately*. You certainly have no obligation in this matter either to the J. P. Society or to me. - Very truly yours, Louis Ginzberg."

My father advanced his contemplated schedule; his first letter from Europe to Miss Szold is dated May 9th. It is filled with forebodings about his father's health, but contains references to his own work and to the American scene. "What are the new developments in Cincinnati? If you find something in the Jewish press of America which you think may interest me, please send me it. My interest in American affairs increases in inverse ratio to the distance in which I find myself from the country. The farther away from it the more American am I."

The following week, he informs her that he has been to Leiden to consult his father's physician and that he was told to be prepared for the worst. He remarks that "you can imagine how much I suffer, mentally and physically, to see others suffer" (his father was dying from cancer of the throat). But he is still able to deal with other matters. "I was reading lately my *Legends* and it strikes me as if we had too many references to the Bible in the text. I am of the opinion that the knowledge of the Bible, i.e., the narration part of it, must be taken for granted. Don't you think I am right?—I have received a letter from Judge Sulzberger complimenting me on my lecture on the Primary School, but

adding that he wished I would have gone to Hillel's School
and learned a little patience. He objects strongly to page ten
concerning the mission of Israel. He does not know that if
not for this, I should not write a line in the popular manner.
I think that it is not too egoistic if the writer tries to enjoy a
few lines in his writings."

To this Miss Szold replied:

Judge Sulzberger spoke to me also about your little ironies and
I disagreed and disagree with him wholly. Not only has an author
the right to enjoy a few lines of his own productions, as you put
it, but those are the very lines that make the material most
eagerly studied by posterity. Is it not true that even the dry-as-
dust scholar dealing in the past is pleased beyond the ordinary
when, amid his antiquarian finds, there is one specially well preserved by reason of its Attic salt—its *Lebensanchaung* and *Le-
bensweisheit?* Judge Sulzberger promises significantly that 'you
will get older,' but if his weakness in this particular is the weakness of age, stay young. In fact, stay young anyhow.

In a long letter in early June, L. G. advises Miss Szold, who
was having her own difficulties with the Jewish Publication
Society, "to have your work and duties carefully defined and
if the J. P. S. expects you to be a *maedchen für alles*—secretary, translator, author and collector of statistics—then let
them look for somebody else." And later, in the same letter,
he comments on her apologizing for bothering him with her
problems at a time like this. "This hurt me very much . . . Is
our mutual friendship of the kind that I am to pour out to
you my heart while you are to keep anything important from
me?"

The very next day, he sends off another long letter in
which he tells about the gradual change for the worse in his
father, but adds that when his pain permits, he continues to
study and in fact "called my attention to some facts which
have escaped me concerning the Fragments." The Zionist
Congress was to be held at the Hague, but my father cannot

attend although he inquires about his several friends and whether he can make arrangements for them. In passing, he remarks that "Zionism is dead here! Holland Jewry produces now only *Kosher Käse* and *Yomtov Chokolade*."

The greater part of a month passes before L. G. writes again. This time his letter contains some reflections about scholars who write in a popular vein:

"Let me tell you that neither you nor Judge Sulzberger knows properly what popular is; indeed no intellectual can know what popular is. If you or Judge Sulzberger read something about a matter, the details of which are not known to you, and the representation helps you to understand this matter without studying the details, then you call it popular. I understand by popular to make the populous *feel*—a gift which Dr. Schechter possesses, but which I entirely lack. I reason lucidly and therefore can explain some difficult matter to those who know how to reason, but entirely fail to make people feel. As a member of the J. P. S., I strongly oppose the issue of my essays, which will certainly be a failure, but as the publication committee might make still a worse choice, I will not make known my protest to the public."

The correspondence remains heavy, containing an admixture of family news, manuscript discussions, and gossip. In one letter L. G. remarks that his father was impressed with Miss Szold's learning through her reliance on the legal evasion which permitted her to send greetings to him; and he in turn, making use of the same device, reciprocates.

In one of her letters, Miss Szold reported on the public altercation between Rabbi Silverman and Rabbi Magnes, respectively the anti-Zionist and the pro-Zionist rabbis of Temple Emanu-El, at the time the Hebrew Union College was being torn asunder by the forced resignation of the pro-Zionist members of the faculty. Magnes had informed the congregation about the "deposed professors" and when he

sat down, Dr. Silverman arose to say that this was his colleague's "personal interpretation." The congregation was in a
turmoil. A board meeting was hastily summoned. Silverman
just missed being suspended, and he was officially rebuked.

Many years later, my father ran into Mr. Louis Marshall,
at that time president of Temple Emanu-El. The morning
newspapers had carried the story of Rabbi Silverman's retirement and the liberal terms of his pension. Although my
father had read the article, he deliberately refrained from
commenting on it, knowing that Marshall would bring it up.
When he finally did, he asked my father whether he did not
find the action of the Board highly commendable, since no
other rabbi had ever received such a liberal pension. My
father indicated that he was not impressed, and Marshall
became increasingly vexed with him. Finally, my father
offered the following explanation: "If Rabbi Silverman received $20,000 a year when he preached, he is surely en-
titled to more, not less, if the congregation is henceforth to
be spared his sermons!"

There was considerable discussion in the correspondence
about the best way for L. G. to handle the publication of the
Yerushalmi Fragments From the Genizah. L. G. was uncertain whether he should publish his emendations with or
without a long introduction. Many years later my father told
his biographer, Druck, that when Dr. Schechter first showed
him a few of these fragments from the Genizah and asked
whether they had any value, he had replied that they would
have value when *he* had added his notes and commentary!
Here is the passage from one of Miss Szold's letters: "You are
not in the least wanting in modesty if you maintain that the
value of the fragments' publication will reside in your commentary. I go further and hold that the text may not even
appear without the notes, and that you must not make the
final plan for them when your condition is not normal."

The *Yerushalmi Fragments* were eventually published in

1909 without extended notes or commentary. But Professor Lieberman has told me that this work is of the greatest importance for the study of the Jerusalem Talmud, since it represents a major step towards the reconstruction of the original text. He also told me that my father deeply resented the fact that in the Rome edition of the text, published in Vilna shortly after World War I, full use was made of his emendations without a single acknowledgment.

The last comment suggests the compartmentalization of my father's life and of our relationship; I had never heard him complain about this plagiarism!

In another letter written in July 1907, Miss Szold writes about the idea of a "Jewish University" in the United States propounded by Dr. Adler in a Commencement Address at the Jewish Theological Seminary. Her opinion is "Tommyrot: I maintain that what he said and the way in which he put it was silly verbiage." The same letter contains the following:

"I wonder when I am going to be permitted to help ever so little with that projected Yerushalmi Introduction? You do not say whether it is to be in English. I think it a fine plan, because it will be work worthy of your critical powers and your scholarship. You remember how much pleasure you derived last summer from your "Appendicitis" article (what has become of it, by the way?) and how little you derive from the Fragment work. But beside your own pleasure, there will be the real contribution you will be making to Jewish science. I hope you will continue to nurse and cherish the project and carry it out at an early opportune time."

And shortly thereafter she presented her case again. "I won't understand? Oh yes, I will, if you will have the patience and desire to explain to me. I *will* to understand."

With the death of his father towards the end of July, he wrote:

"The sad news of my father's death will have reached you

before this letter leaves Europe, and I only want to assure
you that I bear up well. Father lived the life of a saint and
died the death of a martyr. His suffering was such that death
came to him as a deliverance from evil. And have I any right
to think of what I have lost?

"Tomorrow the funeral will take place and I'll not be able
to write to you for a week."

When he is able to write again his letters are full of
anguish: "I do not mourn. But suffer indescribably. My father was the embodiment of all the noble and great Rabbinical Judaism has produced and his death takes away from me
the concreteness of my 'Weltanschaung.' You see how selfish
my mourning is! Do you remember our frequent conversations about my relation to my father as a typical case for the
relation between old and young Israel? Now I never realized
the depth of the chasm as I did in the last three months. . . ."

But distressed as he was, he understood that he was placing a burden on Miss Henrietta: "I feel that my sad fate has
awakened in you the old never forgotten grief over the loss
of your father. As you said, our cases are so alike that at this
moment, I feel your loss and I do not doubt that this is the
same for you. Now I am asking myself is it right for me to
cause you such pain and open old wounds. But what can I
do?"

A few days later, in a letter from Berlin, he shows the
depths of his despair: "But I cannot help thinking that my
presence partly increased the mental suffering of my father.
My father was a great admirer of mine, not in that usual
foolish way of parents but in that of a 'connoisseur,' so that
he never allowed me to perform the smallest service for him
because it is against the (law) to be served upon by a great
scholar. And yet how many a time did he suppress a sigh
that this his son did not become a gaon as he could, but a
scholar! In this summer, he also realized more and more that
I am not 'frumm.' I do not need to assure you that I did my

best to avoid anything which might have offended his religious conscience, but you do not know how difficult it was. Here is an instance. We walked once on a Saturday and suddenly we were over the limit of the *Erub*. My father never carried anything with him on the Sabbath, not even when there was an *Erub*, and he told me that I would have to throw everything which I had with me away, so I did. But unfortunately, I had some money with me—about 20 guilder—by a mistake, as I ordinarily take out the money from my pockets before the Sabbath. I told father this, but it pained him greatly that I could carry money on the Sabbath. As I spent most of my time in observing him, I had time and opportunity to observe the effect of my presence upon him, and I doubt whether my presence was beneficial to him. I cannot say more."

Several weeks later, the dark mood is a little lifted; he turns at last to deal in passing with literary matters. He mentions that a nerve specialist recommended that he go to a sanatorium, but he adds: ". . . what will become of my poor mother? She is very weak though she bears her affliction bravely and it is my duty to be with her."

To lighten his spirits, Miss Szold sent her friend news about sundry matters including the death of the *Jewish Quarterly Review* in England, to which Louis Ginzberg had been a key contributor.

"And do you know that you gave the death blow to the *Jewish Quarterly Review*? At all events it is not to appear after the July number. They simply couldn't get along without those Genizah Fragments of yours and when they were not forthcoming, due to your stubborn—I mean firmness, the *Quarterly* had to die of inanition. Isn't this the psychologic moment for the American 'coterie of scholars' to start a Jewish scientific publication?"

She also reported on an anti-Zionist speech made by Mr. Schiff: "By the way, with regard to Mr. Schiff's address, I am in a hopeless minority—I form a party all by myself—the papers are jubilating over its pronouncements and especially over its outspoken anti-Zionism and its equally outspoken Americanism. Several of them wonder how anyone can dare remain a Zionist since the great and only Mr. Schiff has spoken his 'ipse dixit.' I am keeping the clippings for you until you come back. I count it will be in seven weeks—and I hope you at least will join my party."

L. G. responded at length, if bitterly, to this news about Mr. Schiff's speeches:

". . . a great financier and in his capacity as such he knows that in giving money for an object you acquire it, and as he spends large sums of money for Jewish institutions, he believes himself the rightful owner of American Jewry. One would laugh at the stupidity he shows were it not for the grave consequences of his stupidity. It is the tragedy of a small class or religious congregation that the influential individual may cause so much harm. Mr. Rockefeller, the richest man in the world, is of very little importance in the Baptist Church, indeed some of the members of this church even refuse his money, but Mr. Schiff is the greatest power in American Jewry. The reason is the smallness and poverty of the Jews."

Miss Szold was finally affected by the pessimism that for a much longer period had become a part of Louis Ginzberg's assessment of the American Jewish scene. She wrote: "You remember that I used to plague you about your attitude toward the Seminary, the students there, and the work it is supposed to stand for? I think you will admit that I let up on the subject somewhat during the last year and more. I promise you now that I will not bother you any more. I understand better now. It is hopeless—the whole business has no validity, no viability—no spring, no compelling force. Add to this inanition from internal causes, the real pressure of economic circumstances which make Sabbath observance an

utter and absolute impossibility, and what have you? Do you
remember the Galician canvasser who offered his services to
me for the Directory? Some time ago he presented himself to
bid me good-bye. After four years of struggle with American
conditions in the effort to live as a Jew, he was returning
home. He could not make up his mind to bring his children
to this country."

As that disturbed summer drew to a close and as Louis
Ginzberg began to regain his composure, he wrote to Miss
Szold from Amsterdam: "I know my poor father did not die
peacefully on account of my becoming a scholar instead of a
gaon and on account of my bachelorship, and I can assure
you that I do not regret that I did not become a Polish gaon,
and I only mention those facts to you to show you how much
our individual happiness has to do with our relation to Judaism."

After his return home, the friends saw one another almost
daily during the winter and spring of 1908. The next July,
my father went to Copenhagen to attend a Congress of
Orientalists and later to Amsterdam to visit his mother. In a
short initial report on the Congress, he wrote that Professor
Paul Haupt had sought to convince the Congress of the
Aryan background of Jesus, and L. G. entered the fray, although he was "not interested in the least, it is a topic for
theologians and anti-Semites!" However, he sought to demolish Haupt's evidence about the people who lived in the
Galilee. L. G. tells Miss Szold that after he had spoken, "Dr.
Yahuda, an Oriental edition of Haupt, a mixture of humbug
and arrogance, attacked Haupt in a very ungentlemanly
manner. . . ."

Miss Szold, in her reply, wrote: "I am glad that you took
part in the Haupt debate, particularly glad that your malicious emotional opening was followed by a scholarly criticism and most glad of all that you mean to pursue the matter
further. As for Yahuda, you know he is claimed as a particular friend by your friend Dr. Rosenau, who also claims

Haupt in friendship—isn't that a fine triangular collection. I have been wondering whether Dr. Rosenau was a witness of the mêlée."

Two decades later, when I entered Heidelberg for what was my sophomore year in college, my father wrote to Yahuda to ask him to keep an eye on me and to solicit his help in awakening an interest in me in matters Jewish. Yahuda was then living in Heidelberg pursuing the life of an independent scholar. He had no formal connections with the University. My recollection is that he was a man of independent means and had an interesting circle of friends. I also recollect that he was put out with my father, whom he held at least partially responsible for blocking his appointment to the recently established Hebrew University in Jerusalem. I do not know whether this was justified or not, but of one thing I am certain. My father never lost his original skepticism of Yahuda's finding all sorts of Egyptian influences in the Bible; he particularly disapproved of his tracing the most basic elements in Jewish thought and ceremonials to the land of the Pharaohs. My father's attitude was certainly not so rigid that he denied all Egyptian influence. It was Yahuda's extremism that disturbed him. In his article on Rosenau, my father called attention to the fact that the authors of the Talmud, in their critical study of the ancient texts, did not hesitate to declare that the first word of the Decalogue, *Anoki*, was of Egyptian origin.

Paradox of paradoxes, Yahuda did succeed in breaking through my resistances—and they were formidable at that time—and I did begin to take a more sympathetic view towards the problems of the Jews in general and of Jewish scholarship in particular. He was the first of several individuals who helped me to see my father not as an anachronism on the American scene, one concerned with books that only a minority could read and an even smaller minority could understand, but a major figure in Hebrew and world scholarship.

I suspect that my father must have been deeply concerned about my relation to Judaism to have sought Yahuda's aid, and in time, he must have been grateful to him, as I was. On my return to the States in the fall of 1929, I had passed through the crisis of my late adolescence and at least these problems were eased.

The correspondence between my father and Miss Henrietta in the summer of 1908 is different from that of the preceding summer. L. G.'s letters are fewer; they are less personal; and there are long periods during which he does not write. In time, Miss Szold herself stops writing, and L. G. comments as follows: "I see by your letter of Sept. 1, that for two weeks and a half you exercised self-repression. Of course, I do not deny that self-repression is a virtue, but I fail to comprehend why I should be the victim of your virtues. I feel like picking a quarrel with you about it, but I know that one needs two for a quarrel and it would be a waste of time to try to get you to be a party to a quarrel. As I hate to complain, I cannot even complain to you for having robbed me of the pleasure your letters give me and there is nothing left to me but to ask you to exercise self-restraint in some other way or on somebody else."

The last personal letter that L. G. wrote to H. S. is dated September 20, 1908, and it was sent from Amsterdam. It contains much material. There is a reference to Schechter, prompted by an earlier comment of Miss Szold. L. G. writes that "it is too late for him to reform or rather he does not want at all to reform. With him it is a matter of a tactical measure when he despairs of *his* Seminary and *his* Jewry. He was at first naive enough to believe that a handful of bright lawyers and successful financiers are sufficient to create a renaissance of Judaism, and when they fail then he is in despair. *Great* changes are created by *great* minds with the help of *great* masses."

There is a brief recital of a contretemps with Elkan Adler, who proffered the opinion that certain Yerushalmi fragments

are a forgery, to which L. G. remarked that before discussing the new materials, he would like to engage Dr. Adler in
some problems concerning the old Yerushalmi! There is a
report of a caustic interchange with a distinguished namesake who changed his religion and who had the bad judgment to challenge L. G. on changing a letter in his name.
My father often remarked that a gentleman does not change
his name, his religion, or his bank. And he also stressed that
he "liked his theology and his liquor straight."

But in the heart of the letter, L. G. apologizes for hiding
from Miss Szold after his return to the United States his
"never-ceasing bleeding which I suffered for the last thirteen
months." He tells her, however, that he has passed through
the crisis and is "gradually becoming normal."

This long letter crossed a short one from Miss Szold which
conveyed New Year's greetings: "This note has the one purpose of wishing you happiness in the coming year—the happiness that springs from peace of mind and heart, from
successful achievement in your chosen field, and from the
happiness of all dear to you, and if you have any wishes
beyond this, fulfillment of them, too."

We know that her wishes for her friend were in the process of being fulfilled, and in this fulfillment her own secret
hopes and aspirations were shattered. Only by calling on all
of her great resources and through the support of her large
family and many friends, was she able to survive the disappointment engendered by my father's engagement. Once she
had absorbed her disappointment, she was able to function
at a new and higher level of service to her people.

There is no point at this late date in seeking to weigh the
rights and wrongs in this exceptional friendship, and I would
certainly not presume to do so. But a few general observations can be ventured. My father profited greatly from this
friendship. He had years of rich companionship, and he had
years of dedicated assistance. Miss Henrietta was never able

to enter the inner domains of his work, but since he worked in so many different fields and at varying levels of depth, there can be no question that she helped him substantially— as translator, as instructor in English, as editor, as critic, and in many other ways. No wonder that he desired the relationship to continue and in his naivete, he saw no reason why his engagement and marriage should bring it to an end. Certainly he knew that, as in all true friendships, there was a mutuality. He did a great deal to educate Miss Szold in the inner ways of Jewish thought and life that her Baltimore upbringing, even under the solicitous care of her beloved father, had failed to reveal to her.

When the Szold story was no longer taboo, it became a joke in our family to say that Louis Ginzberg was the father of Hadassah. And so he was. Not only in the sense that Miss Henrietta's disappointment in love propelled her to find new meaning and direction for her life, in the service of her people, not in the land of her sorrow, but in the Promised Land. But my father undoubtedly deepened her perceptions and understanding of the essential role of Zion in the long span of Jewish history.

For a brief time it looked as if Louis Ginzberg's hope and expectation that his engagement and marriage would not affect their friendship would be fulfilled. Here is the letter that Miss Szold wrote to Professor Ginzberg's fiancée on hearing the news of his engagement:

Dear Fraulein Katzenstein,

Dr. Ginzberg was just here and shared with me the joyful secret that he has indeed found the woman who will bring light and beauty to his life. He told me so many things I wanted to know about his future wife and companion. He showed me your picture, the intellectual as well as the bodily likeness and thus he convinced even me that you will make my dear friend happy. On the other hand you are the last person I need to tell what a fortunate women you are to have won the love of such an extraordinary man. I have been in almost daily contact with him for five years and I know every fibre of his being for true and upright. A gift of God indeed is his clear, penetrating and richly stocked mind. For you, life at his side will be a sacred and beautiful feast.

And when you come to follow him to America in a short time then you must promise to become my friend even as your fiance has been up to now.

Bear with the strange language if I have expressed myself clumsily; it comes from the heart.

There is no satisfactory way to end this brief account of what was in truth an exceptional friendship. But there is a brief note from my father to Miss Szold, dated February 21, 1909, that says a great deal in a very few words.

Dear Miss Szold,

I have finished my preface to *Geonica*, and I would like to ask you whether you have any objection to my reference to your kind assistance, without which the book would never have been published in English. I do not think I have any right not to mention it; on the other hand, I have no right to mention your name in connection with the book without asking your permission.

Very truly yours,
Louis Ginzberg

And the reader can find the answer in the Preface to this book—Miss Szold is not mentioned!

CHAPTER VII

IN THE HALLS OF ACADEME

IN A LETTER written by Louis Ginzberg in May 1937 to the
Chairman of the Board of the Jewish Theological Seminary, Sol M. Stroock, the following sentence can be found:
"I think it is high time for the leaders of American Israel to
abandon the dogma of the disqualification of Jewish scholars
for practical problems." In talking with his biographer,
David Druck, my father satirized the widespread misconcep-
tions about the essential qualities of the rabbis of old. He
felt that the assumption that the great leaders of the Sura
and Pumbedita academies in Babylonia or the great rabbinic leaders of Spanish, French, and German Jewry during
the centuries of their high productivity were dry book-
worms devoting themselves to minute problems of textual
criticism was far from the truth. The great rabbis were not
scribes, but true leaders deeply immersed in the problems
of their day, making use of the law and tradition to find
answers to pressing problems: how to order the relations
between the Jews and their hostile neighbors so as to protect the integrity of Judaism and still preserve the life of
the individual Jew from the fanaticism of these neighbors.

My father, who considered Spinoza the greatest philosopher that the Jews had produced, nevertheless defended his excommunication as a *force majeure*. The Jews had only recently been accepted by the Dutch. If the Jewish community had been unwilling to discipline a man whose public views were clearly at variance with the religious beliefs of Judaism and Christianity, this tolerance might have been withdrawn. If it had been, the lives and fortunes of thousands of Jews would again have been in jeopardy.

The great rabbis were concerned with many other practical problems: the raising of taxes and the spending of public revenues, resolving conflicts concerning persons and property, the education of the community, and care of the poor. All this and much more occupied them.

This background makes it easier to appreciate the sense of frustration and annoyance that broke through in Louis Ginzberg's letter to Mr. Stroock. While the American environment made it very difficult indeed for a man such as my father to play a leadership role, he nevertheless found some opportunities during his long life to exert his influence in the realm of policy, particularly in the realm of Jewish scholarship.

The first and probably most important arena was the institution with which he was associated for more than fifty-one years, the Jewish Theological Seminary of America. Reference was made earlier to his role in helping to recruit Friedlaender and Davidson. In a letter written in the year of his death to Dr. Leo Honor, we find evidence of another early effort:

"I deeply appreciate your kindness in forwarding to me your study on 'Jewish Elementary Education in the United States.' It is true I am not an educator, but nonetheless, my interest in Jewish matters is of a catholic nature. You may even be interested to know that at the very beginning of the reorganization of the Seminary, I submitted a lengthy memo to Dr. Schechter on the necessity of establishing a school for training teachers. Of course, I knew very little about conditions in New York, but with the help of my late friend, Dr. Abraham Freidus, I managed to get some materials together which must have impressed Dr. Schechter and the Board of Trustees of the Seminary."

This last sentence suggests that his suggested plan was important in encouraging the Seminary to start its teacher training program which has run parallel to the Rabbinical School throughout all these years.

The comment that he was "not an educator" brings to mind the story told by Professor Isaac Kandel, an old friend of my father and myself, who for many years was a leading member of the faculty of Teachers College, Columbia University. Kandel, who had been trained in England, was invited by Harold Laski to address his seminar. Laski introduced Kandel as a "distinguished educationalist," and added that he himself was an educator!

The influence that a man has in an educational institution depends on his relations with the administration and with his colleagues. When my father became engaged in 1908, he told his fiancée that Schechter had told him that he would be his successor. As I reconstruct it, by the time Schechter died in 1915, this was no longer a possibility. In a letter written in May, 1916, Louis Marshall asked my father's recommendations "as to the person or persons who in [his] opinion are best fitted to take up the office." Through this mimeographed communication the Special Committee of the Board sought the advice of both the faculty and the alumni. I have no knowledge of the advice that it received, but a few deductions can be safely ventured. Schechter had not communicated his desire about his successor to the key members of the Board either because he had changed his mind or because he had not found an appropriate opportunity. The Board would surely have given the most serious attention to a clearly indicated preference. Nor did the senior members of the faculty forward to the Board the name of a candidate, or, as far as we know, did the alumni. In any case, we do know that the Board asked Dr. Cyrus Adler of Philadelphia to be the Acting President. According to my mother's recollections, my father no longer expected to be Schechter's successor when the issue came up after Schechter's death late in 1915.

It is not a secret that the faculty found it incongruous not to have Solomon Schechter succeeded by a distinguished scholar. Schechter had been a man of genius, a man of true intellect and great heart. Yet the Board appointed as his successor a man whose skills were administrative and whose influence and power derived from the fact that he had served as the principal adviser on Jewish affairs to the banker-leaders of the Jewish community.

In 1916, it was not yet the practice for large universities to select as presidents men who were undistinguished in scholarship. And my father was disturbed that the Seminary, which had the opportunity and responsibility to play a leadership role in American Jewish life, suddenly had at its helm a man incapable of providing such leadership.

He also found the trustees' decision bitter because he suspected that it reflected their desire to limit their commitments. The new head was a "safe" choice, both from the viewpoint of finances and from a theological point of view. Since Schechter had not succeeded in assuming leadership over Russian immigrants and in building a bridge between their European Orthodoxy and the modernization which their children in America required, there was little prospect that anybody else could succeed. In Adler, the trustees could expect to have a sound executive, one who would not be likely to cause them trouble.

The state of the Seminary and the attitudes of the trustees

is clearly delineated in an exchange of correspondence several months before Dr. Schechter's death. My father had proposed to Mr. Marshall that Dr. Schechter's seventieth birthday in 1916 be celebrated by the publication of five scholarly volumes. Mr. Marshall indicated his interest in the plan but noted the financial straits in which the institution found itself.

My father replied:

I have your letter of June 10, and wish to thank you on behalf of my colleagues and myself for your kind interest in our plan.

We fully realize the difficulties arising out of the financial conditions of the Seminary. But what we had in mind when we addressed you was that the publication, while issued under the auspices of the Seminary, might partly be paid for by friends of Dr. Schechter who at the same time take an interest in the advancement of Jewish learning in this country. We feel sure that if you will take into your confidence other friends and admirers of Dr. Schechter as you yourself suggested, you will succeed in carrying out the plan.

The publication of these Schechter Studies would not only mark in a most dignified way the position of Professor Schechter in the world of Jewish science, but also the place occupied by our Seminary in the front rank of Jewish institutions of learning. It seems to us that under no circumstances can the Faculty afford to allow Professor Schechter's seventieth birthday to pass without distinguishing in some adequate literary fashion this unique occasion. The loss of prestige to the Seminary from such neglect would be incalculable.

We further wish to point out that if the publication is to appear in time printing will have to start in autumn.

To this second letter, Marshall replied:

I am of course very much interested in your plan of signalizing the event which so greatly concerns all who are desirous of the advancement of Jewish learning. The plan which you have under consideration is one of such extensive scope and involves so large an expenditure, that I do not feel personally justified, without taking others into my confidence, to incur the expense. As you doubtless know, the income of the Seminary does not meet its expenditures by at least $12,000 per annum. During the past five years, we have made ends meet by obtaining subscriptions to a Guaranty Fund, but the term of these subscriptions has ended, and it is now incumbent upon me to procure a renewal of the subscriptions, which will be a matter of some difficulty. To add an additional expenditure of $4,000 during the coming year would, under existing conditions, prove quite burdensome, unless I succeed in enlisting the special interest of one or two of the gentlemen who have always been very generous to the Seminary.

In view of the fact that the gentlemen of the Faculty would in any event prepare the volumes of texts and studies which they have in mind, even though they were published, not at one time, but serially in the course of the next few years, I can see no reason why they should not begin the preparation of their literary work, and leave it to be determined during the coming fall or winter whether the necessary funds can be procured to bring about the publication of the five volumes by December, 1916. If there is anything which is not practical in this suggestion, kindly let me know, so that I may take the subject under further consideration.

The leaders of the American Jewish community were finding it difficult to cover a $12,000 deficit. And an additional $4,000 appeared beyond their easy reach. Even allowing for the fact that the value of the dollar at that time was considerably greater, the sums are hardly astronomical. It seems that the few insiders were not too happy with their investment, but at the same time they were disinclined to invite the support of others, since this action would threaten their control. That is how matters stood in 1915 and that in general is how matters remained until the end of the 1930's, when Louis Finkelstein succeeded Cyrus Adler.

The trustees may have been disappointed in Schechter's partial failure. But they had little to criticize in Adler's regime. He avoided problems, including that of how to expand the budget. The Seminary rocked along, carried by the momentum of the Schechter years.

There is no doubt that my father felt frustrated that he had not been made president so that his sense of direction, his will to accomplish, his commitment to a living tradition could have had full play. And his frustration was greater because of Adler's substitution of bureaucracy for leadership.

But it is my considered opinion that my father's frustrations were partial, not total. He knew too much about Schechter's difficulties; he had too low an opinion of the laity; he must have seen the difficulties which would face any president who attempted to activate the alumni. But even very wise men can be ambivalent, their feelings pulling them in one direction and their intellect in another. I do not believe that my father ever fully understood that had he been chosen president his health, always fragile, would have collapsed; his scholarly work would have had to end; and he would have gone to his grave, as his good friend Dr. Solomon Solis-Cohen prognosticated even without these burdens, by the time he was fifty. And worst of all, he would have failed, or at least he would not have succeeded, in accomplishing those goals that alone would have justified such sacrifices. It may be unfair, and even improper for me, to suggest that my father's hypercritical, if always correct, attitude toward Dr. Adler was contaminated by an element of projection. He was so acutely aware of the gap between the needs of American Jewry for effective leadership and the quality of the leadership available that he held Dr. Adler personally responsible for the gap and even for his own inability to contribute to closing it.

Shut off from playing the leading role in directing the Seminary, he nevertheless exercised considerable influence on its affairs. Early in his incumbency Adler appointed, without prior consultation with the faculty, Dr. Jacob

Hoschander Professor of Bible to fill the chair that had tragically become vacant as the result of the murder of Israel Friedlaender while he was on a relief mission in Poland in 1920. Adler had responsibility for two institutions at the time, Dropsie College and the Jewish Theological Seminary, and he found it administratively convenient to move Dr. Hoschander from Philadelphia to New York. This move understandably added to my father's acerbic views about Adler. I cannot find any letter protesting the impropriety of such high-handed action. But I distinctly recall the degree of my father's agitation and his expressed conviction that this serious breach in academic procedure would never be repeated.

During the thirties and early forties, the Seminary added to the faculty four scholars of outstanding distinction: Louis Finkelstein, H. L. Ginsberg, Saul Lieberman, and Shalom Spiegel. In the appointment of each one my father played a key if not determining role. Finkelstein had long been a favorite of his. I believe that he, Louis M. Epstein, and Solomon Goldman were the closest to him of his early students.

In October, 1919, my father installed Finkelstein, who had accepted a pulpit in the Bronx in New York City. This was a synagogue with which my father had close ties since his brother's family worshipped there, but his willingness to participate in the ceremonies reflected his ties to his student. His remarks on that occasion are preserved and several paragraphs warrant quoting:

With the consent of all, you have been chosen out of the people to be the very first one to read the Torah. By electing a rabbi the Congregation declares its willingness to acknowledge the rabbi's authority in everything pertaining to Jewish law, doctrine and custom; he is the very first one to read and to explain to you the words of the Torah. It is true that democracy is the main characteristic of our age, but democracy and authority are contrasts to him only who sees the surface of things without being able to penetrate below it. The fight of democracy is not for lawlessness against authority, but for authority against those who usurp it, be they individuals or bodies of men. It is one of the most grievous misfortunes of modern Judaism that the cobbler will not stick to his last, will imagine himself able to judge of all things in heaven and earth. And yet who will not grant, except in the case of Jewish doctrine and practice, that an experienced eye is an important qualification for understanding the distinction of things or detecting their form and tendency.

The rabbis speak of three partners owning men—God, father and mother. This is only a poetical way of expressing the deep truth that the decisive factors in the life of the individual, as well as of the many, are heredity, environment and individuality. We hear today a good deal about the two first factors, but hardly anything about the third. Yet, while Judaism cannot live without national consciousness, it cannot live on it. If we are further told that life is the power of adaptability of environment, and accordingly, Judaism must, if it would continue to live, adapt itself to its surroundings, we must reply: A life perfectly adapted to its surroundings is a life without mentality. A person lacking individuality is no person at all but a thing. Today more so than at any other period of our history, the foremost task before us is to maintain our individuality, to be a kingdom of priests and a holy nation.

The bankruptcy of a certain religious movement among the Jews of modern times is mainly due to the fact that it was based upon the confused conception of Judaism as a religion into which the different religious ideals fuse, robbing it of all individuality. And the other fatal mistake made by the leaders of this movement was their ignoring the fact that a religion of respectability is the most despicable. A religion which neither irritates the reason nor interferes with comfort, a religion not from love and fear but from good sense, will, in the long run, satisfy neither the heart nor the head of man. We have no apologies to offer for the God of Israel, the God of the Torah. What we need are leaders who will to have the open vision and will then to declare it: men who set themselves to be messengers of God to their generation, who are ready to listen to the small voice that silences ambition, rejects doubt, crushes the flesh, its afflictions and lust, discloses the secrets of eternity, whispers a message that whosoever hears it repeated doubts not that through the words of the human preacher and teacher he has heard the words of the living God to his soul.

He described Louis Finkelstein as "a very dear friend and beloved disciple" and applied to him the dictum the rabbis applied to Joseph: "Father in wisdom, tender in years."

The relationship of teacher to pupil continued. Finkelstein was the first graduate of the Seminary to continue his studies with my father to the point of acquiring the *Hattarat Horaah,* which conveys upon the holder the right to act as judge in matters of Jewish law. For several years, Finkelstein came every Friday afternoon to our home. I frequently opened the door and would shout in a loud voice to my father, "your teacher has arrived." Finkelstein's big beard made him appear, at least in the eyes of one child, much older than his years.

For many years Finkelstein taught on a part-time basis at the Seminary and at the same time held the demanding post of rabbi of a large metropolitan congregation. He must have found the conflicting pressures increasingly irreconcilable. I know that my father interceded for him with the Seminary authorities—I assume it was with Sol Stroock, at the time Chairman of the Board. My father pressed for a decision: if Finkelstein were not offered a full-time position in the Seminary, he would advise him to resign and concentrate on his work in the active ministry. My father carried his point, and Finkelstein became a professor. Shortly thereafter he became Provost and then President.

My father first met H. L. Ginsberg when he visited Palestine in 1928-29 to serve as visiting professor at the Hebrew University. Ginsberg, a Canadian by birth, had started to study medicine, but had shifted in midstream and

had pursued the study of Oriental languages and literature
in England. He later moved to Palestine. As was true of so
many young and able people in Jerusalem at the time, he
had difficulty in finding an appropriate position and was
eking out a living teaching school, translating, and continuing his scholarly researches on the side.

My father had elicited his participation in a large-scale
project that he had agreed to head—a new edition of the
Hebrew and English Bible to be published in Palestine for
the Limited Editions Club in New York. After tortuous
negotiations, my father worked out an agreement with
George Macy, the Director of Limited Editions, for the
scholarly studies required to assure that the text would incorporate the findings of modern scholarship and that the
King James anachronisms would be modernized. The major
responsibility for revising the English text was to be carried
out by H. L. Ginsberg. The others who had agreed to cooperate were Professors Torczyner, Yellin, and Segal of the
Hebrew University, Jerusalem, and Shalom Spiegel in New
York.

As happened to so many projects during the depression,
the project was still-born. But it aroused my father's interest
in helping Ginsberg find a position which would enable him
to carry on his work. This the Seminary finally agreed to do.
My father also was instrumental in the Seminary's extending
a call to Professor Yehezkel Kaufmann but the Hebrew University, hearing rumors, quickly acted to keep him.

In 1928-29 when my father lectured at the Hebrew University, Saul Lieberman attended his classes. Lieberman,
Russian-born, in fact a native of the same town as Chaim
Weizmann (Motele), had studied at Slobodka, even with
Rabbi Finkel, the man who much earlier had won my father
over to the Moralist Movement. At one point, Lieberman
had interrupted his Jewish studies to enter medicine and
was close to completing his medical studies when he shifted

back. When Magnes, the President of the University, suggested that Dr. Epstein, who held the Chair in Talmud and
for whom my father had high regard, assume responsibility
for seeing my father's lecture on the "Significance of the
Halakhah for Jewish History" through the press, my father
said, no, that he would like Lieberman to do this. This left
Magnes more than a little surprised, since until then he had
never heard of Lieberman. There is no doubt that in this
way and others, my father sought to ease Lieberman's way.
However, when Lieberman obtained his MA degree in the
early thirties, there was no opening for him on the University's staff and he became the head of an institute for
talmudic research established in Palestine with funds from a
wealthy Orthodox Jew in New York, Harry Fishel. My father's advice and counsel had been sought by the benefactor,
but he would have no part of it because of his conviction
that Fishel had no understanding of what was really involved in the scientific study of the Talmud and that if he
had, he would be unwilling to support such an undertaking.
Moreover, my father felt the young men whom Fishel
planned to support in the Institute were inadequately
trained to carry on talmudic research. Realizing that
Lieberman was in an unsuitable post, my father convinced
Adler, through Finkelstein, to bring him to the Seminary just
before World War II. Mrs. Lieberman, the daughter of the
religious Zionist leader, Rabbi Meyer Berlin, was the granddaughter of the head of the Volozhin Yeshiva for which my
father had been destined after he had been forcibly removed from Slobodka. But as we have seen, his short detour
to Vilna led him not to Volozhin, but to Holland, Germany,
and the United States. There were many family ties between
Mrs. Lieberman and my father.

I remember my father's discussing with me a possible designation for Lieberman's chair, and if my memory serves, I
worked out a complicated answer: Professor of Palestinian

History, Literature, and Institutions. In any case, my father was content that at long last, after more than two decades of inaction, the Seminary's faculty was on the way to being rebuilt. All that was still required was to find a professor of history who could eventually succeed Alexander Marx. Earlier and later, my father played a part in faculty appointments, but these strategic additions made in this crucial decade were the most significant.

The influence of a key professor is felt both through the support which he extends to certain faculty candidates as well as the support which he withholds from others. My father long opposed loading the Seminary faculty with able and ambitious rabbis who wanted to do a little teaching on the side. Except for the field of homiletics, in which he recognized the need for a practitioner, he insisted that the threat of part-time faculty be met and fought.

The Spiegel appointment also was complicated. Spiegel had come to the Jewish Institute of Religion, of which Stephen S. Wise was president, from Europe via Haifa, where he had taught in the famous *Realschule*, the first and for a long time the only strong secondary school in Palestine. Parenthetically, despite this excellent model, the problem of secondary education in Israel was still very much up in the air at the time of my fourth survey of Manpower Utilization in Israel undertaken at the behest of the Government of Israel in 1963. The Institute had no rigid theological orientation and this fact alone made it a questionable recruiting ground for the Seminary, especially since Rabbi Wise, its president, was a pronounced liberal in his attitude towards Jewish law and tradition. But under the gentle prodding of his colleague, Israel Davidson, and encouraged by his good friend Dr. Israel Wechsler, my father provided the necessary cover for bringing Spiegel to the Seminary.

One of Schechter's important legacies was that he left a faculty characterized by a high esprit de corps, in which within the bounds of human frailty there was little overt jealousy and backbiting. But the Seminary was an institution of men, not a dictatorship, and eventually conflicts arose. The stormy petrel was Mordecai M. Kaplan, who wanted to see the Seminary move more energetically to modernize tradition. My father had an assortment of responses: silence, humor, and on occasion anger.

Educated in the tradition of German academic freedom, my father believed that every member of a faculty is entitled to set forth his views—in fact, that it is incumbent upon him to do so. He believed further that a responsible institution should not embark upon a program of faculty censorship. He wrote to Dr. Finkelstein in 1949:

Yesterday, I received a copy of Doctor Kaplan's paper which will be discussed tomorrow by the members of the faculty. Without passing any judgment on its merits or demerits, I am rather puzzled about this procedure. As I understand, Doctor Kaplan is to read his paper before his colleagues of the Rabbinical Assembly, and I wonder whether it is quite proper for the faculty of the Seminary to supervise the activities of the graduates of the Seminary.

For a number of years, Doctor Kaplan has published books and articles containing views with which the members of the faculty, or to say the least, the majority thereof, do not agree. Why then, should the faculty now change its policy in this respect? It occurs to me that by doing so, we may be the cause of the Rabbinical Assembly attempting to interfere with the faculty.

My father believed in academic freedom, but he had little sympathy for those who sought to alter tradition. Of this he was sure: only those deeply steeped in the knowledge of the facts would be able to differentiate the important from the unimportant in religious thought and tradition. More important, he had reached the conclusion that any effort at reconciling historic Judaism with American life was doomed to failure. It was not possible, he felt, for Judaism to remain within the broad band of tradition while making the compromises that Kaplan and others believed would lead to a quickening of religion among American Jews. In one of his more sarcastic formulations, my father would ask, "What point is there to revise Jewish theology for pants-makers?"

My father also occasionally responded angrily when he was forced to recognize substantial support for radical innovation among the alumni and the student body. This, he felt, was evidence of his own failure. And so, on rare occasions at home when visitors taunted him, in the classroom when a serious if not wise young man asked a leading question, and at an infrequent meeting of the Rabbinical Assembly which he attended, my father would explode. It did not happen often, but it did happen.

In 1945 the tensions boiled over when Dr. Kaplan and his associates issued a revised version of the prayer book. In a public letter to the Hebrew Journal, *Hadoar,* my father, together with Professors Marx and Lieberman, publically condemned the effort as a gross violation of tradition and taste. They had concluded that it was essential for them to give public testimony that the revised prayer book did not reflect the stance of the Seminary. They believed that membership on a theological faculty required acceptance of certain basic principles and outlook. My father saw no reason for the repeated efforts of the administration to hold on to the radicals; he did not believe that their leaving would lead to a sizable depletion in the ranks of the Rabbinical Assembly or in the United Synagogue of America. In any case, the break did not occur, and on balance my father was probably pleased, since their influence diminished rapidly after World War II.

Dr. Moshe Davis tells me that his initiation into Seminary faculty meetings took place on an afternoon when Dr. Kaplan and my father had an acrimonious debate about a doctoral dissertation. When the meeting broke up, my father

went over to Dr. Kaplan and reminded him that the Ginzbergs hadn't seen the Kaplans lately; he wondered if they
might be free to visit the following Saturday. And the
Kaplans came to call.

The place of theology in the curriculum of the Seminary
was an early and continuing concern to my father. In a letter
to Dr. Schechter, he deplored the state of the students' ignorance about the history and philosophy of religion in general
and of Judaism in particular. He said that he devoted more
time and effort to his lectures on theology (he probably took
over the course the year Dr. Schechter was on leave) than to
all of his other Seminary duties.

In an undated memorandum addressed to the Acting President and Faculty, he recommended a sizable expansion of
this phase of the curriculum to include courses in medieval
philosophy, mysticism, ethics, as well as in the history, philosophy, and psychology of religion. A committee of which
my father was apparently chairman, and which included
Alexander Marx and Moses Hyamson, recommended the
appointment of Dr. Julius Guttmann of Berlin to work in
this area. The important paragraphs of the memorandum,
undoubtedly drafted by my father, follow:

Judaism from the very beginning was and continued to be
through its long development an ethical and spiritual movement.
It teaches a way of life and not a theology. The desire, however,
to explain is an outgrowth of the need to understand, a need
which is born of the exigencies of practical life. Hence Judaism is
not an exception to the rule that in highly developed religions
theological systems arise which seek to expound the value and
meaning of their religion in propositional form. Not by an accident but by an immanent tendency of the religious spirit is theology evolved. Theological doctrines are like the bones of the body,
the outcome of the life-process itself and also the means by which
it gives firmness, stability and definiteness of outline to the
animal organism. No spiritual religion could maintain itself

without some doctrinal statement of the principles implied in its own life. The dogma of a dogma-less Judaism shows as little appreciation of Judaism as of religion in general.

The proper office of theology is, however, not to criticize the religious experience out of which it grew, but rather to deal faithfully with that experience and report what is implied in it. Judaism as a religion based on *revelation* teaches that if men are resolved to philosophize about religion, there is only one way to do so to profit, and that is to set out from the Jewish idea of God as scientifically valid, and to develop a world-view in dependence upon it. At the same time Judaism as an *historical* revelation represents a growing experience mediated by great personalities and maintained and carried forward by the movement of the historic life. Jewish theology has accordingly to concentrate its efforts on a representation of doctrinal teachings on their historical development from biblical times to our own day. Bible, Talmud, Liturgy, Midrash, the Musar-books and Cabbala are the literary sources for this branch of study.

Fact, says a great thinker, is the ground of all that is divine in religion and religion can only be presented in history—in truth it must become a continuous and living history. The literature of the Synagogue is the only witness to the religious experience of the Synagogue, and it is with this experience that Jewish theology is concerned. What is called "Speculative Theology," which seeks to raise religious doctrines to a philosophical form by exercising a free criticism upon them, is better ranked with philosophy of religion.

When Judaism passed into the gentile world it encountered an atmosphere impregnated with philosophical ideas. To escape the influence of these ideas was hardly possible. As early as the second century B. C. E., Jewish Hellenists proclaimed that Judaism was the true philosophy and attempted to offer a statement of Jewish truth in a larger perspective.

The attempt at a "rationalized Judaism," undertaken for the first time by the Hellenists, was repeated by the Jewish philosophers of the Middle Ages, when Judaism came for the second time in contact with Greek thought through the medium of Arabic philosophy. The brilliant intellectual achievements of the

Jewish Rationalists like Saadia Gaon, Maimonides, Gersonides and a score of others, form not only a highly important chapter in the history of Jewish culture but one of prominent importance for the historical development of the Jewish religion. Of the Jewish Rationalists one may well say that there are some things that they have shattered which will never be restored; some that they have founded that will never be destroyed; and that they have pointed out the way along which Judaism will have to move.

The most valuable inheritance bequeathed by the Jewish Rationalists is that a religion which ignores the claims of reason, and moves without its guiding light, is apt to fall into fanaticism and superstition or to drift into obscurantism. Religion is more than reason, but it cannot discard reason without failing to make good its claim to be objective and universal. Thought must exercise its critical and selective function, if the essential in religion is to come to its own and receive due recognition. The theory is perfectly sound that you cannot know anything well except you go beyond it and apprehend its relation to other things. He who knows no book but the Bible does not even know it rightly; and it is the same with a religion. No single aspect of reality is cut off with a hatchet from the remainder, and to know any one thing you must see its relations to other things. Only to this large outlook do the characteristic elements in a given religion stand forth, and to understand the ethical and spiritual value of Judaism, one must recognize not merely its distinctive form but its relation to other similar or different spiritual and intellectual movements.

One cannot have two or more watertight compartments and place in one an agnostic or materialistic conception of the world and in the other the Jewish view of life. If a student of theology can ill afford to disregard the interrelations that existed between Jewish religion and Greek thought in antiquity, he certainly must take cognizance of these interrelations that exist in our own day between religion and philosophy.

No branch of modern thought is more important for the student of theology than philosophy of religion, which has as its problem the final meaning of religion as a constituent element in human life and development. Assuming that religion is a normal and constant aspect of human life and the utterance of a permanent need of man's spirit, philosophy of religion, by its investigations of religious development, may furnish the means by which we gradually recognize and make clear to ourselves these essential and determining principles which are implied in the nature and growth of religion.

Religious phenomenon are essentially reactions of the mind upon the experienced world, and their specific character is not due to the material environment, but to the human consciousness. Hence no interpretation of the meaning of religious development can hope to succeed without a sound psychological equipment.

The memorandum was still-born. Dr. Finkelstein is my source for the statement that a bid was extended to Dr. Guttmann but he rejected it.

In June 1919, discussions about theology went beyond the faculty and were on the way to creating a public embarrassment. A Committee of Six, including Professors Friedlaender and Kaplan, issued the following mimeographed invitation to my father as well as to many others:

Dear Prof. Ginzberg,

We address this letter to you in the hope that you will cooperate with us in the endeavor to formulate, in terms of belief and practice, the type of Judaism that we believe you profess in common with us. We have failed as a group to exert an influence upon Jewish life in any way commensurate with the truth and strength of our position, and that, primarily, because we have never made our position clear to the rest of the world.

In view of the upheaval in the world at large, and in view of the changes which will necessarily take place in the spiritual life of our people as a result of the restoration of Palestine, we maintain that the time has come for us to state frankly and emphatically what we believe in and what we regard as authoritative in Jewish practice, and to develop the implications of the Zionist Movement, especially for Judaism of the Diaspora. We feel that no good can come to Judaism either from petrified traditionalism or from individualistic liberalism, and that it is our duty to point the way to a Judaism that shall be both historic and progressive.

If you are in sympathy with our project, we ask you to attend the meeting which will take place at the Jewish Theological Seminary, on Wednesday, June 18th, at 10:30 a.m.

> Israel Friedlaender
> Julius H. Greenstone
> Mordecai M. Kaplan
> Jacob Kohn
> Max L. Margolis
> Herman Rubenovitz.

As soon as he received it, my father wrote to his two colleagues in the following vein (only penciled notes of his reply have been preserved):

"The Board of Directors of the Jewish Theological Seminary at a meeting held on March 2nd have designated me as Acting Chairman of the Faculty and delegated to me the authority of the Acting President for the time of his absence [Dr. Adler was at the Peace Conference in Paris]. I would be unmindful of the responsibility placed upon me if I permitted the meeting planned by the Committee of Six to be held in the Seminary. I trust in your sense of justice and right that you will see to it that the meeting does not take place in the Seminary. To avoid the appearance of friction between members of the faculty, I have decided not to speak to any other member of the Committee."

We did find Friedlaender's reply: "I am in receipt of your letter of today and I do not hesitate to say that the Seminary should not have been selected as the meeting place. I may add that I knew and know nothing whatsoever about the arrangements of the Conference, except that I was asked to sign my name to the invitation—which I gladly did."

Regrettably, this is the only note from Friedlaender in my father's files. The relationship between the two was warm. Aside from a book which he dedicated to Schechter, the only book my father ever dedicated to another member of the faculty was one dedicated to the memory of Israel Friedlaender.

My father was convinced that Friedlaender had largely squandered his very substantial talent by his determination to play an activist role in Zionist and other communal activities which had little use and less respect for the contribution of a scholar. When his widow, Lillian Bentwich Friedlaender, saw my mother after the news of his tragic death in 1920, she cried out: "I should have followed your advice and not let him go." Lillian had asked my mother whether she would permit *her* husband to go on such a dangerous mission, and my mother had flatly answered in the negative. No father of two children, certainly not the father of six as was Friedlaender, should be permitted in my mother's opinion to place his life in jeopardy.

Friedlaender's hope at the end of World War I had been to go to Palestine, but the story is that Professor Richard Gottheil of Columbia University had informed the British Government that Friedlaender had had German sympathies. Hence, the letter from Gottheil to my father when he learned of Friedlaender's death has added significance:

Pavillon deCeres
Vittel   *July 28, 1920*

My dear Professor Ginzberg:
     Jewish news is very rare in this small place, and it is only now that I learn through a number of the *Jewish Chronicle* of London about the tragic end of Professor Friedlaender. I take the first occasion to express my sincere regrets to his colleagues at the Jewish Theological Seminary at this egregious loss suffered by American-Jewish scholarship. I met Prof. Friedlaender first in Francford [*sic*] when he had come over from Strassburg to speak with Prof. Schechter with a view to his joining the staff of the Seminary. I have been associated with him at our Oriental Club and especially at the Educational Alliance; and, despite divergences that public men naturally have in the course of their work, I had never had occasion to doubt the high character of his scholarship and the intensity of his moral and religious view of

life. By showing himself capable of offering up his life upon the altar of his Jewish patriotism, he has contributed much to the elevation of our profession.

Will you kindly take this present note as an expression to his colleagues upon the Faculty of the Jewish Theological Seminary of my sincere condolence with them in their affliction.

Reference to the Friedlaenders' six children leads me to an observation about the offspring of the early faculty. There were more than twice as many girls as boys, thirteen to six, and of the sons, I alone became an academic, although Frank Schechter combined a successful professional career in the law with scholarly research. His pioneering study on *The Historical Foundations of the Law Relating to Trademarks* earned him the first doctor of jurisprudence awarded by Columbia University. Among the daughters there was one archaeologist, a lawyer, a physician, a musicologist, two social workers and a public health worker. Three of the girls were for a time, one for a long time, heavily involved in Communist party affairs, a talented young male musician committed suicide, and one promising female scientist had a complete mental breakdown which required life-long hospitalization. The rest of the sons went into business and the rest of the girls became housewives. While it is not easy to draw any conclusions from this brief outline, one point does emerge with clarity. Not one of the offspring of these six professors pursued a career in Jewish scholarship.

To finish the Seminary story. When Finkelstein became President in 1940, my father had reached the age when professors customarily retire. But further evidence of substantial neglect of Seminary affairs during the long interregnum between Schechter's and Finkelstein's incumbency is presented by the fact that the Seminary had no retirement or pension plan. As far as widows were concerned, the Board acted on each case individually. And until then no professor had reached the age of retirement. And so my father stayed on, continuing to lecture and to give his seminar for advanced students.

As the depression began to lift, Sol Stroock, a distinguished member of the bar and a devoted Jew, was serving as Chairman of the Board and for the first time plans were laid to broaden and deepen the basis of support for the Seminary in connection with the semi-centennial celebration of its reorganization which was only a few years off. The Board wanted to confer a degree of Doctor of Sacred Theology on a distinguished Christian clergyman who had been "most sympathetic and helpful." Mr. Stroock said, "We are endeavoring to broaden the influence of the Seminary in the community at large . . . and Dr. —— has gone out of his way to support those efforts." Mr. Stroock was quick to disqualify himself as a judge of scholarship; he recognized that the faculty should have full discretion in the matter of honorary degrees (a procedure almost without precedent in other institutions), and he sought to distinguish the Doctor of Sacred Theology from the Doctor of Hebrew Letters, suggesting that the former was less directly connected with scholarly endeavors.

After consultation with his colleagues, my father answered Stroock:

May I now state the policy of the Faculty with regard to conferring of honorary degrees. The Jewish Theological Seminary, being primarily an institution for higher Jewish learning, ought to recognize the merits of men who either distinguished themselves by their contribution to Jewish learning or who by their distinguished efforts made Jewish learning possible in this country. The Faculty is broadminded enough not to make any distinction between Jew and gentile, and has therefore conferred degrees upon prominent non-Jewish scholars in recognition of their contribution to Jewish learning.

Doctor ——, a prominent clergyman and leader of his church, does certainly not fit into the same category of men like the late

Professor George F. Moore, the greatest authority on rabbinics in the Christian world, Professor Torrey, the most prominent biblical scholar in the Western world, Professor Albright, one of the leading biblical archaeologists, and Professor MacDonald, a deep and original student of the religion of Israel and the theology of Islam.

The Faculty was and still is of the opinion that there lurks a great danger in conferring degrees upon Christian clergymen and religious leaders, as it might not only be misinterpreted by a great section of American Jewry, but because it also might force our hands to confer more degrees upon non-Jews than Jews.

This is in explanation of the policy of the Faculty. In deference, however, to you and the other members of the Board, who are of the opinion that your efforts in the work of raising funds for the Seminary will be greatly forwarded by conferring the degree upon Doctor ——, the Faculty should be very pleased to do so.

You began your letter with a candid statement and you will permit me to close mine with a statement of a similar nature. May I say that if the Semi-Centennial Committee would have had besides the officers of the Seminary among its members a representative of the Faculty, this matter would have been settled long ago.

And then followed the paragraph previously quoted about the "dogma of disqualification of Jewish scholars for practical problems." Mr. Stroock's reply must be appended for it shows the ease with which slippage can occur among faculty, administration, and board in an educational institution.

May I assure you that there was certainly no conscious effort to affront you nor any of your colleagues by failing to invite a member of the Faculty in addition to Dr. Adler and Dr. Finkelstein to become formally a member of the Semi-Centennial Committee. We realized that the work of the Committee would be arduous and tedious. We felt that we had not the right to engage the time of more members of the Faculty. Apparently, we erred in this regard, and for that error I apologize sincerely.

I do not know the dogma of the disqualification of Jewish scholars for practical problems. But if there be such a dogma it found no advocate in this case.

More representative of the warm relations between Mr. Stroock and my father was an interchange that took place in 1941. Mr. Stroock wrote to him:

I was delighted to learn from Doctor Finkelstein that your book should be published by March 1st.

At that last meeting of the Seminary Board of Directors, it was agreed that the publication of your monumental work should be commemorated as an occasion of great importance, not only for Jewish learning but for scholarship generally, and that it should be marked by an assembly of those particularly interested in Jewish fields of study.

I would very much like to arrange at the Seminary a dinner in honor of the publication and hope that you will consent to our doing so.

If you agree, we would like to hold such a dinner on Sunday evening, March 23rd.

And my father's warm reply:

I was deeply touched by your letter of January 2 in which you informed me that at the last meeting of the Board of Directors of the Seminary it was decided to have the publication of my work on the Talmud of Jerusalem commemorated.

As one whose entire life is devoted to Jewish studies, I greatly rejoice in knowing that American Israel still has among its leaders men who are concerned about the future of Judaism and do not forget it in their worries about the catastrophic situation of Jewry in the old world. If we are not to be degraded, to become a people like the gypsies, we must save the great treasures that the past has bequeathed to us. The only legitimate interpreter of these treasures is Jewish learning.

It is further a source of great satisfaction to me to know that my work has received the distinction to be considered important for Jewish learning. A great Jewish saint once remarked, "I never acted contrary to the wishes of my fellow-men, I know I am not a priest but should I be told to ascend the platform of the priests to give the priestly blessing, I shall not fail to do so." I am not a saint, neither great nor small, but I nevertheless say to you, "I know my achievements do not merit the high distinctions bestowed upon them but I shall not act contrary to the wishes of my friends."

I tried to find out from the printer whether by the date set by you, the 23rd of March, we shall have the publication at hand. I have not yet received his answer but I do not care to delay longer my reply to your letter and hope that he will not disappoint us.

Finkelstein took office after the start of World War II and about a year and a half before America entered the hostilities. For the next years he had to restrict himself primarily to planning for the future, but with the cessation of hostilities in 1945 he was ready to move ahead on a broad front. The gist of his vision follows. It was set out in a letter to my father dated about a fortnight after the surrender of the Japanese.

This brings me to a thought which has been going through my mind during the past week. The end of the war, coming as it does after a period of unprecedented horrors, for Jews and the world, marks, let us hope, the beginning of a new era in Judaism as well as in civilization. I think that our faculty as such ought to take note of this fact, and that we ought to spend a few mornings in considering the question of where we as the faculty, and the Seminary as such, go from here.

First of all we of course have to adapt our curriculum, drop the accelerated program, and proceed to establish a schedule of studies which we may hope will remain more or less permanent, at least for the next few decades. Then, I think, we ought to have a clear idea of how we are going to develop Jewish scholars in this country, and how we are going to encourage Jewish scholarship by importation of promising students from abroad.

I think, too, that now is the time to consider whether our Teachers Institute has been as effective as it should be in molding Jewish education. Projects like the "Eternal Light," etc., ought either to be integrated into the Seminary, or ought to be separated. At any rate, their relationship to us ought to be clarified.

I think that the time has now come when the relationship of the faculty to the Board ought to be straightened out on the basis of several discussions we have had.

Finally, it seems to me that I would like to draw up, first for your consideration, and then for that of the other members of the faculty, a statement to the Jewish people, and to the world, calling for the spiritual rehabilitation of the Jews, no less than for their material rehabilitation. I think that we must take very seriously the fact that millions are being spent on various objectives which, no matter how important and worthy, cannot be compared in importance with that of preserving the essence of Judaism; we have not yet been able to get across to the Jewish community the importance of the spiritual aspects of our faith.

The other day I was told by an eminent Christian professor that he was present at a meeting which a mutual friend of ours addressed, in which he described Judaism in such a way that at the end, one of those present asked him whether his Judaism was in way different from Unitarianism. The speaker said it was not. "Why then don't you join the Unitarians?" the questioner asked. The answer was because we, being the older group are entitled to have them make the approach. I must have looked stunned when this was told me, for he immediately added, "I am not sure that the speaker meant it seriously."

Perhaps the speaker did go a little far because he felt he was addressing a Christian audience, but it does seem to me that we here have failed to use the enormous prestige of the institution, and the scholars connected with it with sufficient effectiveness to build up respect for Judaism and for Jewish scholarship. When you return I would like to talk this over with you in detail.

I have been discussing with Eli plans for establishing here a Research Department in Jewish Social Studies. At the present time, all that is in the hands of the Yivo. You once remarked to me that Doctor Schechter knew all about the Jews in Safed in the sixteenth century, but virtually nothing about the Jews in New York in the twentieth. In trying to work out the book on *Judaism and the Jews,* which you and I discussed, I found to my regret

IN THE HALLS OF ACADEME   [157

that we can get expert information on every aspect of Judaism, except the present. There are Jews who know about the Jews of Pumbedita; there are Jews who know about the Jews of Worms, etc. But I still have to find a Jew who understands the Jews of Chicago.

There is no question that my father was pleased with the fact that the Seminary was now headed by a man who, in addition to being a distinguished scholar, was full of energy and ideas. But he had reached a stage in his life when he was less and less sure if even energy and ideas could accomplish much in the way of revitalizing Judaism in the United States. So he stayed on the side-lines. In connection with certain organizational changes, Finkelstein asked him whether he would agree to become Provost, but he decided not to. In the process of deciding, my father asked my advice and seeing his reluctance, I did not encourage him to accept.

In the eight years between the end of World War II and my father's death, Finkelstein explored a great many avenues which might heighten the influence and impact of the Seminary, from founding the University of Judaism in Los Angeles to taking the initiative in establishing the Conference on Science, Philosophy and Religion. As far as my father was concerned, he questioned whether these undertakings would prove of lasting value. But he had lived in the United States long enough to appreciate that "public relations" was an essential not only for business but also for educational and even religious institutions. While he remained quizzical and occasionally even critical, he was pleased that the Seminary once again had a strong man at the helm who understood and appreciated the crucial role of Jewish scholarship.

CHAPTER VIII

BEYOND THE CAMPUS

IN AN EFFORT to elicit support from the laity, Solomon
Schechter had taken the initiative in establishing the
United Synagogue of America, in which membership was
open to all congregations willing to identify with the basic
orientation of the Seminary. The rabbis of most of these
congregations were Seminary graduates. In 1917-1918, Louis
Ginzberg served as President of the United Synagogue. In
that capacity, he had a platform from which he could set
forth his views about the direction which Conservative Judaism in the United States should take. The following are selections from a very long address which he made as President,
and which included comments on Jewish education, religious observance, the role of women in Jewish life, and
much more.

"Our organization bears the name, the United Synagogue
of America, and it would pay the trouble to examine carefully the meaning of that name. The opening line of the
Sabbath afternoon prayer reads, 'Thou art one and Thy
name is one, and who is like Thy people of Israel, one nation
on the earth.' In these few words, the most characteristic
feature of the mental make-up of the Jew is expressed with

precision and thoroughness. A striving for unity in all realms of the human mind describes the Jew best; in monotheism the religious aspect of this striving is expressed in the doctrine of the equality of men before God. . . . We Jews of America pride ourselves, and justly so, on our solidarity; and to the honor of American Jewry be it said that in these times of distress and sorrow, American Israel does not know parties nor classes. Yet we have to admit that an internal principle of union is wanting, and to quote the words of a great religious leader of the last century, when this is wanting, the principle of life is wanting, and all is outward show. Societies and institutions, however well organized and energetic, will avail nothing without a living principle. Unity without is a result of unity within, but when there is nothing real within, what appears is as little real and substantive as a shadow. Lacking unity, we today live partly on the shadow of the past, and one shudders at the thought that those who will come after us will have to live on the shadow of a shadow.

"Now let us understand the exact meaning of the expression historical Judaism. It does not intend to give you the content of Judaism while you are standing on one foot. All attempts made in the last two thousand years to create an acrobatic Judaism had to fail—one cannot go on forever standing on one foot. Looking at Judaism from an historical point of view, we become convinced that there is no one aspect deep enough to exhaust the content of such a complex phenomenon as Judaism, no one term or proposition which will serve to define it. Judaism is national and universal, individual and social, legal and mystic, dogmatic and practical at once, yet it has a unity and individuality just as a mathematical curve has its own laws and expression. By insisting upon historical Judaism, we express further our conviction that for us Judaism is no theory of the study or school, no matter of private opinion or deduction, but a fact.

Only what happens, do we understand, not what might have happened. Accordingly, a Torah-less Judaism, if such a being could exist at all, would be a thing entirely new, and not the continuation of something given. If we look upon Jewish History in its integrity as a simple and uniform power, though marked in portions by temporary casual parenthetical interruptions, we find that it was the Torah which stood forth throughout the history of Israel as the guiding star of his civilization.

"The development of Talmudical Judaism from Biblical Judaism, while preserving the unity to type, characteristic as it is of faithful developments, became possible only by means of variation. Biblical Judaism was limited to one small country, and to a time of a cultural homogeneity of the Jewish people. Talmudism could not but vary in its relation and dealing towards the world around it. Historical Judaism therefore does not rest exclusively on the Bible, but also on tradition. Or, as our preamble expresses it, loyalty to the Torah and its historical interpretation. If one be weary of the past, let him remember that he cannot shake himself clear of the past. One is in his character and spiritual life as much a child of thousands of generations behind him as he is in mind and body. The part one contributes to his own making, bodily or spiritually, is infinitesimal. The greater part of what we are is due to heredity and the atmosphere of the time and place into which we are born.

"For a constructive criticism of the contents of tradition, however, the first requirement is sympathy. Where there is no love there is no understanding. There is such a thing as learned ignorance, a stir and curiosity of the shadows and trifles. Hence, the attempts of those otherwise learned men, who without love for historical Judaism tried to reform it, were doomed to failure. One does not break with history without darkening it. Reform, that is shaping of new forms for old truths, was turned into radicalism, that is, the uprooting of old truths. But all progress is a deeper penetration into the meaning of old truth, and a larger appropriation of it.

"A novel product of recent development in American Jewry is what one is inclined to describe as vicarious orthodoxy. America was declared by a clever man to be the land of great possibilities, which really means of great impossibilities. Ours is a country where the impossible becomes possible. The conflict between authority and private judgment as old as religion itself has been finally abolished by the spokesmen of vicarious orthodoxy. Their formula is: There is no other guide for you but blind authority; as for us, we are modern men and are guided by our private judgment exclusively. The Prophet Jeremiah, a Jewish legend narrates, succeeded by means of mystic combinations of the Hebrew alphabet in creating a *golem*. But no sooner was the *golem* created, than he took a knife and scratched out the word truth engraved on his forehead. He went out of existence when this word disappeared. By miraculous or only clever combinations of the Hebrew letters, or of any other letters, one may be able to create phantoms, but they will disappear without leaving the slightest trace; the faint imprint of truth on the forehead cannot withstand the slightest touch.

"Another shibboleth of the day is Practical Judaism. We are told we are living in a practical age; what we want is practice not theory; we are after results, not how they came, or how their coming may be philosophically explained. But few minds can remain at ease without some sort of rational grounds for their religious belief. Practical, if it means anything, means capable of achieving a useful end; but of what value is the adjective useful in defining the word practical if there is no such thing as an end? As a matter of fact, our age is far from being practical, as proclaimed by those who know only their own time. They cannot distinguish between the characteristics that are transient and those that are permanent. One is certainly more entitled to speak of our age as an age of reason. What antiquity imagined, the Middle Ages felt, and modern times reason.

"Judaism always abhors the identity of the narrow absolute formal kind. Alexandrian Judaism differed from Palestinian during the second commonwealth, and so did Spanish Judaism differ from Franco-German Judaism in the twelfth century. Nothing illustrates better the liking of the Jew for variation than the history of the prayer book. Within the brotherhood of the Jewish people, the prayer book in Hebrew became the symbol of a closer and more intimate bond of union, fostered and guarded no less loyally and tenaciously than the grand treasures of the race. At the same time, the prayer book became a species of religious dialect which varied with locality and which communities could not forget or abandon even in exile. The secret of this seeming contradiction lies herein that the unity of type must not be pressed to the extent of denying all variations. Judaism always recognized the fact that there are greater truths and lesser truths, catholic truths and individual opinions, forms which are not essential. The policy of the United Synagogue is to apply this principle effectively. Our organization welcomes all those who stand on the solid ground of historical Judaism, who are loyal to Israel, his God and his Torah. To quote the last sentence of the preamble of our Constitution: 'It shall be the aim of the United Synagogue of America while not endorsing the innovations introduced by any of its constituent bodies, to embrace all elements essentially loyal to traditional Judaism and in sympathy with the purposes outlined above.' We wish all Jews to agree with us and are ready to walk with them step by step as far as they would go, and if they should stop, we will go on with some satisfaction that we had brought them so far. A great movement ought to be independent, yet it must not stand apart in isolation."

The following year, in his capacity as Acting Chairman of the Faculty, Louis Ginzberg gave the Commencement Address at the Seminary. After telling the graduates to "hold fast" to their faith in God and in Israel, he defined the term: "Holding fast, however, does not mean standing still. Without being in sympathy with rapid changes and feverish activities of a restless age, one must admit that any institution which tries to remain stationary in a moving world stands at a very great disadvantage. In modern times, our tastes, our habits, our intellectual atmosphere have so greatly altered that it would be suicidal policy for the Synagogue to ignore the great changes. It is your mission, you graduates of the Jewish Theological Seminary, to restate the Jewish message, that it can be understood by modern man. . . . Truth has nothing to fear from free inquiry, and though criticism destroys much, it creates more. . . . But where there is no love there is no understanding, and for criticism to be constructive sympathy is the first requisite."

At about the same time, Professor Ginzberg delivered an address to the ladies at a convention of the United Synagogue: "Jewish religion centers around the home, and at the divine service at home it is the woman who is the priest. A healthy religious life among the Jews is only possible by having an adequate religious training of the youth, and the woman is the best teacher of the child.

"The greatest glories of the Jew, the purity of the home and loyalty, are mostly due to Jewish women. From the beginning of our history down to our own day, the Jewish woman is the standard bearer of Jewish loyalty.

"The often heard remark that Reform put the women into the Synagogue is correct, if by it we want to state the fact that it drove the men out of it so that only women remain there. In old Jewry, woman had her place in the Synagogue. Now she has also the vacant place of the man.

"We who stand on the solid ground of historical Judaism

cannot permit our religious customs and practices to be
turned into spiritual dolls for women to dress according to
their caprice. The home, the school and the exercise of loving kindness, of which charity is only the vulgarized form,
were always the proper fields of activity of the Jewish
woman, and they must remain so if we are not to abandon
our program which calls for the continuation and strengthening of historical Judaism.

"Permit me, however, to add that ladies' societies are not
novel things in Jewish life. The oldest reference found in
Jewish literature to societies is that to one which existed
more than a thousand years ago in Jerusalem, and this was a
Ladies' Society for the Aid of Criminals. This sounds rather
modern! You will perhaps be more surprised if I tell you that
at about the same time there was in Jerusalem a ladies' knit-
ting or embroidering—I really do not know the exact difference between these two noble arts—society. The purpose of
this society was a noble and holy one, as is [the purpose of]
that similar one of today. The House of God was adorned
with the products of the nimble fingers of the ladies of Jerusalem."

Professor Ginzberg was clear in his views about the appropriate role of the rabbi, the lay leaders, and women in the
strengthening of Conservative Judaism, or, as he preferred
to call it, Historical Judaism. And it is likely that many,
though by no means all, in his captive audiences agreed with
all or most of what he had to say. But it required much more
than intellectual clarity and conviction to shape and reshape
the lives of American Jews, even those who proudly identified themselves with the Seminary or the organizations associated with it. And he must have reached the same conclusion. For he quickly withdrew from organizational activity,
partly because circumstance required it, since Dr. Adler returned to assume his responsibilities as Acting President and
shortly thereafter as President of the Seminary, and partly

because he must have reached the conclusion that he could not effectively influence the course of events.

But he did not want to retreat completely into his study. He sought and found one arena that was congenial for him, and that was to work for the furtherance of Jewish scholarship. His major effort expressed itself in relation to the American Academy of Jewish Research of which he was a founding member and its first and long-time president. As the years passed, he also exerted himself on behalf of particular scholars and research projects. While work on behalf of the Academy was an uphill struggle, it was more acceptable to him than to attempt to deal with an inchoate body of American Jewry, even with that segment identified with the Seminary.

The story of the Academy begins in 1919. The setting is the Jersey coast in the town of Avon, where we had a summer home. In addition to my father and his colleagues Davidson, Friedlaender and Marx, the organizing group consisted of Lauterbach and Neumark of the Hebrew Union College; Malter of Dropsie College; and Zeitlin of the Rabbinical College. The original plan was to form an "Association of Jewish Scholars in America."

According to a memorandum in my father's files, the purpose was "to stimulate Jewish learning by helpful cooperation and mutual encouragement as well as to formulate standards of Jewish scholarship." The major activities were to stimulate the publication of research in Jewish scholarship. Membership was to be by nomination by two regular members, to be acted on at the business session of the annual meeting. Three negative votes would exclude the person for that year. Provision was also made for honorary members, whose election would have to be unanimous. One of the ten invited to be charter members, Professor G. Deutsch of the Hebrew Union College, wanted regular members to be elected by unanimous vote "to follow the example of the elite of Jerusalem." He questioned whether it was right to elect Cyrus Adler, Richard Gottheil or Morris Jastrow and not Jacob H. Schiff who, in his opinion, was "entitled to honor as patron above everybody else."

Professor Max Margolis of Dropsie College completed the roster of charter members. In his letter of acceptance, Margolis, on the basis of his editorship of the *Journal of the Society of Biblical Literature and Exegesis,* warned against house publications; he questioned the desirability of publishing articles in Hebrew; and he pointed to the danger of making invidious distinctions between regular and honorary members, suggesting that Adler might turn down an invitation to become an honorary member. On the last point, he was proved wrong. When the Academy was first established, Dr. Kohler, the President of the Hebrew Union College and Dr. Adler, the President of Dropsie College and the Acting President of the Jewish Theological Seminary, were elected honorary members, together with Judge Mayer Sulzberger. The name of the President of the Rabbinical College (Yeshiva), Dr. Bernard Revel, was scratched out from the draft proposal.

The minutes of the first meeting, held on April 7, 1920 at the Seminary, record the name as the "American Jewish Academy for the Promotion of Jewish Research." The officers were President, Ginzberg; Vice President, Deutsch; Secretary, Malter; Treasurer, Lauterbach. Shortly thereafter, the name of the new organization was changed for the last time to the American Academy for Jewish Research.

Louis Marshall, with whom my father discussed the plans of the newly formed Academy, asked for a detailed program and budget. In April 1921 this was forthcoming. It consisted of four undertakings:

1. A Descriptive Index to the *Responsa* of the Geonim.
2. Corpus Baraitorum—a systematic arrangement of the Tannaitic material in both Talmudim and numerous Midrashim.

3. The Jews in Patristic Literature—a work to consist of five volumes to contain all the material in Greek, Latin and Oriental literature.
4. A Supplement to Benjacobs' *Thesaurus Librorum Hebracorum.* This book had been prepared and was awaiting a subsidy to permit its publication.

The budget was estimated at $12,000 for items 1 and 2, $15,000 for item 3, and $3,000 for item 4, or a grand total of $30,000. The letter also contained specific recommendations about which scholars might be willing to take on these several assignments. Marshall's reply follows:

I am very much interested in your program as therein set forth. As I stated to you when you were at my office some time ago, I recognize the fact that your organization has the potentiality of becoming a very useful force in Jewish research. I regard it as being best adapted to carry on my cherished plan of a digest of the Responsa that could possibly be conceived. Your plan, however, merely deals with one phase of the subject in which I have expressed so great an interest.

I should like very much to be of assistance in enabling you to embark upon your project in a practical way. The difficulty, however, is, as usual, in the financial aspects of the subject. The four items of your program aggregate an estimated expenditure of at least $30,000. While under normal conditions, the sum might not be regarded as large, at the present time I am afraid that it is prohibitive. The recent experience of the Seminary is a demonstration of that fact. I am not, however, hopeless. I nevertheless believe that until we have put the Seminary and the Teachers' Institute upon their feet it will be quite impossible to raise the amount of money which is required for your purposes. I am willing, as soon as I shall be enabled to solve the financial problems of the Seminary, to see what I can do toward assisting your organization.

In November 1922, the young organization held a meeting at Dropsie College, at which it voted to raise funds for various scholarly projects and to appoint "a commission charged with the preparation of a plan for an Index to the Responsa Literature." Its rolls showed that it had lost two of its original members (Deutsch and Friedlaender) and had added Professors Blondheim, Husik, Wolfson, Halper and Dr. Kohler's successor, Professor Morgenstern.

The minutes of the annual meeting held in December 1923 contain the following paragraph:

> In his opening remarks, the President, Professor Ginzberg, pointed out that no organized body had ever attempted to prepare a "Critical Edition" of any of the collective Hebrew works (Midrash, Talmud, Mishnah, etc.). A few individual attempts were made but they were unsuccessful. This is a scholastic piece of work which can only be done by a body of scholars and for any individual to attempt the task of that nature would be futile.

Since no progress had yet been made in securing funds, the Academy took steps at this meeting to establish, among other committees, one on Organization. It also established a Committee on the Jewish University in Jerusalem. The minutes note: "Since there is going to be a Jewish University in Jerusalem, the Academy ought to express its views as to what the University should be like." In addition to appointing himself as Chairman of the Committee, my father asked Adler, Lauterbach, Malter, Marx and Zeitlin to serve with him. As the next chapter indicates, the Academy did play a role in the guidance of the Institute for Jewish Studies that was about to be established as part of the newly created Hebrew University in Jerusalem.

The minutes of the meeting in September 1924 disclose that Dr. Morgenstern had approached the Secretary of the B'nai B'rith to interest that body in the work of the Academy, and that Dr. Adler was working on a prospective list of contributors who would be asked to pledge support for five years at sums ranging from $50 to $500 per annum.

With the death of Judge Sulzberger, Louis Marshall was

elected to honorary membership and once again Ginzberg sought his help. The Academy had shifted its focus to some degree and was now stressing support for works awaiting publication. Once again, Marshall responded sympathetically but warned of the competing demands for funds:

> I am in receipt of yours of the 17th instant regarding the American Academy of Jewish Research, with a statement of the works which are awaiting publication, the importance of which I fully recognize.
>
> I shall do all that I can to help you in your efforts to secure the necessary funds to defray the cost of publication. The difficulty, however, is that I have so many other matters of a similar character which are occupying my attention that I must say that it is not an easy matter to get the required amount within any given time. The needs of the Seminary are, of course, entitled to preferential consideration. Then there is the work of the Emergency Committee for Jewish Refugees, the demands of the University of Jerusalem and its various faculties, the claims of the Jewish Publication Society, the agitation in favor of raising a large fund for agricultural work in Russia and in aid of educational institutions in various parts of Eastern Europe, the securing of capital for the Palestine Economic Corporation, to say nothing of ORT, OZE, Keren Hayesod, and a dozen other conflicting movements.
>
> Just at this time we are in a state of chaos. I had hoped that we could start a great educational movement which would deal with every phase of the subject and which would necessarily include the scholarly work of your organization. I must confess, however, that I have been greatly disappointed by the lack of appropriate response from those who one would naturally expect would take an active interest in such a movement.
>
> I shall try to speak with a few gentlemen at the earliest opportunity, and it is my expectation to make a substantial subscription to the fund sought to be raised.

That Marshall had a realistic estimate of the situation is suggested by the following letter of Lewis Strauss to Cyrus Adler on April 8, 1925:

I am just in receipt of one of the letters which has been sent out by the American Academy of Jewish Research. It seems to me that with support so difficult to obtain for existing organizations, we are inclined to over-do things in the formation of new ones, although if you will say that this fills a need not supplied by the Historical Society, the Publication Society and the Bureau of Social Research, I am prepared to contribute whatever I can spare, on your recommendation.

At the suggestion of Dr. Morgenstern, who had opened up the lead to the B'nai B'rith, my father prepared a statement about the Academy which was published in the *B'nai B'rith News* early in 1925.

In May 1925, my father wrote to Sol Rosenbloom of Pittsburgh, whom he had met several years earlier, and enclosed a copy of this article. His letter contained the following paragraph: "I would like to say to you as follows: American Israel has many who understand the demand of philanthropy and primary education. The number, however, of those who know what Jewish learning means to the life of the Jew could be counted on one hand. If, therefore, a man like you should be lukewarm to an undertaking like ours, who can we expect to be interested in it?"

Small sums were obtained from among the carefully prepared list of potential supporters, but no large amounts were obtained either from individuals or organizations, and when the prosperous twenties came to an end, the Academy had such a modest income that it could do little more than make a few subventions towards the publication of important scholarly works.

Despite its financial position or, more correctly, its lack of finances, the Academy embarked on its most ambitious project in January 1930, when it established a Maimonides Committee to publish a critical edition of the great philosopher's collected works in connection with the eight hundredth anniversary of his birth which would occur in 1935.

Dr. Sarton of Harvard University had called the approaching anniversary to Dr. Adler's attention, who shortly thereafter delivered an address on the desirability of publishing Maimonides' collected works. The response was positive and Adler turned the matter over to the Academy, which set about to organize a world-wide group of patrons as well as a world-wide group of scholars who would be willing to cooperate in the undertaking. Several meetings were held, but because of the deepening economic depression and the advent of Hitler, the project was still-born.

My father resigned as President of the Academy in 1947, when he finally convinced his colleagues that they must permit him to relinquish the post. They had been reluctant to release him for fear that there might be dissension in choosing his successor. Although he had failed during his long time in office to secure adequate financial support for the Academy, after his retirement he convinced his close friend and devoted pupil, Rabbi Louis M. Epstein, to name the Academy as the residual legatee of his estate. I was one of the three executors of Epstein's estate and in the 1950's the Academy received almost $100,000 from it.

But long before this, the Academy was able to expand. It did have limited success in acquiring subventions from the various joint appeals for funds by various Jewish communities, and it served as a mechanism to help relocate and for a time support Jewish scholars who were refugees from Hitler. For this activity, it became the recipient of special grants. Early in the New Deal, it sought to interest the Federal Government in a large-scale undertaking—to prepare catalogues of the Hebrew manuscripts in the United States and in other countries and to catalogue by author and to translate into English all the titles of printed Hebrew books in the United States. It was estimated that about a hundred students and scholars could be employed (the length of time was not specified in the plan) on this undertaking. The draft of a letter to accompany the proposal which was signed by a special committee of the Academy follows:

The undersigned, acting on behalf of a group of men interested in the promotion of education and research and in the alleviation of the fate of the unemployed students and white collar men, beg to submit the plan herein enclosed for your kind consideration. Our intention is to supply useful work for the needy students and scholars and at the same time create the facilities for the continuation of their education and the broadening of their intellectual outlook.

Our plan is conceived in a way that money will be spent mainly for labor, as less than 5% will be required in necessary material. About 90% of the employed will be taken from among those listed on the Relief Rolls.

With this view in mind, we plan the compilation of a comprehensive bibliography bearing on history and literature of the Jews from biblical times up to recent date.

A complete bibliographic apparatus is generally regarded as a basic necessity for scientific reasearch in each field. The preparation of such an apparatus would render aid to unemployed scholars and intellectuals, and, at the same time, create in the United States a body of records serving as a center of information for the journalist and statesman, for the librarian and scholar in the United States as well as abroad.

I never discussed with my father his interpretation of why the Academy had such a hard time in gaining even modest support. But the answers are not difficult to construe. Its goals were too diffuse and unspecific. Early in its existence, it outlined several ambitious projects without firm commitments from potential collaborators. Later, it emphasized the role that it might play in subvention of publications. Not until the Maimonides project, which the depression and Hitler nipped in the bud, did it have the type of proposal that could elicit wide-scale support, financial and scholarly. But there is serious question whether it could have carried through successfully so complicated an effort even had the times been more propitious. The organization was too loose and it had no full-time staff.

The Academy ran into trouble on other grounds. It was considered to be a competitor by the supporters of the established institutions of higher learning in the United States. It came into existence at about the time that American support was first sought and obtained for the Hebrew University in Jerusalem. It also had to compete with the new trend of wealthy Jews' establishing chairs and research projects at large universities. And finally, it predated the revolution in philanthropy. It still looked to a few wealthy men for support.

Had it approached the more than five hundred graduates of the two major theological seminaries who held active pulpits, and had each of their congregations been willing to contribute $100 annually, the Academy never would have wanted for adequate money. But such an approach was still a decade or more ahead of the times. Even this approach might have failed—so low stood interest in Jewish scholarship even among the members of the rabbinate.

Nevertheless, modest progress was made. The Academy approved the work of Rabbi Kosovsky in Jerusalem on the *Concordance of the Mishnah,* and we find as early as 1925 the following in a letter from my father to Dr. Morgenstern: "You may be disappointed to hear that I was not in the least surprised by the very handsome check of $1,400 which you sent me towards the fund for the publication of the *Concordance of the Mishnah.* Having put you in the class of those who promise little and do much, I was quite sure that you would do your share in this undertaking.

"With Jewish optimism, I obligated myself personally to guarantee the amount of $7,000, and I am happy to say that I am lacking a little less than $600 of this sum."

As early as January 1922, my father wrote to Mr. Rosenbloom seeking his support for Doctor B. Lewin of Haifa,

Palestine. The Academy had reviewed the plan and had approved it enthusiastically.

"His plan is to make the writings of the Geonim accessible in a critical form to the student of Jewish lore and literature. Next to the Talmud, these writings, extending over a period of about three centuries, are the most important source for the history of the development of Jewish thought and life in post-biblical times. Unfortunately, however, no branch of Jewish literature has come down to us in such a mutilated and corrupt form as the Responsa of the Geonim."

And a year later, in response to an inquiry from Louis Marshall, my father wrote as follows:

I rejoice in the opportunity your letter of the 6th instant gives me to explain to you briefly the plan of Doctor Benjamin Lewin in which I and my colleagues of the Seminary and many others take so lively an interest.

Doctor Lewin has spent the last fifteen years in preparing a critical edition of the writings of the Geonim. It is no exaggeration in saying that without a careful study of the Geonic literature, we shall never be in a position to understand the spiritual and intellectual life of European Jewry during the Middle Ages. Unfortunately however, there is hardly any branch of Jewish literature which came down to us in such a mutilated form as the literary productions of the Geonim. Especially the Responsa of the Geonim are found scattered through hundreds of books and manuscripts. Doctor Lewin's plan is now to have a critical edition of the Geonic works published in fifteen volumes. The average cost of each volume to be about $4,000. I should estimate that it would take Doctor Lewin ten years to complete his work. Within a year, he might be able to publish the first two volumes which are ready for the printer, provided of course, the necessary funds for this publication will be found. I regret to say that as yet Doctor Lewin has not been very successful in securing financial support for this undertaking. If, however, the sum of $10,000 could be secured for the publication of the first two volumes, it would be a pity not to start this work, as there is good reason to hope that the money necessary for the publication of the other volumes might partly be secured by the sale of the first volumes.

As to the qualifications of Doctor Lewin for this work, I can only say that I hardly know any other scholar who would be better fitted to carry it out successfully. His critical edition with commentary of the famous letter by R. Ben Sherira Gaon shows not only his mastery in this branch of Jewish literature, but also his great critical acumen and methodological training.

My father's efforts on behalf of Lewin continued for over two decades; the following paragraphs are from a letter written in the 1940's to Dr. Simon Greenberg:

"I am enclosing herewith the letter to the Rabbinical Board of Philadelphia by Doctor Benjamin Lewin, who, as you very well know, is no more amongst the living. His death is a great loss to Jewish scholarship and I hope that at least the part of the manuscript prepared by him will soon be published.

"By the way, the American Academy for Jewish Research had applied to the Philadelphia Allied Jewish appeal for a grant of $1,000.00, but our request was denied. Do you think that we have any chance to receive a more favorable reply from them if we ask for a special fund towards publication of important scholarly works, as for instance, the publication of Dr. Lewin's fourteenth volume of the Ozar?"

Despite its modest funds, the Academy was able in 1930 to vote a three-year subvention in the amount of $500 annually towards the publication costs of Rabbi Kosovsky's *Concordance of the Tosefta*. While its great expectations never were realized, the Academy was nevertheless able to point to some modest achievements.

My father's efforts to raise money for Jewish scholars and scholarship were by no means restricted to the orbit of the Academy. In March 1924, he wrote to Dr. Adler requesting his help in having the Joint Distribution Committee appropriate $5,000 for the *Yeshiva* in Bialystok. "The leaders of the *Yeshiva* are attempting to attract paying pupils, the number of which is gradually increasing, so that this institution would become self-supporting if means were found to tide them over for a few years."

In March 1926, Rabbi Israel Goldstein sent the following mimeographed letter to his colleagues:

Dear Colleague:

The following appeal has come to the New York Board of Jewish Ministers from Prof. Louis Ginzberg, the Chairman of the A.S. Freidus Memorial Committee.

The members of our Board are probably better able than most people to feel the worthiness of Prof. Ginzberg's appeal.

"A number of friends and admirers of the late Abraham S. Freidus are planning the publication of a volume of Jewish Bibliography in the memory of this great Jewish bibliographer and no less great Jewish character. It is no exaggeration to say that for the last quarter of a century nobody in America was of greater assistance to Jewish authors and scholars than the late Mr. Freidus, who, in complete self-effacement, has given them the best that was in him. Especially among the members of your association there must be many who remember with gratitude the kindness and services rendered by him.

I earnestly hope that our appeal for a subvention will not be in vain."

And before too much time passed, the Memorial Volume was off the press.

A little later, my father joined with colleagues from the Union Theological Seminary and the General Theological Seminary to raise funds on behalf of his close friend, Arnold Ehrlich.

The life of Arnold B. Ehrlich is fast drawing near the biblical limit of three score years and ten. That life has been devoted to one thing, the study of the Hebrew Old Testament. No scholar in this country and perhaps abroad possesses an equipment comparable to him for the task. The results of his labors appeared first in

Mikra Ki Pheschuto, three volumes in Hebrew (Berlin, 1890). On the basis of this work thoroughly revised and augmented so as to be an entirely new production were published in German beginning in 1908 the seven volumes of *Randglossen zur Hebraischen Bibel,* a monumental magnum opus crowded with fresh, original and learned comments on the ancient sacred books of Israel in which insight and erudition are exhibited in a remarkable degree. Supplementary volumes with much valuable material are finished in ms. If these could be published, the venerable scholar would be ready to sing his *Nunc Dimittis.* The kindness of friends and admirers has helped him in the past to finance the publication of the preceding volumes. What little of this world's goods he himself possesses he has already given to the uttermost. The undersigned, some of whom know Mr. Ehrlich personally and all of whom entertain the highest esteem for him as a scholar, are undertaking to raise the $3,000.00 needed that the final contribution to biblical learning of this modern Rashi may see the light, and that in his declining years he may have the satisfaction of knowing that the self-denying labors of a lifetime have not failed to arouse the interest and sympathy and admiration of Jews and Christians alike. Each recipient of this letter will have the privilege of being instrumental in furthering the completion of a great work which is destined to rank conspicuously in the long and noble history of Biblical Exegesis.

In the middle 1930's, my father sent a copy of a work by Rabbi Abraham Schreiber on Don Vidal Solomon's (Meiri) commentary to Mr. Lucius N. Littauer. From a later letter we learn that for years Rabbi Schreiber had been engaged in publishing and editing from Italian manuscripts the commentaries by the "great Talmudist and Sage Meiri." In forwarding Rabbi Schreiber's book to Mr. Littauer, my father wrote:

"Rabbi Schreiber has inscribed the book to you as a token of gratitude for your generous interest in Jewish learning, and in doing so he voiced the feeling of all Jewish scholars. In these days of great material suffering among the Jews, one is apt to forget the agony of Judaism, and there is some consolation in knowing that there still are men like you who are aware of the truth that man doth not live by bread only. May it be granted to you to continue your work in behalf of Jewish learning for many more years to come."

Some years earlier (1926), in his capacity as President of the Academy, my father wrote to Mr. Littauer extending the congratulations of the Academy on establishment "by you of a Chair for Jewish Literature and Philosophy at Harvard University." He wrote:

"The members of the Academy, all of whom have devoted themselves to the study and teaching of Jewish life and thought, have often felt keenly the neglect reflected in the attitude of the American institutions for higher learning towards Jewish studies which are entirely ignored. This ignoring of Jewish learning harbors the greatest conceivable danger to the future of American Israel as it must necessarily lead to create in the minds of the academic youth, Jews and Gentiles alike, the conviction of Jewish inferiority. We therefore greatly rejoice in the splendid example you have given to American Jewry and earnestly hope that it will serve to many as an incentive to emulate your splendid work."

In 1950, my father was still busy collecting funds for Rabbi Schreiber, who then had the "magnum opus of this great scholar of Jewish ethics" ready for press. My father described the work:

"This work by Meiri is, in a certain sense, quite unique in our literature. It was written as a reply to a priest who had chided the Jews for having little interest in the search for the human-mental religious problems of sin, repentance, and penance. The work in reply to these accusations is in the true sense a treasure of the vast material found not only in the Talmudim and Midrashim, but also in the philosophical-ethical literature of Jews and Arabs. Quantitatively, the book is no less imposing, as it comprises about 800 pages,

and, of course, the expense of publication is a very considerable one."

My father's investment in Schreiber was considerable. I
remember that he elicited my help in obtaining an American
visa for him, which I was able to do through a close friend
who was working with the Joint Distribution Committee in
Europe and who had met Schreiber in Greece, where shortly
after the end of World War II he was serving as Chief
Rabbi. In a letter to Rabbi Solomon Goldman of Chicago in
1950, my father commented in passing that Schreiber is a
member of "the most distinguished rabbinical family in
Hungary for more than a century." He suggested that Goldman might find an opportunity to write a paragraph or two
in appreciation of *Meiri's Book of Repentance* by Rabbi
Abraham Schreiber. He further asked Goldman to call attention "to the outrageous behavior" of a certain "Rabbi and
Professor" who decided to appropriate Schreiber's work by
publishing and advertising the book as his own. "If the Jewish press in America were not corrupt, they ought to have
called attention to the outrage. I was, however, sure that not
only would they not do it on their own account, but if requested to do so they would refuse."

One more effort and we are done. In 1949, Ginzberg took
the lead in establishing a committee to seek funds for carrying on the publication of the *Hatekufah,* of which thirty
volumes had previously been published by the late Abraham
Stybel, whom my father called "the greatest patron of modern Hebrew literature." But this effort, despite the distinguished membership of the sponsoring committee, did not
succeed. There is a large element of the personal in philanthropy. When the originator of an idea or an ideal is no
longer alive it is doubly hard to arouse enthusiasm.

While my father always had a picture of himself as a
scholar self-confined within the four walls of his library, the
truth is that he engaged in a goodly number of affairs that

took him beyond the limits of his library. In addition to those already reviewed, brief reference should be made to the other ways in which he sought to exert his influence and extend his help to those in need. Early in the 1920's he was an active member of the Committee on Jewish Classics of the Jewish Publication Society, and there is at least one opinion of his in writing to the effect that the manuscript which he was asked to review "is absolutely unfit to be printed in its present form." I am sure that he found such assignments distasteful. Moreover, he must have been very restive about Dr. Adler, a non-scholar, chairing the Committee, and before long he resigned. He soon had his own difficulties with the Society. After a change in editors brought about by loose financial management, the Society entered upon a period of austerity. The new business manager, who was an expert in railroad economics [*sic!*] saw no point in proceeding with the plan approved by the Trustees in 1924 to publish an Index volume to the *Legends of the Jews*. The decision of the Trustees to proceed with the index had been taken on the basis of my father's letter of October 10, 1924:

In a few months, it will be a quarter of a century since I began the work on the *Legends of the Jews* at the suggestion of your late Chairman, Judge Mayer Sulzberger. My desire to see the work completed within a reasonable time is therefore natural. In view of the fact that the first volume of the *Notes* has passed the state of proof reading and the second volume is now being set up, it occurred to me that it is now time to think of the Index. There is of course, no need for me to point out to you the importance of an Index to a work like the *Legends*. Without exaggeration, one may say that without an exhaustive and thorough Index my work on the *Legends* would be incomplete.

I estimate that the Index will consist of about 400 pages. This volume, however, is to contain the following additional matter:
1. Three excurses, to wit:—
    (a) The pre-Existent Things

(b) The Testaments of the Twelve Patriarchs in their
    Relation to the Rabbinic Haggadah
(c) The Hebrew Original of the Pseudo-Philonic Writ-
    ing *The Antiquities of the Jews.*

I believe that about 100 to 120 pages will be necessary for these
three excurses.

2. A complete Bibliography of the works referred to in the
   Notes.

About 100 pages.

It is interesting to note that in the Secretary's reply, in
which he indicates that the Trustees approved this plan, a
paragraph was added:

At the meeting the suggestion was made that it might be well to
consider issuing a one volume edition of *The Legends of the
Jews,* following more or less in the footsteps of Lady Frazer, who
reduced her husband's monumental work into one volume. No
action was taken, but it might be well to bear this in mind.

The index volume, prepared by my father's former student
and colleague, Boaz Cohen, was not published until 1938
and the suggestion of a one-volume condensation of the
Legends had to wait until after his death, when I worked
out an arrangement with Simon and Schuster.

My father's feeling about the economist-business manager
is reflected in the following comment written in 1947 in a
letter to a friend, who had had an altercation with the gentleman:

"I knew him from the time of his connection with the
Jewish Publication Society, and to be candid, I never
thought that he had enough Jewish interest to be anti-Jewish
and the spokesman for the American Council for Judaism.

"We may not be a chosen people, but surely a very queer
one to have men like Doctor G—— tell us how Jewish education should be conducted."

My father's personal and professional relations with

George Alexander Kohut and the Kohut Foundation were more pleasant. George Kohut was the son of Alexander Kohut, a distinguished American rabbi and scholar who had become a member of the Seminary faculty before its reorganization. In his youth, George had worked on the Seminary's library staff, and in his later years he was a devoted friend of Jewish scholars and scholarship.

In 1927, my father sought Kohut's help in placing Jacques Faitlovich, who for so many years had devoted himself to studying the Falashas—the Jews of Ethiopia who, cut off from the rest of Jewry for two thousand years, believed themselves to be the only surviving remnant of Israel. Faitlovich first arrived in the United States in the year I was born, 1911; I recall that on one of his periodic visits to America he promised that on his next return from Ethiopia he would bring me a monkey! Kohut assured Faitlovich that the Foundation would bring out his volume on the liturgy and folklore of the Falashas, but he was not able to do more.

In 1938, my father wrote to Rebekah Kohut, George's stepmother, of his pleasure and that of his colleagues on the Publication Committee that the Foundation had agreed to continue the financing of Rabbi Kosovsky's *Concordance*, which had earlier received some modest grants from the Academy. One point of the agreement specified that the work would be dedicated "to the memory of our dear George."

My father never permitted friendship to rob him of his critical sense or to lead him into directions where he did not want to go. Kohut was deeply involved in a plan to bring out a popular Jewish encyclopedia, and he thought that he had succeeded in eliciting a promise from Ginzberg to assume some responsibility in connection with it. But in the end Ginzberg avoided any entanglement. It was not an effort that could command his scholarly talents and interests, however meritorious on other grounds.

My father's relations with Kohut often involved Stephen Wise and the Institute of Jewish Religion. The following letter from Kohut to Wise is one illustration of this three-cornered relationship which not only gave my father much pleasure but which also enabled him to help, through his powerful friends, many struggling scholars.

Dear Stephen:

I spent two wonderful hours with Professor Ginzberg and his wife yesterday, talking over various problems in connection with the *Jewish Encyclopedia* we are editing.

He spoke appreciatively of the Institute and declared, without any solicitation from me, that he does not consider it in any sense a rival of any other organization and that he is glad to see it achieve constructive results in the cause of learning.

In that connection, he strongly recommended our inviting Dr. Scholem of Palestine. He is not only one of our greatest authorities on the *Cabbala*, but is well versed in philosophy and could deliver a series of fascinating lectures, in course, on Jewish Mysticism.

That is a subject which calls for the most delicate and sympathetic treatment at the hands of a mature scholar of his stamp, and I heartily concur in Dr. Ginzberg's suggestion, if you think that we could afford to take on Scholem for a full semester.

I promised Dr. Ginzberg to lay this matter before you and to report your views on the subject. I am sure that Spiegel as well as Baron would unequivocally endorse Scholem.

In the 1940's a new patron of Jewish scholarship appeared on the scene—the late Louis M. Rabinowitz, who, among his many benefactions, gave a large sum to Yale University to support the editing and publishing of Jewish classics. Somewhat out of keeping with his general stance, my father, together with his friend Harry Wolfson of Harvard, agreed to be an editor. The third member was Julian Obermann, who was professor at Yale. This was a most trying assignment because Obermann, whom my father referred to in his letters as "Superman," was constantly at loggerheads with most of the contributors. After valiant attempts to help the many unfortunates who had dealings with Obermann, Wolfson and my father resigned.

There were still additional ways in which my father sought to help those who needed funds for research or a teaching position. Henry Allen Moe of the John Simon Guggenheim Memorial Foundation sought his opinion over the years about various applicants, and it was rare indeed that a man whom my father recommended strongly did not receive a fellowship. He was careful in his judgments about people, and Moe, who apparently placed considerable reliance on his advisors, appreciated that my father meant what he wrote.

On occasion he would take the initiative; witness the following letter to his friend, Professor William Albright:

"I understand that you are connected with the American Philosophical Society, and I hope you do not mind my approaching you in the following matter.

"Dr. Solomon Gandz is applying to this Society for a grant in support of his scientific work. I do not know whether you are personally acquainted with Dr. Gandz, but I am quite sure that you must know at least some of his writings. I consider him a scholar of quite extraordinary ability and vast erudition. His proposed researches will be of great value to the Orientalist as well as to the student of the relation of Western to Eastern culture. I hope that you will be able to further his plans."

Perhaps the most unexpected, if not inexplicable, of actions was his writing, together with his colleagues, Marx and Davidson, an unsolicited letter to Judge Lehman in the latter's capacity as president of Temple Emanu-El. My father had known and admired Rabbi Enelow for many years and had helped him in his work. The Academy had honored Enelow by electing him, together with George Foote Moore of Harvard, an honorary fellow in 1929. There were distinguished rabbis in New York, of whom my father said that if they knew they could land on the front page of *The New York Times*, they would not hesitate to kill their grandmothers. Enelow was indeed of different stuff. He was a mediocre preacher, and not given to bolstering the egos of his rich congregants. This provides some background for the following letter:

Dear Judge:

We were shocked to read in the papers of the contemplated retirement of Doctor H. G. Enelow by Temple Emanu-El. As Doctor Enelow is one of the few outstanding Rabbis in this country who uphold the old ideal of combining great learning with a deep interest in the spiritual duties of the Rabbinate, we, who are vitally concerned in maintaining a learned Rabbinate, venture to address to you these lines.

Doctor Enelow, through his very important scholarly work in recent years, has attracted the attention of the entire Jewish learned world. It is a great credit to Jewry to have such scientific work produced by a man who at the same time serves the most influential Congregation in the United States. To retire such a man in his best years might give the impression that scholarship and the Rabbinate do not go together. It is from this point of view that we thought it proper for us to address you.

As we have the pleasure of knowing you personally and realize your deep interest in Jewish learning and Judaism, we feel certain that you will consider it neither presumptuous nor meddlesome on our part.

We may add that we are writing this letter entirely on our own initiative and that neither Doctor Enelow nor anybody else is aware of it.

Very sincerely yours,

LOUIS GINZBERG
ALEXANDER MARX
ISRAEL DAVIDSON

For about thirty years, from the establishment of the American Academy of Jewish Research until the day of his death, my father never slackened his efforts on behalf of Jewish scholars and scholarship. He did what he could for those at home and abroad who were in need of assistance. He had limited success, but I am sure that, while he was saddened when he failed, he found much joy in his modest successes. He never felt that lack of response gave him a warrant to slacken his efforts. He would have been overjoyed had he found two or three patrons who would have helped him. Lacking these, he did the best he could.

CHAPTER IX

THE REDEMPTION OF ZION

ASIDE FROM some poems, the first item in Louis Ginzberg's bibliography is a short piece on Zionism published in a Dutch journal in 1898. But his ties to the Holy Land predate that article by many years; they go back to the beginning of his consciousness, surely to the beginning of his formal studies. A man who had been reared in the shadow of the Gaon of Vilna, the Gaon who had set out on foot to make his way to Jerusalem and was forced to turn back only by the exigencies of fate, did not need to read Hess or listen to Herzl to share the dream of the redemption of Zion. The redemption was in the marrow of his bones. It commanded his soul.

It may be worth pointing out in passing that the millions of Eastern Jews who, for reasons of intellect, economic necessity, or taste broke with the observance of tradition, whether they migrated to the West or remained behind, seldom went so far as to deny their love of Zion. That was the deepest of all their affirmations. When my father's brother Asher died in the early 1930's in South Africa where he had lived and prospered, we learned that his principal bequests, other than to the multitudinous members of the family, many of whom he had long supported, were to the Atheist Society of South Africa and to the Keren Kayemeth, the Zionist body charged with the responsibility to purchase land in Palestine. A man brought up as my father had been could no more be indifferent to the call of Zionism than to the ties of family. In fact, Zion was the home to which all religious Jews looked forward to returning, thereby ending the long years of alienation from the Temple of their ancestors.

In his discussions with Henrietta Szold, Louis Ginzberg may have, for intellectual sport, defended Mr. Jacob Schiff's right to say his many pieces about the incompatibility of Americanism and Zionism, but he could not possibly have taken him seriously. As my friend Walter Teller, the gifted American writer and nephew of Judah Magnes, remarked to me after his first trip to Israel in 1963, Zion means something different to every Jew who goes there to settle or even to visit. I recall a semi-official discussion that I had with one of the senior members of the College of Cardinals in Rome, in 1956, on my return from a visit to Israel: he challenged me first on the anti-religious orientation of the dominant parties in the Israeli Government and complained about the lack of observance of their own tradition as well as a lack of sensitivity for the traditions of the Christian minority. And then he argued in a diametrically opposite direction by complaining about the stranglehold that the Orthodox factions in Israel had on the Government which left little scope for any other religion.

The issue for my father, as for others of his generation and background, was not whether he would be a Zionist—for that question was as meaningless as it would be to ask if he would be a Jew—but simply what ways to manifest his love for Zion, what roles to play in its rebuilding and redemption.

The following letter dated May 1902 was found in my father's file:

I am glad to inform you that the Society "L'maan Zion" of Des Moines, Iowa, has elected you a delegate to the Boston Convention. I received the credential only yesterday, or I would have notified you before. I do hope that you will not fail to come. I assure you that we will do all in our power to make it pleasant for you.

This letter suggests that Louis Ginzberg must have had some relation with the Federation of American Zionists in order to be elected to represent a "rotten borough." (I do not know whether he went to Boston or not.)

He was elected a delegate to the 1905 World Zionist Congress at Basle, but he eventually decided that since he did not represent any constituent body, he had better not attend. He was fond of relating, however, that the first item on the agenda of the American caucus was whether the discussions should be held in German or Yiddish. In 1907, he expected to attend the Congress that was meeting that year in The Hague, but the serious illness and eventual death of his father forced him to alter his plans.

As his correspondence with Henrietta Szold makes clear, Louis Ginzberg had a deep and continuing interest in the problems of Zionist ideology and in the attitudes and reactions of various sectors of the community to the rebuilding of the Holy Land. But he never found an opportunity to play an activist role.

When his good friend Chajes, the Chief Rabbi of Vienna, first visited the United States after World War I, he remonstrated with my father about his lack of active participation as a Zionist, but when Chajes returned some few years later, he no longer complained. He had learned about the intensity of American-Zionist politics, and he appreciated that this was not an arena in which my father could operate constructively. Of course, many men of integrity and ability were participating in the fray, but there were "no holds barred," and many of those in strategic positions were men for whom the end justified the means. Even such a rugged man as Brandeis found it necessary to withdraw from formal organizational leadership and to find other ways to make his important contributions.

I had called on the Justice in 1933 with a letter of introduction which my father had secured for me from Judge Mack, and I had visited the Justice again at his request the following year, when I had completed my field studies of large American corporations on a Cutting Travelling Fellowship from Columbia. I did not see him again until 1941, when I asked whether I might call on him at Chatham on Cape Cod, his summer home, when I was completing my first assignment for the Jewish community as Director of Research for the Allotment Committee of the United Jewish Appeal. I spent an hour with the Justice in what turned out to be one of his last working conferences; shortly thereafter, he became ill and returned to Washington where he died. It was sad to a neophyte like myself to hear the Justice advise on how the money should be spent in and on behalf of Palestine preferably without funnelling it through certain official Zionist organizations.

Dr. Harry Friedenwald, the distinguished ophthalmologist from Baltimore, whom my father knew intimately for almost half a century, Judge Julian Mack, Robert Szold, who later became my father-in-law, Stephen Wise, my father's pupil and friend Solomon Goldman, and many other devoted and able men remained active in the leadership. But it was too rough an environment for a scholar.

In 1919, Dr. Weizmann laid the cornerstone for the Hebrew University, the realization of an ideal that had first been formulated by Professor Schapira in Heidelberg in the 1880's. Dr. Judah Magnes, the gifted rabbi of Temple Emanu-El in New York City, had been chosen the first President. While not a scholar, he had demonstrated marked leadership capacity and he had the additional advantage of being related by ties of marriage and friendship to the top echelon of American Jews. Above all else, he was a devoted Zionist. My father's relations with Palestine centered, as one might expect, around the newly formed Hebrew University. This story falls into three parts: his role as President of the American Academy for Jewish Research in helping to shape the Institute for Jewish Studies at the University; his role as visiting professor in 1928-29; and in 1933-34, his member-ship on the Survey Committee which was charged with making recommendations aimed at improving the organiza-tion of the University.

The first letter in my father's files concerning the Univer-sity is a letter written in Jerusalem in 1922 to Dr. Cyrus Adler, from Professor Otto Warburg, the distinguished German chemist, in which he stresses the importance of moving ahead with plans for a Jewish Institute for Oriental and Hebrew Research. Warburg inquires about my father's views and asks whether the Academy at its last meeting ad-dressed itself to the subject. In his reply, Adler mentions that my father is in Europe and that he therefore had no opportunity to discuss the letter with him. But, he says:

Our religious and learned work in America is being very badly supported and there is no assurance of enthusiasm which can be translated into funds for the Institute of which you speak. I am not writing in this way to discourage you, but simply to give you an idea of the conditions prevailing here.

A year later, however, the matter had moved a good dis-tance ahead. Magnes wrote to Adler that the Zionist Execu-tive in London had made £3,000 available for opening in 1924 what is now called the Department of Jewish and Ori-ental Studies. Dr. Hertz' Committee in London "has taken it upon itself" to appoint three members of the faculty, Samuel Kraus of Vienna, Ludwig Blau of Budapest, and Chaim Tchernowitz of Odessa and Berlin. Magnes complains that

Kraus and Blau are both over seventy and Tchernowitz is in poor health.

He then animadverts to the role of Bible in the new institution and remarks that Dr. Weizmann had hoped to have Dr. Chajes of Vienna become Dean of the new Department. Magnes reports that a representative of the Mizrachi (Orthodox Zionist party) objected to Chajes' appointment, since he was a follower of the Higher Criticism. In any case he, Magnes, hoped that the new department could be given a less theological slant by the appointment of a non-Bible scholar as its head, and by adding some scholars from outside the field of Hebraica.

My father comments at length on the Magnes letter which Adler forwarded to him:

I very carefully read the letter of Dr. Magnes to you concerning the proposed Jewish University at Jerusalem and your comments thereupon. I was especially interested in what you and Dr. Magnes have to say about Dr. Hertz's committee in London. About a year ago in my conversation with you about the plan of studies submitted by Dr. Hertz, I remarked that the amateurish character of the plan stamps its author or authors as being entirely unfit for work of this kind. The judgment shown by this committee in its appointments perfectly matches that displayed by it in its plan of studies, and hence, *nil admirari*. I am, however, surprised to notice that even a man of such high ideals as Dr. Magnes finds fault with Dr. Hertz's committee only on account of its making appointments without furnishing 'the cash.' In other words, he accepts the principle that if you pay the piper, you may choose the music. If this principle should prevail at the proposed Jewish University, its doom is decreed before its birth. Only then may we hope to see such an institution developing into a center of Jewish learning, if its policy is to be guided by Jewish scholars.

Doctors Davidson, Marx and Zeitlin, to whom I have shown your letter, and myself, fully agree with your suggestion to have the Academy take up the matter. Of course, I am well aware of the fact that up to the present, the Academy is only a paper organization. It is nevertheless true that nowhere could a more representative body of Jewish scholars be found, and it would be criminal and stupid to ignore it at the establishment of the Jewish University.

I would even go a step further and suggest that the Committee in Jerusalem put itself in touch with the Jewish Academy in Berlin. German Jewry is at present unfortunately not in a position to give material aid in this undertaking, but this is no reason why Jewish scholars in Germany should not be consulted in a matter affecting Jewish scholarship.

Another point in Dr. Magnes' letter which struck me rather as being extremely strange is his suggestion that Jerusalem be made the real Center of this Organization. The present Committee in Jerusalem is certainly the most representative of Jewish intellectuals in Palestine. Yet, with all due respect to this fine set of men, they certainly cannot be said to represent Jewish scholarship. We all hope that the time will come when Palestinian Jewry will be able to take over the organization, but for the present, it would be almost a calamity to have the management of a scholastic institution placed in the hands of men who, whatever their merits may otherwise be, are neither by training or inclination, men who could be trusted with a task of this nature.

Although agreeing with Dr. Magnes that work at the Jewish University ought to be started as soon as possible, I am not at all convinced of the necessity to proceed immediately with appointments. It occurs to me that it would be far more advisable to invite for the first three years the most prominent Jewish scholars all over the world to the University. This plan offers many advantages. The prestige of the University would at its very start be greatly enhanced by having the most prominent Jewish scholars attached to it. Further, the experience of men of this type would be very valuable for the policy to be followed by the University and finally, their presence would attract a large number of students from Europe and America.

If you think that the above few remarks might be of some use to the Committee in Jerusalem, I would greatly appreciate it if you would communicate them to Dr. Magnes.

We see that despite the fact that his views were extremely critical, my father encouraged Adler to forward them to Magnes. Too much was at stake to worry about people's feelings. Moreover, sound programs depend on more than good academic advice. Money was needed and certain ideological problems, already suggested by the putative appointment of Chajes, had to be solved or at least shelved.

The value of Dr. Magnes' relations to New York Jewry was soon revealed by a gift of $100,000 by Felix Warburg for the new Institute. And Baron de Rothschild donated $50,000. These two sizable gifts made it possible to pursue further conversations with Sol Rosenbloom of Pittsburgh who had earlier indicated a willingness to make a substantial donation if he could be assured that the Institute would be under the control of people committed, as he was, to the furtherance of historical Judaism. The following letter from my father reveals that he had had discussions with Mr. Rosenbloom as early as 1923:

I often recollect with great pleasure the conversations I had with you about a year ago regarding the plans for the establishment of an Institution for higher Jewish learning in Jerusalem. Varying the pithy saying of our sages concerning the two classes of saints in Israel, one might well say of men in general that they are divided in two classes. There are those whose theoretical principles are unimpeachable, but whose conduct is negligible because of their lack of translating thought into action. There are again others, who in their eagerness for elevating sentiments into programs of life, are too rash to examine the nature of their sentiments. You are fortunate to be one of the few selected who combine sound principle with power of action.

I therefore venture to address you today, with regard to the Faculty of Jewish learning at the Hebrew University in Jerusalem. You are very likely acquainted with the steps undertaken in Europe and in Palestine towards the establishment of such a school. If men of your type should refrain from taking an active part in this important undertaking, there is the great danger of its policy being entirely decided by men who have no vision nor the true Jewish spirit.

Prominent scholars in Europe have suggested that the Academy for Jewish Research in America ought to become the main instrument in the building up of an institution like that planned. Though not of a very optimistic nature, I am convinced that the Academy would be very successful in its work if you would put to its disposal the sum you have set aside for this purpose.

Of course, there are many details which would have to be discussed between you and the Academy, but I have no doubt that they can satisfactorily be disposed of at a meeting during one of your visits to New York.

I would greatly appreciate an early reply as I would not like to have the Academy engage in this work before having heard from you.

Later that year, Rosenbloom communicated to Ginzberg his concern about the arrangements that had recently been worked out in London for the management of the new Institute to which in the interim, Rosenbloom had made a sizable donation.

I do not hesitate to tell you that I am not altogether pleased with the selection of the Trustees. As far as my interest in the Institute of Jewish Studies goes, I cannot entrust its well-being to men who are not in full sympathy with the historic conception of Judaism. I have the highest regard and respect for men like Bialik, Ahad Ha'am, Weizmann and Sokoloff in so far as their service to the Jewish people is concerned, but I do not consider these gentlemen as representing the idea of historic Judaism, nor do I think them the type of men which I have indicated in my utterances to be entrusted with the conduct of this Branch. This is not the time to dwell on it at length, but I shall be pleased to see you and Dr. Adler about these matters as soon as possible after the Holidays.

But Ginzberg, who shared many of these anxieties, would not let Rosenbloom too quickly off the hook:

"I noticed with interest what you remarked in your letter

concerning the Institute of Jewish Studies in Jerusalem and I
share your feeling in the matter, as I too would have preferred a people of different brand than those selected as
Trustees. To be candid, however, you are not entirely free
from blame. I am thoroughly convinced that if you would
have announced your donation to the Institute at the time of
the London Conference, you and Mr. Warburg, who, I
understand is in full sympathy with your views, might have
decided not only the policy of the Institute but also the
personnel of the Trustees. I hope that it is not too late for
you to have your influence exercised in the right direction."

On the ideological front, letters were passing across the
seas, particularly between Professor Haffkine of Paris and
Mr. Rosenbloom with copies to my father. In a note of December 9th, 1924, my father sought to simplify the problem
by getting Haffkine's long excurses out of the way. He
wrote to Rosenbloom as follows: "I have been lately so over-
burdened with work that I could not find time to read carefully the suggestions referring to the organization of a school
for higher Jewish learning in Jerusalem by Doctor Haffkine
which you kindly sent me some time ago. After a thorough
examination of these suggestions, I find them to be of little
value for practical purposes, although a good deal can be
said in their favor from a theoretical point of view. To discuss it, however, in full would require a treatise and as I
hope to have the pleasure of seeing you soon in New York, I
prefer an oral discussion to a written one."

The confusion is revealed most clearly in a letter of Professor David Blondheim, a member of the Academy, to Dr.
Adler covering his efforts in Paris to accelerate cooperation
among the scholarly communities.

I also went to see Professor Haffkine. . . . He appears to be
unwilling to be connected directly with a committee for the University if there are Zionist representatives on it; and he also told
me he did not approve of Jewish studies conducted in a way that

would be satisfactory to . . . even Israel Levi (the Chief Rabbi of France). . . . He seems nevertheless to be cooperating . . . (and) I think he could do a lot for the University, particularly as he had administrative experience in India in scientific institutions . . . (and) he is said to be a liberal giver to causes that interest him.

Although almost six years had passed since the end of the war, Blondheim added that the Chief Rabbi does not think that the time was as yet "ripe for association with the Germans in this way."

In the meantime, a conference was held in London attended by sixteen leaders of the Zionist Movement, the religious communities of England, France, Austria, several Palestinians and a stray academic or two. Counting Magnes as a Palestinian, the only American present was Judge Mack. Excerpts from a letter from Magnes to Adler follow:

The conference was held yesterday from 10:30 a.m. to 1:30 a.m. with the result that the Institute for Jewish Studies of the Jerusalem University was instituted. From the enclosed slip, you will see in part what was done. In addition to what the enclosed slip tells, the following was decided upon:
1. The chief seat of the Institute is to be Jerusalem. The next meeting is to be held at Paris.
2. A Committee of 25 is to be in general charge, five each, to be elected by the following Committees: Paris, London, America, Palestine, Central Europe. Poland will be proposed at the next meeting as a 6th committee.
It was one of the most difficult meetings I have ever attended. Or perhaps it is that I am out of practice? No one is entirely satisfied. But I think a good beginning has been made, if everyone will help along; the Institute is on the right path.
Meanwhile, you notice that the meeting accepted your suggestion and this unanimously and with many expressions of appreciation that Prof. Ginzberg come for a year and this year. Will you therefore be good enough to communicate with him and let me know what arrangements are made with him and what we can do in Jerusalem to be of aid. I am leaving for Jerusalem tomorrow,

via Trieste-Alexandria. I am happy to get away from this turmoil. I am also writing to Dr. Ginzberg, notifying him of this choice, officially.

Do you know of anyone who is competent, scientifically, to take up the subject of "Sociology" (Demography, or Demagogy, as Dr. Hertz's lapsus had it); i.e., someone who will examine the structure of the present day Jewish social organism? Such a subject was agreed to if the proper man could be found. In general, the attitude was taken up, that any of the "humanitarian" subjects was in place, as long as the man teaching them treated them in relation to Jewish discipline.

There was considerable correspondence among Magnes, Ginzberg, Adler and finally the key Seminary Directors, Warburg and Marshall, about who would cover Ginzberg's travel expenses. Magnes assumed that the Seminary would defray them and when Adler refused on a matter of principle to do so, Magnes offered £100 and finally £200. The plan for my father to participate in the opening of the Institute foundered on the paltry sum of £400. He must have found the whole matter very distasteful indeed: "I wish I were in a position to make some financial sacrifice to the cause of higher Jewish learning in Palestine. Unfortunately, however, Jewish scholars have not enough earthly goods for sacrifices of that kind."

But the invitation led to his receiving a warm telegram from the institution that a quarter of a century earlier had broken a contract with him.

Please extend to Professor Ginzberg cordial greetings of the Faculty of the Hebrew Union College and of myself and our sincere wishes for a very pleasant and profitable trip to Jerusalem. Judaism in America is highly honored by the appointment of this perhaps our most distinguished Jewish scholar. Godspeed him on his trip and grant him a safe return to us. Letter follows.

Julian Morgenstern

It was still some time before the reconciliation was complete. In the early 1940's, the Hebrew Union College conferred in absentia an honorary degree on Louis Ginzberg, who promised to visit and lecture at the College at the first opportunity. A few months later he did, accompanied by my mother. Professor Heschel, who was a member of the faculty at that time, recalls the warmth of the College's reception for Professor Ginzberg. The past was completely liquidated.

To return to academic matters in the new Institute, Magnes sought approval of two appointments, J. N. Epstein for Talmudic Philology and Klausner for History. My father's colleagues and he were enthusiastic about Epstein, but balked at appointing Klausner to the chair in History. In a long letter to Dr. Adler, my father set out his views with respect to Klausner as well as about some organizational matters that were still pending:

I never met Dr. Klausner, and cannot judge whether he has the personality that makes a successful teacher. But I have read almost everything he has written, and am therefore entitled to pass upon his scholastic qualifications. I must seriously protest against the insult—I do not mince words—to the memory of the greatest Jewish historian, Graetz, contained in the statement of Dr. Magnes, that the future will say the same of Klausner as of Graetz: "A great historian, although committing here and there slips."

Dr. Klausner has been writing for more than twenty-five years, and if we discount his Doctoral Dissertation, did not contribute *one single line* to Jewish historiography. He is undoubtedly the most learned among Hebrew journalists of the day, and if the Institute would consider the erection of a Chair for Journalism, I would not know of any better man for it than Klausner, but to have him, a dogmatizing amateur, Professor of History at an institution for higher learning, would make it the laughing stock of the scholarly world.

One who is acquainted with Jewish historiography in modern times knows that what Jewish historians lack most is methodological rigor. Men who take ignorance and escalate it into knowledge, hypotheses, and turn them into established facts, have produced among us a variety of historical adulteration which might be almost as dangerous as similar experiments with food. It may be very difficult to get a truly great historian who besides learning has imagination and originality. But imagination without learning does not even make a poor historian.

In principle, I do agree with Dr. Magnes that Jerusalem ought to be the seat of the Institute. I doubt, however, whether for the present, Jerusalem is ripe for it. When the Institute will have a well-established faculty, it will be the most natural thing for the seat of the Institute to be there where the Faculty resides. For the present, however, it might be much better to have London as its seat. This however is a matter which I would like to have fully discussed by all the members of the "Academy."

I am, of course, willing to call a meeting of the Academy to consider this matter, but before doing so, I would like to have the Academy recognized as the Advisory Council for America, which according to the Constitution of the Institute, is to choose the five members of the General Committee. Without being in the least biased in favor of the Academy, I boldly maintain that if this Society were not in existence, one of that nature would have to be created for the very purpose of having an Advisory Council. There are no national bodies in American Jewry who could, with good conscience, undertake an Advisory Council. After all, the problems that will confront the General Committee will be chiefly of a scholastic nature, and what is more natural than that a body of scholars handle matters of this kind. I do not mean to say that all the representatives of America should be scholars. I am rather inclined to believe that one, or perhaps two—men of the type of Mr. Warburg, Louis Marshall, Sol Stroock and others —ought to be men of affairs. Yet, there is no earthly reason why the Academy should not be the Advisory Council to choose the representatives with the understanding that not all the represent-atives are to be necessarily members of the Academy. I wish that either you or Mr. Felix Warburg would make this clear to Dr. Magnes and the managing committee in Palestine that the Acad-emy is to be the Advisory Council for America. As long as this question is not entirely settled, it would be difficult for the Acad-emy to act in matters pertaining to the Institute.

It was a long hard fight to get the Academy recognized as the official advisory group in the United States, but once my father decided that it was the only sound move, he kept hammering away at it without let up. He wrote to Adler about a meeting which he had had with Warburg about this:

I just returned from my conference with Mr. Felix M. Warburg and in compliance with your wish, I want to state briefly the upshot of our conversation.

After explaining to Mr. Warburg the nature of the American Academy of Jewish Research, I pointed out to him that this Society considers it its duty to offer its services in the building up of the Institute for Jewish Studies in Jerusalem. Mr. Warburg first replied that in his opinion the management of the Institute ought to be in the hands of those who live in Palestine, as he considers the rule of the absentee landlord very obnoxious. I called, however, his attention to the fact that at the London Conference it was decided to have America as well as several other countries represented on the larger Board and that it is the view of the membership of the Academy that besides one or two businessmen, several scholars ought to be on this Board and that further, the scholars ought to be nominated by the Academy. Mr. Warburg finally agreed to this view, but added that at present he knows nothing about the formation of the different units of the larger Board, but as soon as the matter shall be placed before him, he would advise to have the Academy represented.

In March of the following year, 1925, Ginzberg wrote to Magnes that he had succeeded in these efforts:

"I received with great satisfaction the news communicated to me by Doctor Adler that the Academy has been designated as the American Consulting Committee for the Institute for Jewish Studies of the Hebrew University of Palestine. As the only organized body of men actively engaged in Jewish research and teaching, the members of the Academy accept this assignment as a matter of duty and high responsibility. We are glad to place ourselves at the service of the Institute and are ready at all times to cooperate with the other governing and advisory committees in the discussion of questions of policy and organization."

Although he found it impossible to go to Palestine in 1924 when the Institute was opened, my father made his plans to go at the first opportune moment. This came when he decided to take his first sabbatical from the Seminary in the academic year 1928-29. I had completed my freshman year at Columbia College, and after exploring with his friend H. Loewe at Cambridge the suitability of my spending a year there, my father decided that on balance I would be better off at Heidelberg. I had known German fluently as a child and it was assumed that I could recapture it quickly. Since I was less than eighteen, my father had to rely on his influence as an "alumnus" to get me matriculated. He went along with me to Heidelberg to explore the conditions governing my admission. The plan was to leave my sister in Bristol, England, where she could stay with an American cousin and attend secondary school.

The Ginzberg family set off for Europe early in June. It was not yet certain that my parents would go to Jerusalem, much less spend the academic year there. My father's availability became known, however, and, as can be seen from Rabbi Hertz's letter, the authorities were quick to take advantage of it—though my father had introduced a proviso that he would not go if Professor Albeck of Berlin was free to relocate. The following letter from the Chief Rabbi summarizes the steps that were involved.

I need not tell you how happy I was to learn from your communication to Dr. Kohn that you had kindly consented, in accordance with the cordial invitation which the Basle Conference extended to you, to deliver a course of lectures on the problems of Halakhah during the coming scholastic year, if Dr. Albeck could not accept our invitation. I have now had a reply from Dr. Albeck saying that, while he accepts our invitation for a term of two years, it is not possible for him to go out to Palestine during the present year as the time is too short for him to find a proxy to take his place in Berlin. I hope that in these circumstances you will accept our invitation and inaugurate the Department of Halakhah. Its initiation could not take place under more auspicious circumstances. I am writing today to Jerusalem and in informing Dr. Magnes of Dr. Albeck's reply, shall also send him the good news that you have expressed yourself as ready to accept the invitation of the Council. I should be grateful if you would be so kind as to let me know when you think of arriving in Jerusalem so that the necessary arrangements can be made in the organization of studies at the Institute.

All that need be added was the unconscionable delay because of the uncooperative attitude of the British consulate when my father sought his visas. But at long last, everything was in order and my parents took off for Palestine with a planned stop-over in Egypt.

This is my father's recollection of this trip:

"In 1928, on my way to Palestine, I stopped off at Shepheard's Hotel in Cairo. I didn't eat much normally and coupled with keeping kosher, I ate even less. Nevertheless, I got a violent attack of dysentery. I said to myself, tomorrow we go back. We are only at the gate of the East and I already have trouble. But it so happened that a group of specialists attending the International Conference of Tropical Diseases were stopping at the same hotel. My wife went to see a very nice German physician. He came over to see me and said that I would be in good shape in a day or two. He promised to look me up in Jerusalem. He persuaded me to go ahead with my plans. He actually did fix me up. I was miserable, however, in Jerusalem, but not from dysentery. There was a particular fish—bura—and I was apparently allergic to it; three hours after I ate it I got violently sick. In 1933, on our second visit, we were offered fish, guaranteed fresh, and ex-

actly three hours later I got violently sick. The third time
was in Tel Aviv, with Bialik, who said, 'My wife knows how
to cook it.' So I ate it, and was left with no ill effects. My
explanation is that in Jerusalem, there was no refrigeration,
but in Tel Aviv, it *was* fresh."

The Chief Rabbi of France, when he heard that at long
last my father was finally on his way to join the faculty of
the Hebrew University, wrote him a lyrical note.

Le Dr. Herz m'apprend que vous avez bien voulu vous rendre à
nos instances répétées en acceptant, pour une durée dont vous
êtes seul juge et que nous voudrions très longue, la chaire de
Halakha à l'Institut des Hautes Etudes Juives de Jérusalem. La
nouvelle me remplit de joie. Notre rêve, en fondant cet etablisse-
ment, était d'y appeler les maîtres les plus estimés, universelle-
ment connus pour leur savoir et la rigueur de leur méthode, et
capables de former des disciples d'élites. Votre entrée dans notre
maison sera la réalisation de ce voeu. Aussi, quelle reconnaissance
ne devons-nous pas à votre dévouement, dont nous mesurons
l'étendue! Puissiez-vous en trouver recompense dans la formation
d'élèves dignes de leur maître, qui, à leur tour, seront l'honneur
de la science juive!

Some random events occurred during this visit which,
while they do not provide a rounded or a balanced view, do
give some indication of his reactions to the country and of
the reactions of the country to him. Although a "Litvak,"
long resident in the United States, he was able to deliver his
inaugural lecture in "Sephardi" Hebrew as a result of the
years that he had spent in Amsterdam. It was probably his
ability to speak pure Hebrew that made it possible for the
barber in the King David Hotel to identify my father in a
conversation with me more than thirty years later.

Of more substance was his relation to the Chief Rabbi of
Palestine, Rabbi Abraham Kook. Not wishing to embarrass
him, my father was careful not to make the first move, and
he was more than a little surprised to learn that the Chief

Rabbi wanted to call on him, one far beyond the pale of Orthodoxy—for in the Palestine of that day, as in the Israel of this, chief rabbis are subject to a great many pressures which restrict their freedom of action. My wife has not yet overcome the shock and chagrin when Chief Rabbi Herzog, to whom she brought greetings from her father and father-in-law on her first visit to Israel, ignored her outstretched hand and turned his back. She had not known about such anachronisms. To her, Louis Ginzberg was the acme of piety and she knew that he could never have acted in this way.

Rabbi Kook had an urgent problem to discuss. Dr. Magnes and his friends played tennis on the Sabbath and Kook could not persuade them to stop. He suggested that my father, a Western man, write an opinion on the subject; if he disapproved strongly, perhaps this desecration of the Sabbath in the Holy City could be brought to an end. My father asked Kook whether he had been correctly informed that the rate of interest in Palestine was 20 per cent and more. When Kook admitted this, my father reminded him that it was a direct violation of biblical law. He suggested a deal. As soon as Kook wrote against the prevailing usury, he would write about the impropriety of playing tennis on the Sabbath!

Another less serious story relates to the time my father was invited to be present at a circumcision of a Yemenite child. Although he tried to persuade my mother to remain at home, he failed. After the ceremony, he was introduced to the rabbi, who inquired how his grandmother was. My father was puzzled until he realized that this word also meant the "old one." Since my mother was much younger than my father, the rabbi had asked him whether "the old wife" was at home!

My father made it a practice to read the daily papers printed in Arabic, and I recall receiving long, pessimistic letters from him about the political future of the country. He understood the British game of playing off Jew against Arab, but he also appreciated the rising nationalistic power of the Arab leaders and the potentialities for trouble. He wrote me that the Zionist leadership was "blind." Of the Zionist leaders whom he met, the man who impressed him most was Berl Katzenelson, the intellectual leader of the labor group.

His friendship with Bialik was the high point of the trip, but even though both became deeply attached to one another, Bialik was unable to convince my father to remain in Jerusalem. He found living conditions there a little too difficult and he probably weighed the disruption it would cause for my sister and me. My mother, with her extroverted personality and great physical strength, would have been happy to remain. Bialik thought it important for my father to remain because, among other reasons, he could contribute to the sound modernization of the Hebrew language. So much of what was corrupt in modern Hebrew resulted from ignorance of rabbinic Hebrew. In later years, when Bialik visited us in New York and found that I knew no Hebrew, he was deeply shocked, so shocked in fact that I do not think he even asked my father for an explanation.

In accordance with Magnes' policy that every visiting professor deliver a major public lecture which would be published by the Hebrew University, my father put together what has come to be generally recognized as one of his principal minor works—an essay on "The Significance of the Halakhah for Jewish History"—the one that he left for Lieberman to see through the press. Having had Lieberman in his class was another of the highlights of his year in Jerusalem.

Regrettably, the full impact of his Palestinian visit was clouded by the fact that shortly after his return to Europe in the summer of 1929, he became seriously ill as a result of a questionable diagnostic procedure followed by a German professor of urology. He had to make a strenuous fight for his life in a hospital in Frankfurt, and I think he would have lost had not my mother's cousin, Henny Posen, a general practitioner, fought every inch of the way to prevent his being operated on. He won and twenty-four years were probably added to my father's life.

Prior to his becoming ill in Frankfurt, my father had planned to attend the meeting of the Academic Council of the University that was scheduled to meet late that summer in Switzerland. Although he was unable to be there, he was appointed a member of a five-man group to review the structure of University's doctoral degrees and to bring some order and uniformity into the system. One interesting aspect of this Committee was its diffuse membership, which provides a concrete example of the horrendous administrative difficulties of operating the new, but fast-growing institution. In addition to my father, the Committee included Dr. Magnes, Palestine; Professor Selig Brodetsky, England; Jacques Salomon Hadamard, France; Leonard Salomon Ornstein, Holland; Joseph Horowitz, Germany. Progress depended on the preparation of good draft documents and on the members communicating their views *in extenso* to the Secretary. Apparently this system worked, for at a subsequent meeting of the Board of Governors, the Committee's proposals were acted on.

But the University faced other difficulties. The next letter indicates that the fears that my father felt while in Palestine about the drift in Arab-Jewish relations had been justified. Shortly after his departure, the bloody riots of 1929 erupted.

I am directed by the Chairman of the Governing Council of the Jewish Institute to inform you that owing to the disturbed state of conditions of Palestine and the consequent inability of the Administration to carry out the new developments decided upon last year, it has been agreed between him and the Chancellor that no meeting of the Governing Council shall be held this year.

It would have been difficult to keep all the interested parties cooperating even under the best of circumstances and, as we know, circumstances were frequently far from the best. And they worsened as far as the crucial matter of financial support was concerned with the onset of the depression in the United States, which was soon paralleled by serious weakening of the European economy. Another important cause of trouble was the long-standing dissatisfaction of Dr. Weizmann and Albert Einstein with the Magnes regime. Einstein, to whom the University was very dear, refused to lend his active efforts to its support because he believed that the ex-rabbi from New York was not qualified to be the head of a major academic institution; moreover, he felt that neither the Board of Governors nor the Academic Council could effectively control Magnes, since he failed to carry through on his commitments to these bodies, not once but repeatedly. There were rumblings of dissatisfaction in Jerusalem. A number of disappointed and disaffected people—and there were many of them, for the University was constantly short of funds—blamed Magnes, who was after all the administrator. At its meeting in the fall of 1933, the Board of Governors decided to act to stem these difficulties by appointing a Survey Commission of three. The Chairman was Sir Philip Hartog, a distinguished British educator and one of the builders of Punjab University in India. Dr. Redcliff Salaman, the distinguished Cambridge biologist and head of its Experiment Station, was the second member. An invitation was extended to my father to join and complete the group. As Hartog's cable indicates, a major new development affecting the University had been precipitated by the success of Hitler. Many German scholars suddenly wanted to relocate.

Have just accepted from Weizmann and Board of Governors Hebrew University Jerusalem Chairmanship Commission of three for investigation and constructive report including measures for absorbing German Refugee Teachers STOP Will you act as member STOP Other member Salaman Biologist STOP Commission should leave London if possible by middle November FINISH

With his customary caution, and his concern about conserving his time, my father did not accept immediately. Hartog sent a second cable:

Investigation not purely administrative STOP Terms of reference as follows to inquire generally into affairs of Hebrew University with view to such reforms as may be found desirable to the framing of plans for development of university and especially to strengthening by inclusion of suitable number of teachers excluded from German universities under present regime STOP Your presence specially needed to report on Jewish studies sincerely trust you will accept appointment as your name mentioned for commission by recent Conference of Governing Council Jewish Institute at Geneva.

I was not in New York when these cables were exchanged, but I do recall that my father talked to me about the proposal and that I encouraged him to accept. I based my judgment on what he told me about the background of the two British members. I am sure that he was also encouraged to accept by his colleagues in the Academy, who must have been concerned that an expert in the field of Judaica be on the Commission.

My father's membership on the Commission made it necessary for him to consult with Einstein, whose dissatisfaction with affairs in Jerusalem was one major factor leading to the appointment of the Commission. Among the stories that my father told about his visits to Einstein preparatory to his leaving for Palestine was of Einstein's meeting him at the front door and insisting that they go into his bedroom, where he could lock the door to insure that their conversation would not be overheard. Then, when it was time for my father to return to New York City, Mrs. Einstein, in good German tradition, gave him a package of sandwiches for the journey. Train-time from Princeton to New York was about one hour!

In a more serious vein, my father told my wife about those visits:

"I have seen Einstein three or four times, and each time have been amazed at his simplicity. He is naive and childlike and has no sophistication. The first time I saw him we were discussing the relation of Poincaré to Planck. Accordingly, I had asked him whether he had read Poincaré, whose work was a first step for Planck's quantum theory. In all seriousness, he assured me that he had, and was quite amazed that I understood these theories. He could not believe that I had been able to give up mathematics. Although this was the first time that I had met him, he started talking about people in a most ingenuous way. He warned me not to be taken in by any tricks which they might play at the university. I told him that I had no doubt that there were very clever men at the university, but I said that when it comes to shrewdness, I doubt whether anyone can take me in.

"Humility is relative. With great men, especially great scientists, the more they know, the more aware they become of the fact that they do not know anything. A man of really great knowledge will understand that in relation to what we do not know, we know very little. At the same time, he may be fully aware of his own contribution to the knowledge we do have. The difference between a great scientist and the average man is that the average man's ignorance is infinite, whereas knowledge is finite.

"Many people think that I am very proud, but really proud people have no vanity. A man of a critical mind who measures the achievements of others by high standards must surely apply the same to himself."

The Commission began its hearings in Jerusalem on the 8th of December and concluded them, according to the schedule that my father retained, on the 21st. Although they held no meetings on Saturday, they undoubtedly worked a seven-day week, since they must have talked informally about University matters with friends and acquaintances even on their day of rest. It was a strenuous effort, particularly for my father, who was the only member of the Commission who could interrogate witnesses in Hebrew.

The members of the Commission developed a high order of mutual respect for each other which greatly facilitated their work, and my father developed a deep friendship for Sir Philip and his wife Mabel which lasted for the rest of his life.

The Commission published a "white book" and a "blue book" incorporating its findings and recommendations. The conclusion of the Survey was that Dr. Magnes, who had no basis for independent judgment about many academic matters, particularly in the sciences, had come under the domination of a few advisors who were men of little vision and less heart. They were primarily concerned, as academics frequently are, with their little empires which they ruled as tyrants. The careers of many young people were being made unnecessarily hard. To break the stranglehold of the Chancellor's coterie, the Survey Commission made a series of temperate, but nevertheless far-reaching, recommendations, the eventual upshot of which was to save Magnes' face but to strip him of most of his authority over academic matters. But the Commission took a more kindly view of Magnes than had Einstein and Weizmann. They understood that he was severely handicapped; many of the problems were a direct consequence of the University's penurious state.

My father found the trip exhilarating and, since he had undoubtedly accepted the assignment with the expectation that only a little could be accomplished, he was not disappointed. However, despite Einstein's generally favorable response to the Commission's report, he never became vitally concerned with University matters, although he was always willing to lend his name and to give advice.

Many years later, in the late 1940's and the 1950's, I became heavily involved in the affairs of the American Friends of the Hebrew University and served for two terms as a member of the Board of Governors of the Hebrew University sity although unfortunately, I was never able to attend a Board meeting. From these vantage points, I was able to observe first hand, especially with the vast improvements in communications that had taken place in the interim, the problems of managing a university which has and should continue to have, close ties with Jews throughout the world. The problems have not been solved, but the difficulties are slowly being mitigated by the ever larger role that the University must play in the development of Israel and the corresponding willingness of the Government of Israel to cover a high proportion of its budget.

At the conclusion of the Commission's work, the High Commissioner of Palestine, Sir Arthur Wauchope gave a reception in its honor. In addition to the opportunity that this offered my mother, as previously noted, to arrange a hand clasp between my father and Miss Szold, it also was the occasion for an amusing contretemps between the Arab mayor of Jerusalem, Nashishibi, and my father. The mayor was in high spirits and my father asked him the cause of his merriment. "Oh," he said, "I'm much relieved. For years we Arabs have had it dinned into us about how smart the Jews are and we have seen enough evidence to believe it. But today I met one of the leading members of the American government, and I now know that it is not true that all Jews are smart!"

My father's interest in the welfare of the University remained strong to the day of his death. I am sure that few things gave him more pleasure than the congratulatory note which he received on his seventieth birthday in which the University saluted him as the *Doyen* of Jewish scholars. And it was my good fortune to be in Jerusalem as his eightieth birthday was drawing near and to be asked by the then president, Professor Mazar, what action the University might take that would please my father. On the spur of the moment, I suggested that the University establish a chair— the Louis Ginzberg Professor of Talmud. The University did this and my father, though he died a fortnight before his birthday, knew of this gracious act.

CHAPTER X

FIRST AMONG THE JUDGES

FROM THE AGE of twenty-one when he earned *Semikhah*—the right to judge under Jewish law—until his death at the age of eighty, Louis Ginzberg devoted considerable time and effort to this task. He never held a position in the Jewish community which would have required him to decide matters of law, as was the duty of an active rabbi or a member of the law courts; Louis Ginzberg's concern with law had a different origin and motivation.

As knowledge of his reputation as a talmudist spread, those who wanted to know the law on any difficult issue sought his opinion. His major decisions were in the nature of advisory opinions, although he was drawn into a few cases where active conflicts raged, usually between an individual or group of individuals and the rabbi or the board of directors of a congregation.

His legal opinions covered a wide range of subjects, including those on which he could bring his sense of humor to bear. He was fond of telling the story of being asked by his colleague Dr. Marx, shortly after the latter's arrival in this country, whether one was permitted to use an elevator on the Sabbath. My father replied that it was not permitted, and Marx started his climb of six stories. My father, always restive when confronted with the rigidities of German or-

The Young Professor (1906) with his brothers Abraham and Asher.

Louis Ginzberg's father: Isaac Elias Ginzberg

Louis Ginzberg's mother: Zippe Jaffe Ginzberg

With his favorite nephew—Sol Wiener Ginsburg
(1905)

Summer in Tannersville (1906) with Drs. Schechter, Marx, Magnes, Benderly and others.

With his fiancée—Adele Katzenstein, Berlin (1908).

With his former students: Crescent Country Club, Milton, Vermont (1927). Epstein, Solomon, Levinthal, Minkin, Goldman.

Summer in Maine with Judge Goldberg, Harry A. Wolfson, Alexander Marx, and Louis M. Epstein (early 1930's).

Reading on the shores of Snow Pond, Oakland, Maine (early 1930's).

A meeting at home with Baron, Morgenstern, Kohut, Husik and others (early 1930's).

With Yemenite children in Shiloah, Palestine (1933).

In the Harvard Yard during the Tercentenary (1936).

Birthday celebration, late 1940's with his life-long friend and colleague Alexander Marx.

Michael Gould (right)—his first grandchild—with Sula Peterfreund and Jimmy Lawrence (1947).

Speaking at a Seminary Convocation (late 1940's).

With Louis Finkelstein at the same Convocation.

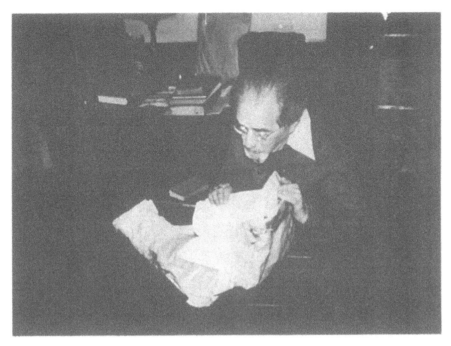

Working on the *Yerushalmi*—Maine (late 1940's).

Still working, early 1950's.

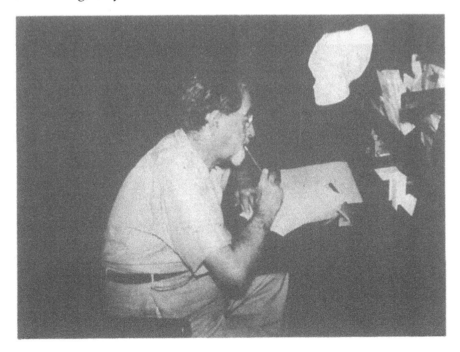

Faculty and students—J.T.S.—*circa* 1912.

Faculty and graduating class—J.T.S.—late 1930's.

thodoxy, awaited the return of the elevator to the ground floor, stepped in, and rode up. Marx, astonished, reminded him that he had just stated that using an elevator was not permitted. He replied: "I didn't ask for an opinion!"

For many years, from 1914 until 1929, the Ginzberg family lived in the Washington Heights section of New York City, an area which for most of this time did not have any rabbis qualified to judge matters of law—at least they were not qualified in the eyes of the Orthodox kosher butcher from whom my mother bought her meat. As a matter of noblesse oblige, my father agreed from time to time to examine poultry with a defect or blemish that might make it non-kosher. While my father was not bothered unduly, women carrying a chicken or a duck showed up at our apartment at least once or twice a month. Finally, if my father passed such a woman in the lobby, he could guess her mission.

In this connection, he was fond of telling the story of the German lady who sent her maid to the rabbi in Berlin for an opinion about a duck. The maid rang the bell and was asked by the housekeeper who opened the door whether she wanted to see the *Herr Doktor*. She replied, "Oh no, the duck is already dead!" Another was about Dr. Schechter, who was once asked whether sturgeon was kosher. He replied, "Some learned rabbis say that it is; other learned rabbis say that it is not. Who am I to say that the learned rabbis who say that it is kosher are wrong!"

It was convenient for my sister and me to grow up in a house with a one-man Supreme Court, where there never was any delay in obtaining an opinion that was final and not subject to further review. In fact, some of our friends benefitted from this accessibility of final opinion. I recall one *seder* night when our friends, the children of Rabbi Jacob Kohn, called in great excitement. They had hidden the special matzo which had to be found or ransomed before the second half of the service could proceed. There was some argument about the procedure for ransoming it; they asked and received an opinion forthwith.

They were more fortunate than Clarence Darrow, who also sought telephone help. In the middle of the famous Scopes trial, being conducted in the summer of 1925, the telephone rang one Saturday afternoon. My mother answered, as was her wont, and informed my father that Mr. Darrow wanted to speak with him. There was a brief delay, occasioned by the fact that my father hated to use the phone and did so only under compulsion. Since he customarily did not talk on the phone on weekdays, he decided that he would not use it on the Sabbath—although his objections were not doctrinal. It was decided that my mother would relay the questions and the answers.

Darrow wanted to know whom Cain had married: Was it not his sister? Apparently he was attempting to make the story of evolution more palatable than the scriptural account of the beginnings of man. My father was quick with his reply. He told my mother to inform Mr. Darrow that he didn't like to discuss scandal, surely not by phone, and still less on the Sabbath. But, he said, he would drop Darrow a line with some leads to the *Legends of the Jews* which he might find useful!

I will order his more serious opinions in chronological fashion, since a man's opnions are likely to be affected by age and experience.

In 1910, at the time of the blood accusation trial of Beilis in Kiev, Russia, Louis Marshall obtained in advance a draft of the testimony of the "expert" whom the Russian Government would introduce to prove (!) from Jewish sources that it is a religious necessity for Jews to use the blood of Christians. He asked Professor Ginzberg to prepare a reply to Monk Paranaitis in a popular style that would help to demolish his expertise. Ginzberg's reply ran to twenty-three closely typed pages in which the whole sad story of Blood-Accusation is reviewed.

Since Ginzberg's "Reply to Mr. Paranaitis" has never been published, I will select a few paragraphs to show how he went about his task of demolishing the claims of "Russian experts," which included such preposterous accusations as the fact that Jews frequently say they are gentiles to gain advantage; that the Talmud inveighs against Christians; and that the Jews have no respect or regard for any religion other than their own and act accordingly.

A Jew is not permitted to say that he is a gentile, not even if he can save his life by it.

The Talmud never mentions Christians, but twice makes reference to the Christian celebration of Sunday.

The rabbis in post-talmudic times decided that talmudic laws against heathen do not apply to Christians or Mohammedans.

"Proselytes at the Gate" are to be treated as brethren if they adhere to the following seven laws:

1. Not to worship idols.
2. Not to blaspheme.
3. Not to commit incest or adultery.
4. Not to murder.
5. Not to rob or steal.
6. Not to tear an animal's hide while it is still alive and cut the meat thereof.
7. To establish Courts of Justice.

Here is Professor Ginzberg's anguished conclusion:

So we are at the end of the expert opinion of the ritual murder offered to the world by the Russian Government. It will be understood that we are not engaged in a refutation of this abominable lie. Our pride as Jews prohibits us to defend ourselves against accusations of cannibalism. We, the descendants of prophets and saints, wise and holy men, have no need to do it. If the promoters of pogroms of inhumanity, equal to if not worse than cannibalism, want to excuse themselves in the eyes of the civilized world, let them, this is our candid advice, choose other defenders than Paranaitis. The atrocity and barbarism of the Russian Government had been known to the civilized world before now. Its stupidity is revealed by the manner in which it tried to use a half-witted babbler as its spokesman. Truth may be silenced for a time, but "Truth will spring out of the earth."

We found in my father's files a four-page typescript without a date—I suspect it formed the basis of an address in the 1920's—which outlines in concise fashion his understanding of the historical development of Jewish law.

1. At the establishment of the Second Commonwealth under Ezra-Nehemiah, the Jews solemnly obliged themselves to regulate their life, public and private, in accordance with the Torah of old. Thus the Pentateuch became, if one may say so, the constitution of the Jewish people.

2. The Torah provides for an authoritative body to interpret and explain the law and there can be no doubt that such a body did exist—for convenience we shall call it Sanhedrin—and functioned during the Second Commonwealth.

3. There is no record nor is it at all likely that the Sanhedrin ever abrogated a biblical law, although some of the old interpretations of law looked to us like abrogations, as for instance, the limitation of the *jus talionis* to the case of homicide.

4. The same authoritative body that was entrusted with the interpretation of the biblical law had at the same time the power of promulgating new laws and ordinances. These later laws and ordinances, however, unlike the biblical ones, could be abrogated by those who ordained them or by their successors. We may also safely assume that even among the Pharisees the observation of the rabbinical law was not as general as the biblical law, nor did the Pharisees' leaders ever attempt to enforce their regulations with the vigor they displayed in enforcing the biblical laws.

5. The final complete loss of national independence of the Jewish people meant the end of the power of Sanhedrin. Some of its functions were taken over by the leading schools of the Tannaim. But even the most important one among them, presided over by the Patriarch, never replaced the old Sanhedrin.

6. The great centers of Jewish learning that arose in Babylon about two hundred [C. E.] became the most formidable competitors of the Palestine academies and finally superseded

them. On account of certain historical conditions, however, Babylonian Jewry never produced a central body for the regulation of its religious life.

7. The Talmud is not a code since it contains thousands of conflicting opinions. The normalization and codification of these decisions is mainly the work of the Geonim. At no time, however, was the authority of the Talmud proclaimed, like that of the Bible. The authority of the Talmud is the result of a gradual process. The Geonim, the successors to the masters of the Talmud, were for several centuries the recognized spiritual leaders of the Jews. Whenever questions of law were addressed to them, they naturally looked to the Talmud for their guidance, and thus, the Talmud became the standard authority in matters of law for almost all Israel.

8. The post-talmudic scholars never claimed authority for themselves, nor was it ever given to them. To speak of the *Shulhan 'Arukh* and similar works as codes is incorrect—the sole basis of law for all these authors is the Talmud.

It was much easier for Professor Ginzberg to set out in brief context the nature of authority in Jewish law than to find acceptance of this authority among American Jews. Each rabbi was an authority unto himself and those who were willing to follow him. As in Gresham's law, which says that bad money tends to drive out good money, so bad law had a tendency to drive out good law. In general, the denigration of the law followed when rabbis with little learning decided that certain fundamental precepts no longer were binding since life took precedence over the law, and life could flourish only if the law accommodated itself to reality. Hence, at the extreme, some Jews, with their rabbis in the lead, ignored the Sabbath and worshipped on Sundays; they disregarded all the laws of *Kashruth;* and they paid scant attention to the laws governing marriage, divorce, and death.

In one instance in which Professor Ginzberg became directly involved, the matter of authority related not to the disregard of precedent and tradition, but to the opposite: to an insistence that the law was even more demanding than it actually was. When the Volstead Act barring the sale of intoxicating beverages was passed in 1919, special exceptions were made for those who required alcohol for religious or medicinal purposes. It is worth pointing out in passing that despite the efforts that the medical schools and the medical profession made to establish and maintain a high level of ethics among the members of the profession, it was common knowledge that many a young physician covered the costs of setting up his office by selling prescriptions for liquor.

The proviso that wine could be sold for "sacramental purposes" led to much wider abuses, since for Jews these purposes include the use of wine for ceremonials at home. These ceremonies include benedictions at the beginning of the Sabbath and at its conclusion; similarly, for services for each of the festivals; and a much heavier requirement for the Passover service, which stipulates the drinking of four cups of wine by each individual. Other occasions on which wine is used are weddings, circumcisions, and the redemption of the first-born male. The total requirements per annum per family were considerable and a lively bootlegging trade based on the sale of certificates for obtaining wine for sacramental purposes quickly developed in which unscrupulous rabbis, and men who called themselves rabbis, joined forces with the underworld. Not many years ago, I visited one of the largest wineries in California that had carried on business with governmental sanction throughout the Prohibition Era to meet the needs for sacramental wine. And there were several others. It was big business, and most of the output quickly came under the control of nefarious interests.

The responsible leaders of American Jewry were sickened by these developments and the Rabbinical Assembly formally put the following questions to Professor Ginzberg:

1. Is there any reason why fermented wine should be preferred to unfermented in the performance of Jewish religious ceremonies?
2. Is there any reason why grape juice may not be used in the performance of those ceremonies?

It was Louis Marshall who first asked Professor Ginzberg for an opinion that would help to guide the federal authorities.

Professor Ginzberg wrote an opinion which ran to thirty-nine printed pages under the title, "The Use of Wine in Jewish Ritual." The burden of his findings was that "The Sages of Israel never intended the drinking of wine as a religious custom. They merely gave a religious sanctification to the use of wine which before their times had been drunk in a freely secular way. . . ." He then points to the three concepts in Jewish law involved in the performance of a commandment: in certain instances, the ceremony is invalid; in others, it is valid, but not preferable; and then there is a "best possible way" of complying with the law. After a critical review of all the authorities, he concluded that "from the point of view of Jewish law and custom, there is no preference to be given to fermented wine over unfermented."

The opinion was attacked by many on sincere grounds and others who were insincere. Emanuel Hertz, a New York attorney and Republican politician and the brother of the Chief Rabbi of England, did not hesitate to argue against Ginzberg's conclusions even though he had no competence whatsoever in matters of Jewish law. This eventually became more than a duel of words. My father received threatening letters warning him to mind his own business. During these months, my mother did not want him to go out alone. The opinion also brought him an opportunity to make some money. The producers and distributors of grape juice wanted permission to use his name in a large-scale advertising campaign, which of course he refused.

During World War I, the Federal Government sought my father's opinion on the problem presented by a selectee who insisted that he should not be drafted because, since he was a member of a priestly family, he was forbidden by Jewish law to come into contact with the dead. Professor Ginzberg in this instance had a very brief opinion: he pointed out that Judas Maccabeus came from a priestly family!

Shortly before my father's death, while the Korean War was under way, I involved him in another military problem which I called "The Case of the Bearded Soldier." General Schultz, President Eisenhower's Military Aide, called me at Columbia to inquire whether it was true that Jews couldn't shave. He told me that the President had received a letter from a soldier who had been forcibly shaved by the Army and who was threatening to bring a suit against the Army. A reading of the file revealed that the case had been dragging along for months and it came to contain all sorts of opinions and letters, including one from the Adjutant General's Office to the soldier, quoting the Talmud and other Jewish works, signed Mary Quinn, 1st Lieutenant, WAC (!) The soldier contended that he was a member of a Hasidic sect in Brooklyn, that he served as a part-time rabbi, that cutting his beard was against his religious beliefs, and that his future had been jeopardized by the Army's forcibly shaving him.

I sought my father's advice, and he took the position that the Army had the right to require the soldier to remove his beard (by cutting, not shaving), and that there was no merit to the soldier's claim that he was a member of a sect, since Jewish law recognizes no sects. My father felt that if the soldier's position were upheld, and since the Army insisted that soldiers be clean shaven, a draft loophole might develop. My own recommendation, which was eventually accepted, was to avoid the issue by sending the soldier overseas to an out-of-the way assignment and forward advice through the Chaplains' Corps that he was to be permitted to grow a beard.

Louis Ginzberg's opinions only now and again involved the civil authorities. For the most part, they were written for the guidance of those who held leadership positions within the Jewish community and who raised questions concerning primarily synagogal practices; ceremonies and practices governing marriage, divorce, and death; and medical issues such as autopsy, euthanasia and artificial insemination. I reported earlier that he never held an official position in which he was required to render opinions and judgments concerning the law, but this might be misconstrued. For many if not most of his opinions were rendered in his role as the Chairman of the Committee on The Interpretation of Jewish Law of the United Synagogue of America, a position which he held for many years. Even after he resigned the Chairmanship, he remained influential in its later work as well as in relation to the work of a similar committee that came to be established under the aegis of the Rabbinical Assembly.

One of the earliest (1920) and most interesting exchanges of letters in my father's file relates to a question posed by the principal of a public school in the Williamsburg section of Brooklyn, who asked whether it was necessary to excuse children who were in mourning from attending assemblies where music was part of the program. The principal pointed out that it was difficult in a crowded public school to provide adequate supervision if children were to be excused. Professor Ginzberg's brief opinion follows:

. . . if the assembly periods and music hours are parts of the regular curriculum of study, there is no harm in having the children attend. The only objection will arise if the main function of these assembly hours were amusement, which I do not take to be the case.

A later opinion (1947) summarized the relationship between Jewish and civil law in matters of divorce. It was in reply to an attorney who was attempting to facilitate the remarriage of his client:

Marriages and divorces are according to Jewish belief religious institutions, and their validity is dependent exclusively on their being performed in accordance with Jewish law. People married according to the "law of Moses and of Israel" can only be divorced by a Bill of Divorce known as a "Get." Once the "Get" is properly executed the husband and wife are free to marry whomever they wish. Of course, it is understood that a Jewish court would never perform a divorce as long as the law of the state in which it resides has not declared the couple divorced according to the state law. The validity of the "Get," however, is not dependent upon civil law.

Whether according to French law the rabbi of Paris who executed the divorce of the Polish woman residing in France acted in accordance with French law is a matter to be decided by French lawyers and not be me. As far as Jewish law is concerned, the divorce is valid.

May I add that according to Jewish law, the woman claiming to have been divorced must prove her statement by reliable witnesses or by her former husband.

Unscrupulous members of the rabbinate and pseudo-rabbis were granting Jewish divorces without first determining that the marriage had been civilly dissolved. The Association of Reform Rabbis in New York City requested the United Synagogue to pass a strong resolution to the effect that no rabbi should grant a Jewish divorce without unequivocal documentary evidence that the parties had already secured a civil divorce. While the Committee on the Interpretation of Jewish law was sympathetic to the intent of the proposed resolution and was particularly eager to contain the evil of easy divorces, it pointed out that the resolution would have to be amended for otherwise it would make it impossible "for a rabbi to forward a Get to a country where Jewish divorce is recognized by the state."

In a report as Chairman of the Committee, Professor Ginzberg told of his reactions to having been called as an expert witness before the Court of Domestic Relations in the State of New York:

. . . I cannot help mentioning the distressing effect it had upon me in bringing home to me in a very tangible form the laxity with which Jewish divorce law is practiced. Judaism never taught the indissolubility of marriage; of the Torah it is said 'Her ways are ways of pleasantness and all her paths are peace.' Hence rather peace without union than union without peace. But only one entirely ignorant of the spirit of Judaism as developed in the course of its glorious history could sanction such laxity in the domain of law as practiced by some of those who claim to hold the monopoly upon the true guardianship of Judaism. It is time that the rabbis who are members of the United Synagogue call a halt to this disgraceful practice.

When the graduates of the Seminary sought to find a legal answer to one of the more perplexing problems in the domain of marriage and divorce law, Professor Ginzberg moved with great circumspection. At one time, his close friend and devoted pupil, Rabbi Louis M. Epstein, attempted to find an acceptable solution to the problem of the "deserted wife." According to Jewish law, if a man deserts his wife, she cannot remarry unless he divorces her or he dies. And a presumption that he has died because he does not return at the end of a war is not sufficient. Proof of death is required. It was this difficult situation that Rabbi Epstein sought to resolve.

In response to a paper presented by Epstein at the Rabbinical Assembly on the subject of the *agunah* (deserted wife), my father advised against any discussion in the general press because it would tend to alienate the Orthodox rabbis. He was concerned that one of the proposed solutions might mean "the annulment of wedlock" which in turn would mean the children in these familes would be "illegitimate."

Some years later Dr. Julius Greenstone, a senior member of the Rabbinical Assembly and the then president, found it necessary to write to my father:

I was very much grieved to learn that the Committee on Jewish Law of the Rabbinical Assembly failed to consult you about the proposal regarding the provision to obviate the *agunah* evil that was to be presented before the Convention of the Assembly at Rockaway Park last May. Personally, I was under the impression all along that Dr. Epstein had had your approval of his plan as elaborated in his pamphlet. At the meeting of the Committee prior to the Convention, Rabbi Drob suggested that your formal approval be obtained before the Convention. In some way, this was neglected, but since every one expected you to be present at the sessions, it was thought that the matter would be explained to you there and that you might even participate in the discussion and give the members the encouragement of your undisputed authority and the weight of your opinion.

I am sincerely grieved that this was not done and am willing to take my share of the responsibility and humbly apologize to you for this omission. I hope, however, that you will realize that the negligence had no reason and the entire matter was unintentional. The Assembly has undertaken a most important and far-reaching task and it needs your encouragement and cooperation. In fact, it cannot expect to succeed in this, especially in view of the opposition which this matter has created, without your support and authority.

However, the looked for support never was forthcoming. Since my father did not find a solution that appeared to be a clear improvement, he preferred to let others take the responsibility for modifying the law. The fact that many Orthodox rabbis refused to acknowledge the authority of the Rabbinical Assembly helps to explain Louis Ginzberg's caution. He saw little point to developing a solution that would not be acceptable beyond the confines of the Rabbinical Assembly. He wanted no part in further splintering authority.

Another subject on which my father wrote had to do with the removal of bodies. These questions usually arose when men and women who had grown rich wanted to do honor to their parents by reinterring them in a mausoleum. This was his view:

Death, to the Jew, is the great leveler. The distinctions of life must not be carried into the earth. All Jews must be buried simply, in a plain coffin, without ornamentation, fine garments, or other displays of vanity in death. Rabbi Gamliel the Elder made a special decree to that effect, at a time when funerals had become more ornate than many joyous functions of the living. To seek new burial grounds under the conditions advanced to our Committee is not a commendable attempt. Of course, there are legitimate exceptions. Bodies may be moved when the land containing them has been condemned for some public purpose—though even here we must interpose every possible exception—or when there is danger of their being washed out or otherwise desecrated, or when proper burial has not taken place in the first case, or for certain other limited reasons. But to move the remains of parents solely to satisfy the new-grown vanity of their descendants is hardly an honor to the Jewish dead. The Jewish viewpoint is now, and always has been, that the money spent for costly mausoleums—which will only slightly outlast the lesser memorials of the dead in the passage of time—might better be employed in supporting schools and institutions for the cultural enrichment of mankind. The result of such expenditures will be lasting, for the impress on a living soul is transmitted forever, while inanimate stones only await the ineluctable change that befalls all visible matter.

More complicated aspects of the law with respect to burial are dealt with in the following brief reply to a series of complicated problems submitted by Abraham Neuman, who at the time (1927) was the rabbi of one of the oldest and most distinguished congregations in Philadelphia, Mikveh Israel:

. . . the conception of "consecrated ground" is entirely foreign to Jewish Law. The strict rule that nobody who has left the Jewish fold is to be buried in a Jewish cemetery is based upon the statement of the Mishnah, Sanhedrin 46, 2, with regard to the cemeteries for criminals. On the basis of the law referred to in the Mishnah, the Talmud draws the inference that the wicked and the just, the sinful and the pious, ought not to be buried in the same cemetery.

1. The Christian Science Church is undoubtedly a part of the general Christian communion, and any Jew who had become a member of this Church severs his connection with the Synagogue. In an address delivered before the annual convention of the United Synagogue several years ago, I strongly emphasized this fact. I have no copy of my address and doubt whether the United Synagogue has one.

2. I fully agree with you that the Ethical Culture Society is neither a religious or anti-religious society and, hence, membership in it could not be considered as a break with the Synagogue.

3. The answer to question three is contained in my general remarks at the beginning of the letter, according to which it is against Jewish Law and practice to bury a person in a Jewish cemetery who had left the Jewish fold.

4. and 5. There is, of course, only one answer to questions four and five, and that is, that one who has not been formally converted to the Jewish faith is not to be regarded as a Jew in relation to burial.

6. I would strongly advise against leaving out the customary burial prayer and the Kaddish in the case of one who is opposed to ceremonial religion, as it might be interpreted in a wrong light.

7. I would, however, not raise any strong objection to the reading of a poem or a prose composition, which in themselves are non-sectarian.

The questions put to Professor Ginzberg about the synagogue concerned, as the following excerpts suggest, a wide range of considerations. He was asked whether a congregation had to face the East:

The high antiquity of this custom can be seen from Daniel 6.11 which biblical passage forms the basis for the regulation found in the Talmud and in the later Codes. . . . It is also highly interesting to notice that the old church has adopted this custom, see Riet-schal, *Liturgik* 1, 88, 124. That this custom was strictly and gen-erally observed among the Jews of antiquity and the Middle Ages can be seen by facts that Mohammed at the beginning of his career ordained to have the kibla facing Palestine as a concession to the Jews.

A congregation about to build a larger and more com-modious synagogue desired to sell its old building for com-mercial purposes. Was this in conformity with the law?

I would say that the Jewish Law is explicit on this point, dis-criminating between a community synagogue and a congrega-tional synagogue. A community synagogue cannot be sold for commercial purposes; a congregational synagogue may. By the first, we understand a synagogue erected by the contributions of the Jewish inhabitants of a city or town for the use of all. A congregational synagogue is one which is erected by the contribu-tions of members of a society, primarily for their own use. Al-though I know nothing about the history of your synagogue, I assume that it is a congregational synagogue, as there are hardly any community synagogues in the sense of the law in this coun-try. If my assumption is correct, there is nothing against the sale of the synagogue building for commercial purposes.

One question was repeatedly asked: a minority usually sought to interpose its veto on a decision to obviate the necessity to separate the sexes in the synagogue. Here is a late reply (1947) when a conflict broke out over the issue in Baltimore, Maryland:

1. While there is no written prohibition against the mixing of the sexes during worship, there can be no doubt that for thou-sands of years the separation of sexes in the Synagogue was an established custom all through Jewry.

2. The origin of this custom was to emphasize Jewish opposi-tion to the pagan immorality which held sway over the idolatrous neighbors of the old Hebrews like the Phoenicians and Assyro-Babylonians.

3. The custom of separating the sexes in the Synagogue was modeled after that of the Temple, yet occasionally, even in the Temple, this rule had its exceptions. For instance, in one of the most solemn ceremonies, on the most solemn day of the year, the Day of Atonement, the High Priest read the biblical section of the day in the "Women's Court" before men and women. Similarly, the reading of the law by the King at the end of the Sabbatical year took place in the "Women's Court."

4. If conditions of a congregation are such that continued separation of family units during services presents a great danger to its spiritual welfare, the minority ought to yield to the spiritual need of the majority.

Time had left its mark. Material in the files indicates that Professor Ginzberg earlier expressed the hope that "where there is a minority in a congregation which protest against such an innovation, the others should respect their wishes, not on the grounds of law but of true liberalism. The question is out of the reach of the law; it is a matter of sympathetic judgment of conditions." A period of about a quarter of a century separate these two views and in the interim Professor Ginzberg had become a wiser man. He no longer expected the majority to respect the views of the minority.

The question as to whether late Friday evening services were in harmony with the law led to the following judgment:

I understand that in some places voices of protest have been raised against this so-called innovation. This only corroborates the truth of the observation made by many that humanity could easily be divided into two main classes, those who maintain that whatever was good enough for our fathers is not good enough for us, and those who proclaim that whatever was not good for our fathers cannot be good for us. There is not the least objection to late Friday evening services even from the strictest point of view of the law, but certain people will nevertheless object to it because it was not known in the time of their fathers. Yet, they forget that what might have been unnecessary and even obnoxious in the times past, may become very necessary and advisable in our days.

Professor Ginzberg's effort to move circumspectly in all matters which could divide rather than unite Jewry is revealed in the following comment about the desirability of having an organ in a synagogue:

> I am at present not interested in the question of whether Jewish Law sanctions the organ or not. But far more important is the fact that the question of the organ does not and will not exist in those countries where the non-Jewish mode of worship knows of no instrumental music. In other words, the Jews living in Greek-Catholic Russia and in Mohammedan countries would never admit the necessity or even the desirability of the organ in the synagogue. You, who as I am firmly convinced, have outgrown provincial Judaism and are working for United Israel, could never solve the question of Jewish Law satisfactorily as long as you approach it from the point of view of American Jewry.

This same sensitivity for the feelings of other Jews is revealed in the following letter from Louis Marshall to Professor Ginzberg. It was prompted by the fact that Temple Emanu-El was to be rebuilt on a new site.

> A question has arisen in connection with the construction of the new house of worship of Emanu-El Congregation as to the limitations upon decorations imposed by the practices of traditional Judaism. There is a desire to establish memorial windows. Questions have also arisen as to carvings upon stone and wood. I have assumed that the "Lion of Judah" is an entirely permissible decoration, but that the representation of a human figure or of any other figures which may be suggestive of ancient idolatrous practices, or of certain symbols which have a non-Jewish connotation, is forbidden.
>
> I would greatly appreciate your views upon this subject. It is our desire to avoid the use of any decoration which would offend the sensibilities of the most Orthodox.

Some excerpts from Professor Ginzberg's full opinion follow. They help to provide not only an answer to the specific questions posed by Mr. Marshall, but they also illustrate the approach which Ginzberg used in developing an opinion of law. He was always concerned not only with the decisions of his predecessors but with their underlying attitudes. Most of all, he was concerned with the spirit of Judaism and its fundamental orientation to God and life.

The biblical prohibition against fashioning of idols, especially that found in Exodus 20.4, was at an early time understood to include the making of all images of living things and for all purposes; for worship as well as for the sake of beauty. It is not without interest to note that Philo, the Jew most deeply imbued with Greek culture known to history, is the oldest authority for this sweeping prohibition. In his work, *De Gigantibus* 13 he remarks, "Therefore, our lawgiver—Moses—excluded from our commonwealth the pleasing arts of fashioning human or animal likenesses because they falsify the truths and cause the souls of those who are easily misled to accept falsehood and sophism made acceptable to them by the charm of art."

We are, therefore, not in the least surprised at the rigor with which the Jews of the first century of the common era applied the law against images. To mention only a few facts referred to by the Jewish historian, Josephus. The two great leaders of the Pharisees, Judas and Mattathias, died as martyrs at the stake by the hands of Herod for having torn down the golden eagle that he had erected over the great gate of the Temple, "contrary to the law that forbids to erect images or representations of any living creature" (*Antiquities* XVII, 6.2). A sedition of the Jews arose against Pontius Pilate when the Roman soldiers that were stationed in Jerusalem unfurled the standards upon which were Caesar's effigy, "whereas our law forbids us the very making of images" (*Antiquities* XVIII, 3.1). The first act of Josephus as Governor of Galilee during the revolution was to ask the Senate of Tiberias to demolish "that house which Herod, the Tetrarch, had built there and which has the figures of living creatures on it, although our laws have forbidden us to make any such figures" (*Life* 12).

It is difficult to say how long the strict interpretation of the law against images continued to prevail among the Palestinian scholars. . . . Attention must, however, be called to the fact that in the remains of ancient synagogues . . . were found representations of animals; eagles, lions, etc., not only in mosaic but also in plastic designs. We meet with pictures of animals and other objects in mosaic also in the ruins of the recently discovered synagogue in Jericho—beginning of the fourth century—and further in the famous ruins of the synagogue at Hammam-Lif, near Carthage, from about the same period.

. . . With the gradual increasing influence of Babylonian Jewry not only upon the other parts of the Diaspora, but even on the Holy Land, the rigor of the law against images was greatly lessened. In Babylonia, a considerable part of the gentile population with whom the Jews came in contact were Zoroastrians and like the Jews abhorred the worship of images. The close connection between art and religion that the Palestinian Jew could not help notice among his gentile neighbors did not exist in Babylonia. Whatever art the Persians had developed in Babylonia or taken over from the Greeks was entirely divorced from religion and hence the quite liberal attitude taken by the Babylonian scholars towards the law against images. According to the Babylonian Talmud (main passage Abodah Zarah 42b-43b) this prohibition is restricted to:

1. Representations of the human form but only in relief, not otherwise.
2. Representation in relief of the four figures—as a unity—seen by the Prophet Ezekiel on the Divine Throne (Ezek. 1. 1 seq.)
3. Representation of sun, moon and stars, whether in relief or otherwise.

The historical reasons for these rulings of the Talmud may be said to be the following ones. Not only was the human form the most favored by the Greeks and other nations of antiquity for the representation of their gods but the Jews had not yet forgotten their sufferings because of their refusal to pay the divine honors to the statues of the living or dead Caesars. The phenomenal development that Christianity took about the time of the rise of the Babylonian academies to importance could not but strengthen the aversion of the Jew against images of man. The fear that gnostic and syncretistic sects who often mistook symbol for reality, ideas for hypostases, might misinterpret the symbolic vision of the Prophet Ezekiel led the rabbis to prohibit the representation of the four figures in the Divine Throne. And finally, the old astral worship of the Semites was not yet quite dead among large numbers of the gentile inhabitants of Babylonia and Palestine and hence the unqualified prohibition against representation of the heavenly bodies.

On the whole, one may state that with very few exceptions, as for instance, the famous lions supporting the Ark of the synagogue at Ascoli, later removed to Pesaro (comp. Kaufmann in *Jewish Quarterly Review*, Old Series IX, 254) no designs in relief were used, the decorations of the synagogue being limited to mosaic engraving or painting, and that representation of animals was restricted to lions. In accordance with this practice, I have frequently rendered the following decision:

1. No designs in bas relief are to be used.
2. Representations of animals to be limited to the lion.
3. That of the Heavenly Bodies to be excluded entirely.
4. The walls and windows of the synagogue should not contain any figures whatsoever.

It may not be out of place to call attention to the fact that the Christianization of art in the Middle Ages and at the time of the Renaissance could only discourage the artistically inclined Jews.

It is indeed very humiliating for us Jews if we consider that the one truly great religious reform of modern times, that of the sixteenth century among the Christians, began with the removal of statuary and painting from the churches; while some of our brethren know of no better way of expressing their advanced ideas than by returning to forms of worship discarded by the Jew thousands of years ago as not being compatible with the spirituality of his religion. It would be a sad day for the synagogue if it should fail to proclaim by external forms the inner truth that the only acceptable worship of God is of the heart, and that the intrusion of any material attraction is a degradation of this pure service. We must uphold the ideal that the best worship is to penetrate to that region where the things of sense cannot accom-

pany us. Neither in life nor in worship should freedom be dependent upon more material succor.

In the United States, where affiliation with a congregation
was a matter of individual choice, and where the synagogue
depended on contributions from its members, a question
would arise from time to time as to whether a rabbi was
justified in "refusing religious services to those who are not
affiliated." This was Professor Ginzberg's reply:

With very few exceptions, Jewish life up to recent times had
as its center of gravity the community and not the congregation.
One who did not belong to the community put himself—or was
put by others—outside of the Jewish fold. The ideal thing would
be, of course, to have the synagogue in America take the place of
the community of old. Economic as well as other reasons, however, have prevented so far the realization of this ideal plan.
There are certainly thousands of Jews who do not belong to
congregations because of their inability to contribute to them and
at the same time who do not want to be treated as beneficiaries of
the synagogue. On the other hand, there are many more who are
too indifferent to bother about anything Jewish as long as they
are not forced to do so. It seems, therefore, to me that while the
policy of a congregation should be in the direction of excluding
"outsiders," a hard and fast rule would be dangerous.

There remains the complicated question of conversion.
Here are Professor Ginzberg's general views as well as one of
his specific opinions. "Judaism is not a proselytizing religion.
At the same time, it is not a closed corporation and heartily
welcomes those who, for the sake of the God of Israel, wish
to enter its fold. The ceremonies connected with conversion
to Judaism have been established for thousands of years.
These ceremonies must not be trifled with, though Judaism
never turned them into sacraments . . ." In reply to an inquiry as to whether married women can become converted,
Professor Ginzberg replied:

1. Married women can become converts to Judaism under the same conditions as unmarried ones. If one were to insist upon the strict talmudic law, it would be the duty of the rabbi to advise the Jew who had lived with a gentile woman to divorce her immediately upon her conversion. No less an authority, however, than Maimonides has decided a practical case against this talmudic regulation, and notwithstanding the fact that in his code he has incorporated this talmudic regulation. In a case where there are children that were born by the gentile mother and one is quite sure that divorce would be out of the question, we may be guided by the decision of Maimonides. Another regulation is that sexual relations are not permitted for ninety days after conversion. Of course, I do not know what kind of people you have before you and whether an advice of this nature would be listened to. You may, of course, explain to the husband that this abstinence is commanded as the first step in the Jewish life of holiness and discipline. If the woman is pregnant, the period of abstinence is not required.

2. I strongly advise against hurrying a matter of this kind. You ought to have the opportunity of meeting the woman several times, and talking to her concerning the steps she is considering to take. She also ought to read some books on Judaism, as for instance, Morris Joseph—*Judaism As Creed and Life;* Dembitz—*Home and Synagogue Ceremonies,* published by the Jewish Publication Society. It may also be advisable to have her read selected chapters in Graetz's *History of the Jews.* In my opinion, at least three months' preparation ought to be insisted upon. I suggest three months because in that case we may expect the couple to comply with the three months' abstinence. It is true that talmudic law insists on the abstinence after conversion, but from a psychological point of view, abstinence before conversion, during the time of preparation, can more easily be expected.

3. The children need conversion and their conversion is the same as that of adults and the instruction is to be adopted to the mind of the child. Of course, for male children, the circumcision must precede the baptism.

There is very little to add to the method of conversion to that given in *Shulhan 'Arukh, Yoreh De'ah* 268. May I however remark that for the baptism she may use a loose bathing gown. To carry out literally the regulation of the *Shulhan 'Arukh* would be very awkward in our time. You need three learned men to witness the baptism, preferably rabbis and if unavailable some laymen who have Jewish learning.

In addition to his suggestion about the shift in the period of abstinence, Professor Ginzberg approved a modification of the law which stated that the woman would be permitted to wear a loose flowing robe for her baptism.

Three decisions were related in some fashion to the practice of modern medicine. The first was an answer to the question under what conditions autopsy may be permitted. After reviewing the attitude of Jewish law toward the treatment of the dead, Professor Ginzberg concluded that *the prohibition against autopsy is clear*. And yet, he sought to specify the conditions which would justify the performance of autopsies in view of their crucial role in the advancement of human welfare. Key passages from his opinion (probably dating from the late 1920's) follow:

Permission is sought (*Noda' b'Yehuda, ibid.*) on the ground that autopsy is necessary in the interest of advancing medical science which involves the saving of human life. It is granted that whatever offers even a doubtful saving of human life is permitted, save idolatry, adultery, and murder. The argument is offered, however, that there must be a direct relation between autopsy and the saving of human life, i.e., when the autopsy performed on one person is expected to suggest a possible cure for another definite person who is afflicted with the same disease and for whom physicians seek a cure. Only, therefore, when there and then another person's life is to be saved by the autopsy of the dead person may the autopsy be performed. The advancement of science in general does not constitute saving of life, else we would argue that medical students may violate the Sabbath in the study of their vocation.

The argument is not altogether conclusive in itself in view of the leniency of the law in all cases where danger to life is in question. To prevent danger, not only is the actual act of prevention permitted, but as many links in the act as may be necessary to reach the final prevention (cf. *Orah Hayyim* 328 ff). Possibly even the desecration of the Sabbath for the study of medicine would be permitted if the study of it could not be done without the desecration of the Sabbath. The distinction between an act that has direct bearing on the saving of a life and the one that has an indirect bearing is logical but not based on or supported by any Talmudic or Geonic authority.

There may be another consideration for permitting autopsies, namely, the moral right which the hospital has to make certain demands from the patient. If it is part of the moral code of the hospital that in return for treatment given to the patient by the hospital, the latter expects the advance of the medical science and the patient's cooperation in that direction; if, for example, the hospital reserves the moral right—if not the legal right—to permit students to be present at an operation, contrary to the will of the patient, in the interest of the progress of medicine as part of the terms under which the patient is given the hospital service; and if that interpretation of the agreement between the hospital and the patient can apply also to the treatment of the body after death, though this interpretation is not explicitly stated, though a court would not honor such an understanding of the rights of the hospital over the patient—so long as there is a semblance of a moral obligation on the dead person himself, the law of the disrespectful treatment of the dead is suspended.

I would draw the following conclusions from the above. In hospitals whose function is a double one—the cure of patients and the advance of the medical science—and if that duality of function is publicly known, an autopsy may be made on a body of a Jew who died from a certain disease, with the expectation that the autopsy may help to bring relief or to lessen the danger of other patients known to the physicians to be suffering from that or a similar disease. The knowledge of one patient in existence within reach of the physicians is sufficient from the point of view of Jewish law. Under these conditions, the autopsy may be made against the will of the family, and the family is commanded by the law to permit autopsy in such instances. Unnecessary scarring, delay of the funeral, and leaving parts of the body unburied must be avoided.

In January 1936, Professor Ginzberg set out in writing his views about euthanasia which he had earlier discussed with his nephew, Dr. Sol W. Ginsburg, a distinguished psychiatrist. The critical paragraphs follow:

The earliest Jewish authority who discusses this problem directly and explicitly is Rabbi Judah of Regensburg, Bavaria (died 1217), who in his work *The Book of the Pious* no. 315 (ed. Berlin, p. 100) remarks as follows: "If one who suffers excruciating pain says to his fellowman, 'You see yourself I shall not live—not much longer, and as I cannot bear my pain any longer, I beg of you to kill me,' he (the one asked to do so) must not as much as touch him." The author, one of the most famous scholars and saints of the Middle Ages, quotes Bible and Talmud in support of his decision and is particularly interested in the correct explanation of the two cases of euthanasia mentioned in Scripture—one of the judge Abimelech (Judg. 9.54) and the other of King Saul, so graphically described in the opening chapter of the Second Book of Samuel. Rabbi Judah is not quite certain whether the arm-bearer of Abimelech was as wicked as his master and slew him in defiance of the law or that the exigencies of war justified his death; the speedy dispatch of Abimelech ended his attack on the tower and thus saved hundreds of people from sure death. He has no doubt whatsoever that the Amalakite committed murder in slaying Saul at his own request after he had wounded himself fatally. It is true Saul was justified in committing suicide (this is stated in as early a source as Genesis Rabba 34.13); the honor of Israel required that its first King should not permit himself to be captured alive. But the Amalakite had no justification for hastening the King's death and since shortening human life, even for a few moments, is punishable by death, he suffered by the hands of David the punishment he deserved.

The following few quotations from the authoritative sources of the Mishnah, Talmud and Codes will suffice to corroborate this view.

"One must not close the eyes of a person in agony of death—to hasten the end and thus save pain—and one who touches or moves his body 'sheds blood.' "

Said Rabbi Meir (the most famous doctor of the law about the middle of the second century), "A person in agony of death is like a flickering candle, it extinguishes as soon as one touches it, and similarly the closing of the eyes of a dying person is like pulling out the life from the body." This statement is found in all codes of Jewish law from the Mishnah composed about 200 to the *Shulhan 'Arukh* composed about the middle of the sixteenth century.

In this connection reference should be made also to the statement found in Talmud Sanhedrin 78a that he who kills a person in agony of death is punished with death. This is an application of the general rule found in many old sources (Semahot 1.1 and parallel passages given on the margin) that according to Jewish Law a person is considered as living as long as there is some life left in him.

Very instructive is the story told in the Talmud Abodah Zarah 17b about the death of the martyr Rabbi Hananiah ben Teradion, a victim of the Hadrianic persecution about 140. Wrapped in the scroll of the law, he was placed on a pyre of green brush; fire was set to it and wet wool was placed on his chest to prolong the agonies of death. His disciples asked him to open his mouth that the fire might enter and thus put an end to his suffering, but his answer was, "it is best that He who had given the soul should also take it away; no man should destroy himself."

This story about the gruesome death of the Rabbi might be a legend but it nevertheless expresses the Jewish view of the sacredness of human life. "Our life," remarks Maimonides (Laws Regarding Murderers, 2.2 and 1.4) "belongs to the Giver of Life —and nobody has any right to dispose thereof."

This does not mean, however, that according to the Jewish view a physician is not to try his utmost in alleviating pain. On the contrary, this is one of his main duties even if through certain pain-soothing medicine, the resistance of the patient might be weakened and finally cause his death.

My father was pleased that shortly after he had written the above opinion, Dr. A. A. Brill, one of the leaders of American psychiatry, came out against euthanasia. Even those whose profession was centered on the relief of pain and suffering saw vast complexities if the door were opened to "kill people for their own good."

In his autobiographical comments, Professor Ginzberg summarized his last responsum, which dealt with artificial insemination: "I found this to be illegal. And the legality was my only concern. I never entered into a moral discussion. At the end of 36 pages of discussion proving that a child born as a result of artificial insemination would have no legal status, primarily because of the Jewish family consciousness which would not permit a stranger to become a member of the family, I moralized only to the following extent: 'In addition, how reproachable it would be from the point of view of morals and purity of married life to have the woman become pregnant by a man not her husband.' 'And thou shalt be a holy people unto the Lord of thy God.' "

For at least thirty years and probably for nearly a half century, Louis Ginzberg was responsive to requests about how a higher degree of reconciliation could be achieved in the United States between Jewish law and Jewish life. He never failed to answer any question put by a responsible person, rabbi or layman. But he did not take any initiative to modernize the law. He saw no point in venturing on such a task, for whom could he hope to persuade? Those among his own students who found the law too burdensome did not hesitate to modify it for themselves or to tolerate the modifications introduced by the leaders and members of their congregations. And he had little inclination to disturb the beliefs and convictions of those who belonged to the more orthodox strand of the Conservative Movement.

His was a vision of Judaism with an honored past and a future that was still to be unfolded. He had no patience with those parochial leaders of American Jewry who thought it important to solve the problems of their own day without consideration for the problems of Jews in others lands or of those not yet born. He knew, beyond any question of doubt, that it was the authority of the law which alone had made possible the survival of the Jews and Judaism, and he had no intention of helping to shrink or confine further its domain already diminished as a consequence of the inroads of emancipation and reform.

Here was a man who appreciated better than most the inherent flexibility of Jewish law and yet he moved with great circumspection when it came to altering any of the dogmas and doctrines of the past. He hesitated at change because he knew that no matter how great his own learning, he would never be able to convince the great rabbis of Eastern Europe whose life and experiences differed so greatly from his own. And he saw little point in developing new law for American Jews, most of whom had long ago denied its authority.

The disruption caused by two wars and the Hitler holocaust added to his caution and constraint. Contact with Eastern Europe became more difficult to establish and maintain. The confusion generated by the irreconcilable groups in Palestine and Israel was also clearly before his eyes. He once entertained the idea of a world assembly of great talmudists to see what might be done to modernize the law, but this remained more a dream than a plan.

Cut off from effective dialogue with the great talmudists of the old school, he found himself almost alone on this side of the Atlantic. A few of his students had developed into serious talmudic scholars and were productive research workers. But none of them was a colleague. They were disciples. And so Louis Ginzberg remained a lonely man, more determined with each year to be a vigilant keeper of the law since he could not effectively reform it.

CHAPTER XI

THE GIRL FROM BERLIN

SHE HAD been known as *Die Amerikanerin* during the years of her youth in Germany, because of her independence and refusal to conform. She was not actually a radical in her thought or in the way she lived; the nickname described her personality. Her mother had died as the result of a ruptured appendix when Adele was eight, and her father had moved her family some years later from Frankfurt to Berlin, where he continued to deal in real estate with more gusto than luck. He went through a considerable amount of family funds, with only an occasional good year among many bad ones. He bought heavily on the outskirts of Berlin, convinced that the capital would expand. It did expand, but in the opposite direction. But business did not circumscribe his life. He was a devout Jew with a deep love for Israel, and worked hard on behalf of the poor.

At one point after World War I, my father put up several thousand dollars of his modest savings to protect the family investment, but the only result was that after World War II a small part of the total was recovered from the West German Government. The land was in East Berlin, and the settlement was only a fraction of what the Katzenstein family had invested in this real estate.

The girl Louis Ginzberg became engaged to, after having seen her three times during the course of one week-end, had had a modest formal education. She attended a finishing school until she was about seventeen or eighteen, and then sought permission to study nursing, since she had developed a young girl's infatuation with Professor Heinrich Finkelstein, the distinguished Berlin pediatrician, who had taken care of her step-brother. I recall Finkelstein's visit at our home in New York after World War I, during which my mother sought to evoke memories about times past which may have had more meaning to her than to the distinguished professor. She was refused permission to study nursing, and so she stormed her father's office and secured a modest place for herself there. She was not the type to sit home and crochet.

As a matter of fact, in all her adult life, Adele Katzenstein Ginzberg undertook only a few pieces of needlework. She knitted a vest of many splendid colors as an engagement present for her fiancé, which he never wore out of the house since he did not ride with the hounds; and it took an appeal to patriotism during World War I for her to knit me a sweater which must have had many unusual qualities—I was asked so many questions about it that I learned a simple response that I still remember: "knit one, purl one, and reverse."

Since her father was not very successful in his business, and her stepmother, who had earlier been her governess, was greatly depressed by the loss of her only child, the family environment was not a happy one. Just as Louis Ginzberg was ready to find a wife in 1908, so Adele Katzenstein was ready for a husband, although she had already turned down several suitors.

Since my father had been remiss in taking out his citizenship papers—or did he entertain for some years the possibility of returning to Europe?—he was not able, as a Russian citizen, to obtain permission to marry in Berlin except after a considerable delay. So the nuptials took place in London, for British regulations were less sticky. My father explained to the rabbi of St. John's Woods Synagogue that since his bride did not understand a word of English, it would be an act of mercy if he would keep his remarks to a minimum, which he did to the gain of both. In harmony with her Orthodox upbringing, my mother wore a wig when she was married. When my father discovered it shortly after the ceremony, he ripped it off and off it stayed. My parents spent their honeymoon in England, and arrived in New York during a heat wave in the early summer of 1909.

My mother was alone in a strange land where she did not speak the language; married to a scholar whose work she could not understand; a member of an academic community that felt she had usurped another woman's place; the aunt of a considerable number of American boys and girls (the children of my father's brother and sister) who were not much younger than she and whose ways were completely strange to her. Had it not been for the love and understanding shown her by her sister-in-law, Libby Ginsburg, with whom my father had earlier lived, she would have had an even more difficult time, and the one she experienced was difficult enough.

But she was young, beautiful, strong, and outgoing, and she quickly made her way. And by April, 1911, she had borne her first child. My mother insists that during her pregnancy my father threatened her with all sorts of dire consequences if it did not turn out to be a boy. I give some credence to this, since when our own first-born arrived I telephoned my parents' home shortly after midnight to announce that my wife had just given birth to a girl. In the early hours of the morning my father suggested to my mother that she might have misunderstood the message— perhaps the child was a boy after all!

When my mother wrote proudly about her baby boy to her aunt in Berlin, she added that he would be named after his paternal grandfather, Isaac Elias. Her aunt wrote to congratulate her and remarked in passing that such a name might not be suitable for an American child and suggested an Anglicized version. My father was outraged that this pseudo-Teutonic aunt, who came originally from Rumania, should question the appropriateness of his son's carrying the honored name of his father. The name stayed, but from the beginning I was called Eli. The oversolicitous aunt had made her point.

When I was a few months old, my mother's only sister was sent to visit her in the hope and expectation that she too might find an American husband. The visit lengthened from six months to a year to two years and then three; then came World War I, and Martha became a permanent member of the household. In 1914 my sister Sophie was born, and that completed the family. It is likely that my mother would have been willing and happy to have more children, but my father probably wanted a small family. His health had always been fragile, and his friend Dr. Solomon Solis-Cohen of Philadelphia had serious doubts whether he would survive his fiftieth birthday. The Seminary salaries were modest and there was no established pension fund. My father's anxieties about his health, reinforced by a world war, help to explain why he had only two children.

Although I was born and brought up in New York City, English was not the language I first learned. We spoke only German at home until I went to kindergarten. There were enough other children with German-speaking parents in our neighborhood so that I had companions. Even after I learned English, German remained the language spoken at home until the United States entered World War I. At that point, I returned home from school with my own ultimatum: either we stop speaking German or I would leave home.

My mother took at least partial revenge. We used to spend

the summer along the Jersey coast and I recall how she insisted on singing her favorite German *Lieder* in a loud voice, not because she loved and admired the Germans—which she didn't—but because she refused to be intimidated by anybody. A more nerve-wracking recollection is of her swimming far out in the Atlantic just to show the lifeguard—and us, I suppose—that she would obey no law. The fact that my father's good friend, the distinguished University of Pennsylvania Assyriologist, W. Max Müller, who was an excellent swimmer, drowned one summer while we were vacationing at the same seashore town added to my apprehensions.

The war was an important turning point even for my mother. With two young children to care for, she had so far confined her activities in America to homemaking and child-rearing. She added to these activities in connection with a Liberty Bond campaign. She won first prize in her district and from then on, that is from 1918, she was able both to run an active household and to participate in many community undertakings.

With his marriage, my father made a radical shift in the patterning of his life. He substantially restricted his participation in social and community affairs. He was pleased to have people at his home, but he developed all sorts of rationales for not going out, particularly in the evening. We always had guests on Friday evening and at Saturday lunch, and my father frequently brought home one or more guests during the course of the week, almost always without any warning to my mother. She was never flustered. In fact, it became a challenge to her to see how many unexpected guests she could take in stride. I believe the high point of this came many years later when my parents had shifted their summer residence to the Belgrade Lakes in Maine, when a group of twenty-five former students and their families dropped in to see my parents, and my mother insisted that they stay for lunch.

In harmony with the practices that prevailed in his native

land, my father turned over to my mother all responsibility for running the household and caring for the children; he retained control only over finances. I recall that every Saturday night my mother received a check for household expenses for the week. For many years that check was for $25, and we ate very well on that. When it came to finding a summer cottage, making travelling arrangements, or solving other household problems, routine or special, my mother attended to them.

The only exception to this was in 1922, when my father decided to take the family to Europe so that my mother and he could see their families and friends after the long separation caused by the war. He went downtown to arrange certain financial matters. He was on Wall Street just a few minutes before the bomb explosion, and he used to speculate about the theories the newspapers would have advanced had he been a victim. What was a Professor of Talmud doing on Wall Street?

We spent four months abroad. I remember several different aspects of this trip. For the first of only two times in his life, my father took some action with respect to my schooling. He went to see the principal of Speyer Junior High School, to which I had just been admitted, to inquire whether my late entrance would cause any difficulty. He found that I could enter after school started if I would read extra books. Speyer required that all students read and report on three books a week. And I, up to this point, had steadfastly refused to read anything. My mother, who was almost totally free of any anxiety about my scholastic progress, even consulted our family physician about this. After his visit to the principal, my father sought to impress upon me the need to alter my ways. I did, of course, but I don't think that at that time he had much faith that I would.

I was also a recalcitrant student of Hebrew. My mother had started to teach me when I was five, but she soon retired in favor of my father. He made several valiant attempts, but I was much more interested in playing ball than in learning Hebrew, and I soon discovered that an attack of acute cramps would permit me to escape from my father's study. I would lock myself in the bathroom for thirty to fifty minutes and when I re-emerged there was only a short period left for instruction.

To return to that European trip, it was a near fiasco. My father, cut off from his books, became very nervous, particularly since he was exposed for so many hours a day to my sister and me, who found Germany a most undesirable place. Food was short, milk was not obtainable, and above all, there were no youngsters to play with. But there were a few highlights. We were in Berlin on the day that Walter Rathenau was murdered, and I suspect that my deeply ingrained view of the instability of German political life stems from that early impression. Then, I recall as if it were yesterday the train ride from Berlin to the South (we spent several weeks at Wildbad in the Black Forest) during which a German officer explained to us that he had just returned from eighteen months in Russia where he had been helping to establish relationships between the Reichswehr and the Communists. That, too, stayed with me. My unhappiness with the Germans was such that I prophesied to my relatives and to all others who would listen that the German inflation was just beginning—the value of the mark would go much lower. It was currently 300 to the dollar; I warned that it would go to 3,000 and even lower. They recalled in later years their regret that they had not acted on my forecast!

There are two stories that relate particularly to my mother. She had wanted to take us on a trip down the Rhine. My father agreed, but he wanted no part of any sightseeing, so it was decided that we would join his train from Frankfurt at Cologne and proceed together to Amsterdam. While on the Rhine steamer, my mother learned that there was not a hotel room to be obtained in Cologne and that we had better disembark at Bonn, which we did. But Bonn too was crowded. After a long search, we were still without a room for the night. At one point, my mother asked the taxi driver about a large building and she was told that it was the former palace of the Kaiser. She told the driver to stop, she got out, found the caretaker, and persuaded her to put us up for the night! At breakfast the next morning we found milk on the table—a rare delight that summer. The caretaker had made a special effort to secure it. But when we tasted it we spat it out immediately; it was goat's milk. I can still hear the old woman's plaintive question: Are all American children so spoiled?

The climax of our German visit came a few hours later. Some time after we had joined my father's train, it pulled into the station at the frontier where everybody had to get out for customs' inspection. We were herded into a small room with sealed windows. After an unbearably long wait, one American took his cane and smashed the window, to the utter consternation of the local officialdom. But they were soon to have their revenge.

Nothing could be taken out of Germany unless the purchaser had obtained an *"ausfuhrbewilligunsschein"* (export permit). To make room for their many purchases, most travellers had bought additional luggage—many of them had filled big trunks with the inexpensive merchandise which they had bought with depreciated marks. When the German customs officials, annoyed at the Americans, found that they did not have export certificates for their trunks, they emptied their contents onto the floor and confiscated the luggage. The place was bedlam. We, however, were relaxed, because as a matter of principle, my mother had refused to exploit the currency situation. We had bought nothing of consequence.

Finally, we were ready to go back to the train. At that

point, men went one way, women another. Soon my father and I were back in our coach and after a while it appeared that everybody had returned. Only two were missing, my mother and sister. Shortly thereafter, we heard a great commotion at the far end of the station. My mother was gesticulating in the midst of a large number of German officials, including, it later turned out, the Commandant of the Border Garrison, to whom an appeal had been made. In the final inspection, my mother, who had a pair of Zeiss binoculars with her, had been asked to surrender them. She insisted that she had not bought them, which was true, that they had been a gift from her brother-in-law. Having been careful not to take advantage of the depreciated currency, she was determined to save her binoculars. The Commandant, with the wisdom of Solomon, finally made his decision on the basis of whether my mother had tried to conceal the item during the inspection. When he learned that she had worn them openly, he let her keep them. The international express could now proceed—twenty minutes late. But my mother had bested the German bureaucracy.

My father did not die at fifty as his physician had warned he might, but at eighty. The credit for these extra years and for the basic tranquility of his home belongs to my mother. She arranged everything to protect her "Schatzie," the only name she ever called him, and sought to make his life more pleasant and productive. In forty-five years of married life my father spent only five nights away from her, four of these occasioned by the need to work out a last minute arrangement with the printer prior to going on vacation. The only other time they were separated was when my father went to Chicago in 1922 to deliver the second Zunz Memorial lecture at the University of Chicago.

Printers and vacations suggest the following story that my father told: "Once, when I left Bradley Beach, New Jersey, on a train that departed at 8 a.m., I met Daniel Guggenheim.

He asked me why I was going to the city. I told him that I had to look at some proofs of a book. He asked why this was necessary on such a hot day. I said, 'May I ask you a question? Why are *you* going?' He, the richest Jew in the country, said, 'I have to be at the office.'"

"His father had been a very simple man. He used to peddle lace. When the boys grew up, they went West and made a fortune in copper. One of the brothers later became Senator from Colorado. Schechter and I were invited to spend a weekend at the Guggenheims' in Elberon. Driving to his home, Guggenheim pointed out the beautiful estates, the church, the school. I pointed to a large building and asked what it was. This was a building for Guggenheim's servants!"

My father had little if any talent for recreation. His New York physician used to encourage him to take up a hobby, but he insisted that study was his hobby. He could swim on his back for long periods of time, and once he swam from Bradley Beach to Asbury Park. He taught me chess and pinochle. But his major pleasure was in talking with people he liked, and my mother was willing to adjust to his severely constricted life. During World War I the distinguished archaeologist, Immanuel Benzinger, lost his professorship in Toronto and found himself without money or friends in New York. My parents befriended him. He came weekly, if not more frequently, to our home. He became our *Shabbas Goy*. He was astounded at the freedom of American children, and remarked that the decalogue should be amended: an eleventh commandment should adjure parents to obey their children. Nevertheless, when I got into some kind of trouble through petty shoplifting, he proved very reassuring to my parents, who I believe were disturbed but not unnerved.

My father's concern about my future was more deep-seated. During my youth he had a vision of his only son becoming a shortstop, although he didn't know a shortstop from a pitcher, since he never saw a baseball game in his life. And when I grew up, he had serious questions about my underlying attitudes towards Jews and Judaism. His worst fear was that I might marry a "*schicksa.*" His position on intermarriage was adamant and inflexible. A step-niece of his had married a Brahmin. Thereafter, he had refused to let her in the house and made the entire family sever connections with her.

The relations between my father and my cousin Sol were exceedingly close. My father had lived with Sol's parents during the first ten years of Sol's life. My mother was told that he had cried inconsolably when he learned of my father's approaching marriage. I can still recall the anxiety that prevailed when Sol brought a beautiful red-headed nurse to dinner one Friday evening. She had been born and had grown up in a small town in upstate New York. The conversation was very guarded and constrained until my father slowly maneuvered it and discovered that she knew Yiddish! Then everybody relaxed.

During my bachelor days, my parents knew that I kept company with young ladies who were not Jewish, and while my mother may have had an unhappy moment or two, this was a source of deep concern to my father. As I have said, on intermarriage, he had no flexibility. He considered it odd, but nothing more than that, when a good friend of mine, a Christian, who was a distinguished economist, decided to marry a Jewish girl. But when one of his own good friends, a Jew, after many years of unhappiness, was married for the second time and this time to a Christian, he broke off his relationship with him. Not even the suicide of this friend shortly thereafter led him to question his own behavior. Judaism could not survive if Jews married non-Jews and the survival of Judaism remained of primary importance for my father.

Family life tends to be more or less uneventful between

crises, external or internal. On the external side, World War I came quickly, and ended quickly, and as far as I can reconstruct it, its effect on the Ginzberg family was not pronounced. A part of my father's notes to an important scientific work was lost by a European printer in the turmoil which attended the war and the dislocations that followed. The war also unsettled his plans to complete and publish his study of *An Unknown Jewish Sect*. However, as far as my father was concerned, World War I also had its constructive and even comic side. This is his account of his first meeting with Harry Wolfson, who later became one of his most intimate friends: "He was drafted towards the end of World War I. He came to see me in his uniform: one sleeve was too short, one was too long. One shoe was too wide, one was too narrow. He was good only for KP. I told him that it was fortunate that the war was almost over—that we would lose it if it depended on him."

And this is what my father told his daughter-in-law of Wolfson's struggles at Harvard.

"He came to this country at the age of sixteen in 1905-06. Conditions in Russia were bad—*very* bad for Jews. He went to high school in Scranton, and to college at Harvard. He has a truly elegant English style, but he continues to speak English with an accent. It is also difficult to learn German if you speak Yiddish—they are too similar. This is especially true of Lithuanians. I am one of the very few who learned how to speak German fluently. When I first came to Strassburg I had a conversation with Noeldeke. He said, 'You are not a native German, are you?' I said, 'How do you know?' He said, 'No German speaks perfect German—listen to me.'

"Judge Mack, a graduate of Harvard, and at one time an Overseer, had an interest in Semitics. Wolfson became an instructor. Later, Wolfson came to see me about a call from the Hebrew Union College. I said, 'Stay where you are.

Don't go. There is no future there from any point of view. If you remain at Harvard, something will happen.' He listened to me and remained. After some time, he became an assistant professor. He published an important work on Crescas. Meanwhile, Littauer, a prominent Harvard graduate, gave several million dollars to the university. At the Tercentenary, when he was nearly eighty, he was an usher. Littauer became interested in Wolfson, but his real interest was Harvard. But he gradually got to like Wolfson. He established a Chair of Jewish History and Philosophy, and Wolfson became its first occupant."

There was one summer when Wolfson fled from his room in Cambridge to our family in Maine because of an invasion of bats in his old dormitory room. Once he came north after being released from the hospital, and my mother held on to him long enough to feed him up. It was not easy to hold on to Wolfson; many times after he had telephoned from Boston that he was coming down to see my father, he would telephone a few hours later from Grand Central Station that he had just arrived but that he had decided to go back on the next train. Sometimes, my mother, who handled most of the telephoning in our house, managed to persuade him to come to the house before going back, but just as often she failed. On one of his visits to Maine, I took Wolfson and my father fishing, and while they were heavily engaged in an esoteric philosophical discussion, Wolfson hooked a fish. He became so excited that it was difficult to keep the boat from turning over. There is no question in my mind but that the one person who was a regular visitor to our house for whom my father had unconditional intellectual respect and regard was Wolfson.

The Great Depression of 1929-33 had little if any direct impact on the family. The Seminary reduced salaries a little but in the early thirties, my father's brother, a wealthy bachelor who lived in South Africa, died and left twoseventeenths of his estate to my father and to each of his other siblings. The family's financial position, which had always been modest but never strained, now eased.

Although the Depression left few if any scars on the Ginzbergs, the coming of Hitler cast a shadow that turned into a dark cloud that settled over all Jews. From the first, my father feared the worst. He had lived among "cannibals," as he described the Russian perpetrators of the blood ritual, and he knew that beneath the intellectual anti-Semitism of the Germans was a seething cauldron of twisted emotions. Moreover, he did not believe that any of the civilized Christian countries would come to the aid of Jews even in their hour of dire need. Although the following note was written many years later to Dr. Grayzel, in fact in the year my father died, it is relevant here:

"Many thanks for your kindness in forwarding to me your essay on the relation of Pope John XXII to the Jews, which I read with great pleasure and profit.

"It is extremely interesting to note how little the attitude of Roman Catholicism to the Jews and Judaism has changed in the last six centuries. The policy of the Vatican with regard to Israel is exactly the same as that taken by Pope John XXII and several of his predecessors: '. . . the Jews are to be kept alive as a witness to the truth of Christianity, but let them beware of trying to compete with the true religion.'"

Even the Hitler tragedy had a positive side-effect: it awakened and reawakened the interest and concern of many Jews in the welfare and destiny of their brethren. Among those who felt compelled to play a more active role was Professor Morris Raphael Cohen, who for several decades had been trying to turn his students at City College from believers into skeptics. Shortly after the rise of Hitler, my father, who had seen very little of Cohen in earlier years, quickly developed a warm friendship with him. One evening when he and my teacher and friend, Robert Morrison Mac-

Iver, were at my parents' home for dinner, they got into a heated argument which kept up for a considerable time. My father sat quietly enjoying the debate. Suddenly my mother jumped up and shouted at my father, "Schaffskopf, why don't you say something! Don't you know anything?"

My mother usually said what she felt or believed. Early in my graduate studies, I invited Professor Roswell McCrea to my parents' house. He was then Chairman of the Graduate Department of Economics, as well as the head of the School of Business at Columbia. Early in the evening my mother asked McCrea what he did; he replied that he was an economist. "Oh," said she, "another faker like my son." We were in the middle of the Depression, and as far as my mother could see the economists were not making any significant contribution to ending it.

When I brought the young lady in whom I was seriously interested to my parents' house for the Passover *seder* in 1944, my mother fortunately kept her opinion to herself until after we left, at which point she announced to all who were still there: "She'll never do: she's too quiet and she drinks too much!"

In the latter period of my father's life, my mother used to attend his course on Festivals and Ceremonies. While my mother sat towards the back of the room, she was not unobtrusive. If my father ran beyond the hour, she would borrow a pocket watch from one of the students nearby and begin to swing it to remind him to close his lecture. From the day I began to teach in 1935, I have been comfortable and relaxed in the classroom, but during my early years as a teacher I had a dread that my mother might decide to audit my course, and that was a challenge I preferred to avoid.

My sister and I grew up free of serious illness, and my mother was never bedridden, not even for one day, throughout the years that I lived at home. But my father's health was poor. His correspondence is shot through with references to his having recently been ill or to the current unsatisfactory state of his health. As I have mentioned, a real crisis occurred in Frankfurt in 1928, when he developed a serious bladder infection as a result of a cystoscopy. When he was finally released from the hospital, the German specialist told him that he must never be operated on—that he would not survive surgery. Within a few years, in New York, his prostate difficulty became worse, but his physicians hesitated to recommend an operation on a patient who was in delicate health, and who in addition had deep anxieties about surgery. Matters dragged on until at last some kind of action could no longer be postponed. My mother opposed surgery and her opposition further intimidated the already cautious physicians. I finally intervened in favor of an operation after I learned that further delay could lead only to debility and death. While surgery held risks, it also held out the promise of many good years.

My cousin Sol had the foresight to anticipate that in a two-stage operation good nurses would be very important for a patient as anxious as my father, who had been explicitly warned to avoid surgery. Dr. Edwin Beer, a leader in his profession, was his surgeon. Stage one of the operation went well, but after twenty-four hours my father went into shock and hovered between life and death for the next several weeks, proving once again the wisdom of surgeons who hesitate to operate on apprehensive patients. They finally brought him through, and the second stage of the operation proceeded without difficulty. When he was convalescing, Beer said that he would personally bring him a "big lobster from Longchamps," and it took a little explaining to convince Beer that the gesture would have to suffice for the deed. It is interesting that my father began his autobiographical recitals with a recollection of this operation.

"In 1937, when I had a bladder operation, Wechsler was upset. Silver, who had been putting off the operation for years, finally agreed—mainly at Wechsler's instigation. After the operation, I went into shock and was in the hospital for ten weeks. Wechsler felt tremendously responsible. At one point, I was in an oxygen tent and as I was going to sleep for the night, I said to the nurse, who was a very pretty girl from Providence, that I would surely pull through the night. She said, 'Of course you will, but why do you feel so sure tonight?' I said that if I had been able to live through the visits of the fourteen doctors who saw me that day, I could live through anything.

"Later that night, Scotty Schapiro came to see me at 2 a. m. He said, in order not to alarm me, that he had just been in the neighborhood. I knew that was not so, but I told him he was welcome. I had been so uncomfortable in the oxygen tent that they were trying a mask, but this needed the constant attention of a doctor and Scotty had volunteered his services."

From the time he returned from Germany late in 1929, almost until the time of his trip to Palestine as a member of the Survey Commission in the winter of 1933, my father had been in indifferent health. And after his return from Palestine, his condition and particularly his mood worsened. He knew that he was approaching a crisis. But there were happy events. A long letter from James Bryant Conant made 1936 an exciting year.

I dropped in late one afternoon, as was my wont, and my father handed to me a long letter which he had just received from the President of Harvard University inviting him to participate in the forthcoming Tercentenary activities. There would be two weeks of public lectures and symposia, and Conant suggested that L. G. might be willing to prepare a paper within the broad area of "Europe and the Middle East." I read the letter through, which he had not done, and on the third page, I found the following sentence. "Should you find it possible to attend the Conference, it is hoped that you would remain as an honored guest at the concluding ceremonies and then accept the Honorary Doctorate in Theology which the Governing Boards of Harvard University have authorized me to confer upon you if you can be present."

My father's acceptance follows: "I deeply appreciate the great honor conferred upon me by your invitation of January 15 to attend the Tercentenary Celebration of Harvard University.

"Ever since its foundation, Harvard University has played a predominant role in the development of American culture; it has contributed to every advance in the arts and sciences. The galaxy of scholars who shall participate in the Celebration will honor themselves by expressing homage to the institution which for centuries has guided the intellectual and cultural life of America. I consider it, therefore, a rare privilege to add my small mite to this large offering.

"In accordance with your suggestion, I shall prepare a paper within the field (II,b) *Europe and the Near East;* it will deal, granting your approval, with *Folk-Lore: East and West.*

"I hope to be able to attend the concluding ceremonies of the Tercentenary and there accept the Honorary Doctorate in Theology which the Governing Boards of Harvard University have authorized you to confer upon me.

"I beg to express to the Governing Boards and to you my sincerest gratitude for this signal distinction.

"With the assurance of the highest esteem, I beg to remain—"

In recalling the event my father said: "Wolfson was very excited about the award—first because Jewish scholarship was recognized, and second because of his personal liking for me." His recollection was sound; Wolfson was excited. He sent a large number of suggestions about alternative papers and titles. At the end, my father decided to stay with his original choice.

But a crisis soon developed. The climax of the Tercenten-ary coincided with the Jewish New Year. Wolfson took the initiative in arranging a special Orthodox service which about 200 people attended. Professor Nathan Isaacs of the Harvard Business School and my father took turns officiat-ing. Because my parents did not use their tickets, my sister and I heard one of the three special concerts that Koussevit-zky conducted in honor of the occasion. It was the only time that I sat in the close company of twenty or so Nobel Prize winners and an equal number of distinguished humanists.

It was a festive two weeks and my father was in good spirits. He even granted two interviews to an attractive lady reporter of the Hearst Syndicate—the first on Russia and religion, in which he flayed the Communists for their materi-alistic outlook and made them responsible not only for their own misdeeds but also for having been models for Hitler. The second dealt with Jews and Arabs in Palestine and was much more constrained, although he did accuse His Majes-ty's Government of seeking to profit from the miseries of others. This was the period of the "United Front," and I remember my chagrin at what I considered my father's red-baiting.

I attended the Tercentenary as a member of the Sympo-sium on the Social Sciences, and in addition to my pleasure in my father's honor, I saw Harvard give honorary degrees to two of my favorite teachers, Wesley C. Mitchell and Robert M. MacIver. I recall my father's telling me that he had helped to succor Jean Piaget who, knowing no English, could not make known his need for a sleeping pill. My fa-ther's French was adequate and he always travelled with sleeping pills. Among the most famous of the Tercentenary stories was the introduction of Carl Jung. After many flowery statements, the chairman said, "I now have the plea-sure of presenting Professor Freud to you!"

My father had some other amusing recollections of the Tercentenary: "About sixty degrees were given and only two of these were for Doctors of Sacred Theology; the other one went to a theologian. The ceremony was held in a frightful rain. It was just pouring, but since President Roosevelt refused an umbrella, the rest of us perforce had to. After the ceremony they held a reception. A friend of mine plied me with whiskey, but I had rarely had any until then. I said to him that I didn't like whiskey, and he said that was because I never drank it. Lunch followed immediately and we all checked our diplomas. When I retrieved mine after lunch, Peggy Gresser, the granddaughter of Rebekah Kohut, asked to look at it. I showed it to her, and it turned out to be the diploma belonging to a Norwegian who was honored for his work in oceanography. He was rushing for a train, and we had just enough time to exchange diplomas.

"At the ceremony I also represented the Seminary, and in the procession we walked according to the age of the institution. The first was a representative of the University of Cairo, and then the University of Salonika. Next to me was the delegate from Stanford University. The most amusing of the delegates was the one from the Académie Française. He had a green hat and a gray robe all beautifully embroidered, and he carried a little sword. No one could help smiling at him."

So appropriate was Conant's citation that it suggested the title for a posthumous collection of my father's essays. He had called him "A profound scholar of the laws and legends in talmudic literature."

These years, 1936-37, marked the dividing line between my father's years of maturity and the years of his old age. The years immediately following saw the preparation for publication of the first three volumes of his magnum opus, *Commentary on the Palestinian Talmud,* which appeared in 1941.

Then came the war. For millions of young people it meant the disruption of conventional patterns and the taking on of new ones. But persons like my father, who was sixty-eight when the United States entered the war, were forced to the sidelines by the world conflagration. It robbed their lives of any composure and tranquility, but it didn't make new demands on them. They lived more or less in suspense.

My sister Sophie, after graduating from Hunter College in New York in the middle 1930's, had gone to Cambridge to study Public Health at M.I.T. There, in 1938, she fell in love with and married one of her professors, Bernard Gould, a member of the Department of Biology. He specialized in micro-biochemistry. Her first son Michael was born in 1942, and she gave birth to twin boys in 1944. My sister Sophie added much to the contentment of my father's later years, not only because he enjoyed her, her husband, and their children, but because long before her marriage she had brought into my parents' orbit two young women with whom my father developed a deep and affectionate relationship. When they married, the Ginzberg family also adopted their husbands: Florence and John Lawrence and Helen and Irving Peterfreund. Although my father made it a point not to perform marriages or otherwise act in an official rabbinical capacity, he broke his rule for Flory. He officiated at the ceremony which took place in my parents' home.

At the end of the war, I was still in Washington, serving as the principal logistical advisor to the Surgeon General of the Army. My parents came, as they said, to pay me a visit, but in point of fact their aim was to become better acquainted with the young lady whom I was courting. In order to ease the strain all around, I took along to dinner one of my good friends, whom my parents knew and liked, Professor Abrahamson of Bowdoin College. During the course of the evening my parents succeeded in eliciting considerable information about the young lady's physical health; my father removed her glasses and remarked how strong they were. Finally, my friend Jim leaned over and said, "And how are your teeth, my dear?"

When Ruth first announced to her family that she was

keeping company with me, they and others recapitulated for her the story of the "Exceptional Friendship" of four decades earlier. But she was willing to test the fates a second time. We were married in July 1946, in the presence of assorted notables that included several Army generals, distinguished academicians, the elite of Jewish scholarship, many prominent physicians, lawyers, and other professional and business and labor leaders—and David Ben-Gurion, who happened to be in the United States at that time and who gave the bride competition as the center of interest for amateur photographers. According to *The New York Times* three rabbis officiated: Max Maccoby, Louis M. Epstein, and Stephen S. Wise. In point of fact, Wise was ill and did not attend. And as far as my father was concerned, Alexander Marx and Louis Finkelstein were the witnesses.

My father had changed his regime after recovering from his operation in 1937. No longer was he denied liquor. No longer did he stay away from movies and theatre. No longer did he refuse to go out at night. He developed all sorts of fanciful explanations as to why he was now able to eat, drink, and be merry, while earlier he could not. I never had any doubt that the explanation was psychological, not physiological: he had finally shed the tremendous tensions associated with his productive work. He had reached a point in life when despite the continued sharpness of his mind, he could no longer muster the strength required for major architectonic efforts. He began to relax a little, and then a little more.

A big part of the credit for his relaxation during these last years goes to his daughter-in-law, for whom he quickly developed a deep love, which was quickly reciprocated. She had the quickness of mind and subtlety of humor that could not fail to bring out the best in her father-in-law, who had always had a way with the ladies. And they both enjoyed the added exhilaration that came with conversation aided and abetted by alcohol.

In the summer of 1948, Ruth and I vacationed on East Pond, Maine, not far from where my parents had their camp. This was the summer when I spent each day talking through with my father what later became my *Agenda for American Jews.* I never would have been able to put together that book but for his help. During those days and weeks, which coincided with the anniversary of the death of his father and the Fast of Ab, he revealed more and more of the doubts that had begun to plague him anew about the road that he had taken in pursuing a "scientific" approach to the study of Rabbinics. Not that he had had any choice in the matter. He knew that. But he was concerned about the breach which his approach and method had caused between his father and his father's father and himself. He told me regretfully that he could never have published his *Commentary* during his father's lifetime.

And then the blow came. He received the following letter:

Levi of Neistadt:

Your life has been a failure. Not only have you made the Torah a *Kardom Lachpor Bo,* and you glory in the designation of Professor of Talmud and great authority on "Halakhah," when you know that there are scores of men superior to you in Talmud in this city; not only have you helped produce "Rabbis" who are in almost every single case *Boale Niddot* and *Chot'im* and *Machti'im et Harabim;* not only are you a *Poresh Min Hatzibur* of the real *Talmidei Chachamin* who toil for the welfare of *K'lal Yisroel;* but you have cast aspersion on the Talmud and supported the *Kofrim:* you declared at least twice (once in your Legends and once in your Students, etc.) that the Rabbis of the Talmud uttered their Hagadic statements on the spur of the moment (May the Almighty forgive you), and you support Weiss in his denial of the authenticity of a great part of *Torah Sheba'al Peh.* Your works are full of echoes of the *Kofrim.* Remember your childhood hopes, and now see yourself not only as an associate of

M. Kaplan (*Yimach Sh'mo*) but also in part responsible for him and for others like him. For you, the authority, have undermined the faith of these *Am Ha'aretz*. May the Almighty open your eyes and help you to recant, to recall the harmful books, to repudiate your associates the *Kofrim*, and to return to the *Tzibbur* of *Talmide-Chachamim*.

Yours sincerely,
A Friend.

Within twenty-four hours he had a severe case of *herpes zoster* (shingles), and although the acute infection subsided after a time, he was left with an aggravated neuralgia which plagued him every day and night until he died. He had the best medical care, but the greatest contribution of his able physician, Dr. Solomon Silver, was that he encouraged my father to try any therapy that might prove beneficial as long as it had no prospect of hurting him; at the same time, he interdicted any radical therapy that held a potential for harm. Dr. Silver and his wife were close friends; Sol shared my father's pain and suffering, but he held firmly to a conservative approach against the anguished outbursts of my mother. This was just one of many situations where the best of physicians could do little more than stand by and watch. He could not even relieve the patient's pain.

Some months following his attack, my father wrote to a former student, Rabbi Abraham Goldberg, who was living in Jerusalem: "There is little to report about ourselves. You very likely know that my son was married three years ago to a Miss Szold, daughter of Robert Szold, and a cousin of the late Miss Henrietta Szold. My son is a very busy man: in addition to being Professor of Economics at Columbia University, he is still a consultant of the War Department and besides these two jobs, is also engaged in a number of literary undertakings. My daughter is now the mother of three boys. As the sister of an economist, she managed to cut down expenses and work by giving birth to twins, and thus she is now the mother of three boys, one livelier than the other, whether you start from the top or the bottom. As far as I am concerned, I am sorry to say that for the past fourteen months, I have suffered a great deal of pain. First, I had a severe case of neuralgia, which was the aftermath of the shingles, which I contracted last summer. I am still suffering a great deal of pain from the neuralgia. The physicians do not consider my case as a serious illness, but I am sure that none of them ever had it, otherwise they would change their minds."

The following two letters written to his friends at the Jewish Publication Society, asking them to send on copies of his books so that he might inscribe them for physicians who had treated him, tell us a little about his last years. The first, written to Dr. Jacobs, is dated June 1949: "One of my two baker's dozen physicians who treated me in the last few months is a typical southern gentleman. After treating me for almost a month, he dismissed me with the parting words, 'There is little that the physicians could do for you. You will have to carry your cross till nature will take its course.' Knowing, of course, that I am a Jew, he quickly apologized for using the phrase 'carry your cross,' whereupon I said to him, 'We Jews dance with the cross—carrying it for thousands of years would have exhausted us completely.' You see, I am an average Jew who does not lose his sense of humor in suffering. It is one of my favorite theories that Jewish humor kept the Jews alive, notwithstanding all their troubles and suffering.

"The purpose of this letter, however, is not to tell you a story, but to thank you for your kindness in having forwarded to me a copy of my essays which I needed as a gift for somebody who was exceedingly kind to me while I was in Boston."

The second to Dr. Grayzel is a year later: "Though a student of oral lore all my life and a teacher thereof for half a century, I nevertheless believe in the old Latin proverb *scripta manent.* I wish, therefore, to thank you again, and this time in writing, for your kindness in sending me a set of *The Legends,* which I presented to my physician.

"I know one might maintain that my book is a poor compensation for the time spent on me by the physician. In view, however, that he did not succeed in his efforts, and hence can only claim reward for good intentions, and as to good intentions, I put claim to them in writing *The Legends.*"

No man can assess another's suffering and surely a son cannot assess his father's. I believe it is correct to say that for the last five years of his life my father was in constant pain, and the pain prevented him from doing any constructive work. But I cannot repress the very strong impression that I had at that time and that I still have, that much of my father's pain during the last years of his life stemmed from his inability to continue working as he had ever since his early youth. And so the circuit was closed: pain—inability to work—pain.

But his life was not completely bleak. My father had much joy from my sister's growing family and from mine. He had my mother to care for him solicitously every minute of the day and night, during those last years as during all the years of their marriage. He had the company of many attractive young women and particularly the company of his daughter-in-law. And above all else, the Lord granted him his most cherished wish: he was in full control of his faculties until he suffered the cerebral hemorrhage from which he died.

CHAPTER XII

OLD FRIENDS AND NEW

I N LOUIS GINZBERG's study there was a very limited amount
of wall space between the end of the bookshelves
and his modest desk. But as a clue to the man, it is interesting to recall the pictures that occupied that limited space.
First, there was a very small snapshot of Professor Noeldeke
taken in his very advanced years. There was a somewhat
larger snapshot of George Foote Moore, taken while he was
on holiday in the New Hampshire mountains. There was a
formal portrait picture of Solomon Schechter. And there was
a photograph of the tombstone marking his father's grave in
Amsterdam. Relatively late in my father's life, his colleague
Israel Davidson presented him with a formal photograph
and my father found room to hang it.

The following anecdote, which was recalled by one of his
students, conveys another facet of his life.

I came to his study for a consultation on my doctoral thesis.
Sitting in the study was the late Professor Zvi Diesendruck, of
Hebrew Union College. I showed your father an interesting document which had come into my possession, an agreement drawn
by a Philadelphia rabbi for a sexton and a widow, in which for a
certain consideration of money paid to the sexton, he would recite
Kaddish for a year in memory of the deceased husband.

Your father glanced over the document quickly and then handed it to Professor Diesendruck. After perusing it for a few moments, the Professor commented: "Isn't it strange, in this document written in the rabbinic idiom of the sixteenth century, to find a phrase like this (regretfully, I do not recall the phrase!) which is found only in modern Hebrew." Whereupon your father smiled and said, "I think you are mistaken, Professor. If my memory serves me correctly, this phrase was current in the rabbinic contracts of the sixteenth century." When Professor Diesendruck expressed doubt, your father went to his bookshelves, and without a pause, picked out a slender volume, unerringly turned to a particular page, glanced at it for a moment and then said: "Here it is, look." And sure enough, in this little volume which was written in the sixteenth century, and which dealt with rabbinic contracts, the phrase was there.

Professor Diesendruck shook his head and then said, "Tell me, Professor Ginzberg, when did you last have occasion to look into this book?" And with that subtle, quizzical smile which we all loved so much, your father said, "about forty years ago."

Diesendruck was a great favorite of my father. They quickly established an excellent rapport, which was somewhat unusual since my father was already in his sixties when Diesendruck migrated to the United States. Whenever the opportunity offered itself, which meant whenever Diesendruck came East from Cincinnati, they spent some time together. When he died prematurely from Berger's disease, my father was terribly upset.

Jacob Klatzkin was another Jewish philosopher with whom my father had close ties of friendship. But friendship did not stop him from being critical about the way in which Klatzkin had failed to make productive use of his great talents—as the following comments show.

"Klatzkin had quite unusual ability. He wrote the best Hebrew of today. He was a first-rate essayist and was especially able in popularizing philosophy. He was uniquely qualified for this, since most modern writers do not have enough Jewish background to enable them to combine the necessary knowledge with the necessary ability. Modern writers have read the Bible—probably no more—but since the Bible is eighty percent lyrics and ten percent codified law, it is not exactly a model for modern writing.

"Klatzkin had had a very good talmudic training and he knew a great deal of post-biblical literature. In addition, he undoubtedly had a fine philosophical mind. If he had stuck to one thing or the other—merely writing good Hebrew or philosophy—he would have excelled. But in his early Berlin days, he was—to be very kind—a man who liked life in all its ramifications, day and night. He was a gourmand, and these proclivities undoubtedly killed him. He died at seventy of Berger's disease, which he had had for several years.

"Although intellectually Klatzkin outgrew his Rabbinic and Talmudic Judaism, he maintained a love for this kind of culture. His admiration for Jewish learning did not disappear; it was merely suppressed. Time and time again, his emotions gained control over him. He must have had a continuous fight between his emotions and his intellect. While not a poet, he was an artist in his writing, so his emotional capacity was not solely a burden.

"His relation to his old father was quite unusual. When he first came to Germany, he shaved. This had been unknown in Lithuania where, since the law precluded shaving, any man who did so openly announced his divorce from custom. From time to time when he planned to visit his father, he would start to grow a beard six weeks before he left.

"In 1929 he spent Passover in Palestine. Klatzkin's father was living there and he, Jacob, came to spend the holiday with him. I visited the old man the second day of the holiday, at which time he said to me, 'I really don't know where my Yonkeleh is. You don't think he is traveling on this day, do you?' I knew that Klatzkin had gone to Tiberias the day before, but I answered, 'I am sure that your Yonkeleh is as strict in observing the second day as he was the first.'"

In 1947, my wife and I spent two months at La Tour de Peiltz near Vevey on Lake Geneva. Klatzkin lived there. He had great warmth for Louis Ginzberg's son and daughter-in-law, and we saw much of him. There were few conversationalists who surpassed him.

Of the Jewish philosophers with whom he was intimate, Wolfson held an unique place in Louis Ginzberg's life. In writing to Mrs. Bertha Badt-Strauss, a German writer of distinction who lived in the United States for a time, my father commented on the difficulties that her son was experiencing in making contact with Wolfson:

"Philosophy might be stable, but philosophers are the most unstable persons I know. My friend, Doctor Wolfson, remained in Cambridge Yom Kippur, though he had promised me orally and in writing, to spend the holiday with us. I have, however, written to him, and I told him of your son's stay in Harvard, and I am sure that the written word will have as much weight with him as the oral one. Tell your son at the same time that he should not get frightened by certain external idiosyncrasies of my friend, Doctor Wolfson. He is really a very fine and good fellow, if you know him well."

A short paragraph in a letter to Mr. Rabinowitz, written a few months before his death, more accurately states the warmth of his feelings toward his Cambridge friend.

Rabbi Harold H. Gordon, the General Secretary of the New York Board of Rabbis, has informed me that "due to the generosity of a great benefactor of Jewish learning, Mr. Louis M. Rabinowitz, the library of the New York Board of Rabbis will be named the Louis Ginzberg and Harry A. Wolfson Library." May I therefore extend to you my sincerest thanks and deep appreciation for the honor bestowed upon me. It is certainly very gratifying for a layman to be connected with the activity of the clergy, and the only reason I can find for your choosing me among the laymen is the "merits of my fathers"—my belonging to a family many of whose members have distinguished themselves for their learning and saintliness over the past three centuries.

To have my name coupled with that of my friend, Harry A. Wolfson, is a special delight, as I admire him not only for his great learning but also for his truly humane spirit.

No one except relatives called my father by his first name. His friendship with his colleague, Alexander Marx, covered a period of half a century. Marx, being a full head taller than he, usually called my father "*der Kleine.*" And my father always called his colleague by his last name. The ties between them were close and became even closer in the 1930's when the Marx family had to carry the burden of the chronic illness of their only daughter. The following letter provides just one insight into this long and rich relationship.

I was very happy to learn that your fiftieth anniversary as Librarian at the Jewish Theological Seminary of America will be celebrated on June 7th, 1953.

I wish I were able to be present on that occasion, but you know how difficult it would be for me to attend a long session, and I hope that you will accept my written good wishes as if they were given orally.

The bonds of friendship that have tied us for half a century are such that it would be complimenting myself if I were to compliment you on the great achievement of building up the greatest Jewish Library. May I, however, say that the little I have achieved in that period I could not have accomplished if not for your kind assistance. May it be granted to you to continue your splendid work for many and many a year to come.

Friedlaender, the other member of the original trio, had died in 1920. There were warm and intimate relations between the Friedlaenders and the Ginzbergs, especially after the Friedlaenders moved back to Manhattan after their sojourn in Fort Lee. Louis Ginzberg admired and respected

Israel Friedlaender for his many qualities of mind and heart, but he deeply regretted that Friedlaender had become so enmeshed in communal affairs, which led only to frustration, and that he was not able to pursue the life of the creative scholar for which he was so well endowed.

The relationship with Davidson was cordial but not intimate, and this characterized his relationships with his other senior colleagues.

As I noted earlier, the Seminary faculty expanded substantially in the thirties and early forties, and my father soon developed a close relationship with his new colleagues, particularly Lieberman, Ginsberg and Spiegel. Few people acquire close friends late in life, especially friends who are much younger than they. And Louis Ginzberg did not invite intimacy.

I want to note at least briefly those other Jewish scholars with whom my father maintained a long and close relationship. Jacob Lauterbach of the Hebrew Union College was one of his very good friends, as was Henry Malter of Dropsie College. The Ginzberg and the Malter families used to vacation as neighbors on the Jersey coast. Malter was a highly nervous person with very strong opinions. He had a mortal fear of dogs, and one day while I was carrying cold cuts from our house to theirs for a shared supper, a big dog, attracted by the smell of the meat, followed me and I could not shake him. When he ran up Malter's porch after me, the professor beat a hasty retreat. Another incident arose because I used to let the door slam both in his house and in ours. Malter told my mother that I would doubtless end up in Sing Sing, and I suspect that he half believed it.

David Blondheim of John Hopkins and Isaac Husik of the University of Pennsylvania were frequent visitors in our home. Solomon Zeitlin of Dropsie College came often and became a close friend. My father early developed a great personal liking for Zeitlin and helped him get settled academically. And Zeitlin always treated my father with a deference that he showed no one else. They talked shop for hours on end, weekly or fortnightly, from the time Zeitlin first settled in the United States during World War I. My father was very indulgent about Zeitlin's theories and his altercations with other scholars, although I am sure that he was more than once astonished by them. As is so often the case, sympathy is the key to understanding which in turn is the key to acceptance.

Among the Europeans and Palestinians, there were his good friend Chajes of Vienna; Perles of Königsberg, who was visiting professor for one year at the Jewish Institute of Religion in New York, the man who said of Irma Lindheim who was a student of his in a course in homiletics—"Oh, I have seen her skeleton and it is beautiful!"; Ismar Elbogen of Berlin who in his late life had to flee to the United States to escape from Hitler; Gershom Scholem of the Hebrew University whom my father saw much of both during his visits to Jerusalem and during Scholem's visits to New York. These were the men whom I remember being in and out of our home. About their relationship with my father I have no doubt. There were undoubtedly a great many others to whom he felt close, even though he saw them infrequently and corresponded with them erratically.

In his later years, my father had two especially close relations, one with Ralph Marcus, who after long years of academic stagnation was finally rescued by Robert Hutchins and became for the rest of his short life a professor at the University of Chicago; and one with Judah Goldin, who had originally been a student of my father's and then had joined the faculty at the University of Iowa, to return later to the Seminary as the Dean of its Teachers College, and who is today Professor of Classical Judaica at Yale.

Marcus had originally been a student of Wolfson. After finishing his doctorate during the depression at Harvard, he came to New York where he tried to eke out a living while pursuing his scholarly research in the Judeo-Hellenistic field by dividing his time between Columbia University and the Jewish Institute of Religion. At one point, I tried to convince some of the powers at Columbia to offer Marcus a regular appointment so that he could more fully exploit his great talents, but to no avail. The Columbia budget at that time had no room for luxuries, and a Hellenistic scholar definitely fell into the category of a luxury.

Marcus served for many years as Secretary of the American Academy of Jewish Research while my father was president. This explains why he talked of and wrote to Professor Ginzberg as the "Boss." The following is taken from a congratulatory note that Marcus wrote the Boss on his seventieth birthday in November, 1943.

I must add a passage from Philo on the mystical value of the number 70:
De Migr. Abrahami 169
"Come up, O soul, to behold the Existent One, come with thy being in harmony, that is, with thy speech and reason active, come willingly, fearlessly, affectionately, come in the holy and perfect measures of seven multiplied tenfold." (Commentary on the seventy elders in Ex. 24. 1.)
I'm delighted to hear that you and the Frau Professor are coming to Chicago next month, not only because we'll be glad to see your cheerful faces and hear the latest gossip, but also because I want to pump you dry about the Pharisees and Sadducees and such matters. What's the good of knowing a walking encyclopedia if I don't waylay him and make him talk?
P.S. Don't you think that now that you're 70 years old, you can afford the luxury of calling me by my first name?

After many hints, Professor Ginzberg finally shifted his salutations. He used "Dear Ralph" only once, but he did unbend a little. The following letter shows the warmth of feeling and intimacy that he had for Marcus.

Dear Friend Marcus:

If I were to follow in the footsteps of my nephew Sol and my son Eli, I would find a psychoanalytic explanation for your letter of October 19th. *We* psychoanalysts speak of transference and that is what happened to you. You must have been dreaming a good deal of Ann Sothern and transferred your desires and wishes to me. However, not being a psychoanalyst like the rest of the Ginzbergs, I assume that you wished to write to me on the occasion of the New Year, and were it not for the fact that Hoshanah Rabah was a week ago Sunday, your letter would have reached me on the very day when the heavenly powers register and file our accounts for the coming year.

There is nothing particular to report about "the Boss." He is neither bossing nor being bossed, in other words, a plain human being. I have done some work during the summer in Maine, and continue to do so since my return to the city. I hope that by the end of this month I shall have the copy ready for the fourth volume of my Commentary.

The Bostonian Goulds spent a part of the last Festival with us. They are all well. The youngsters are growing up strong and healthy—a little too lively for their grandfather; but very likely the same remark was made by my grandfather concerning his grandson. Eli is working very hard, and as a matter of fact worked very hard while he stayed in Europe. In contrast to his father, he seems to have somewhat of a Messianic complex, trying to improve the world and especially the Jews. When he reaches his father's age, he will have learned that where the good Lord has failed, no human being can do better.

I can hardly believe that Dan is now of military age. I am, however, almost convinced that the trouble in Korea will soon be over and there is nothing to fear about the youngsters being sent to the battlefield. I assume that he still remembers me, and give him my best regards. I am, however, doubtful whether Philip has any recollection of me. I was very happy to know that he is making good progress in his study of the piano. I wish my grandchildren were in Chicago and would attend the Sinai Temple Nursery School under the direction of your wife.

It was not quite clear to me what you meant when you said

that you were finishing Philo. Does this refer to a new edition or to a translation of some of Philo's works?

The Frau Professor is busy as ever, and discounting a bruised knee, which she very likely caused by her over-zealous desire to empty the lake of its fish, enjoys good health.

With kindest regards to Mrs. Marcus, yourself, and the boys.

Professor Ginzberg thought very highly of Marcus' scholarly activities. He felt that Marcus was one of those rare fortunate-unfortunate human beings whose talents are so many and so diverse that they find it difficult to specialize, which is the *sine qua non* for a high level of accomplishment. Here are excerpts from one of Professor Ginzberg's last letters to his friend Marcus:

I greatly enjoyed your discussion of the Sebomenoi, and especially your reference to Xenophon, which supports the interpretation given by Jacob Bernays of the famous passage in Josephus. I never had any doubts as to its correctness, especially in view of the fact that the rabbis quite often use the Hebrew equivalent of Sebomenoi to describe gentiles, who without accepting Judaism fully, gave up idolatrous practices. Your reference to Xenophon, however, establishes the true meaning of the term used by Josephus.

Your essay on the Pharisees is excellent, and I only regret that it was not published also at least in a Jewish magazine. Ignorance of the Christian world is excusable, but how many of our so-called Jewish intellectuals know more about the Pharisees than that found about them in the New Testament? By the way, I do not agree with my late friend, Lauterbach, in all respects. He went even further than Geiger in overemphasizing the anti-priestly element in the Pharisaic movement. He even misunderstood the phrase "Chachme Israel," which he takes to mean 'the sages of Israel,' in opposition to "the sages of the priesthood." In my forthcoming fourth volume of the *Commentary on the Palestinian Talmud,* I have pointed out that the phrase always means "the leading scholars in Israel," in contrast to the average scholar, and has nothing to do with priestly or anti-priestly tendencies.

I do not belong to the Jewish "cave dwellers." All that I know is that a good deal of trash has been written on the scrolls found in the caves—so that I decided not to read anything bearing on this subject. Of course, now I will have to change my decision and go carefully over your remarks.

The ties between the two men were not ended even by my father's death in 1953. Among his unpublished works was the second part of *Eine Unbekannte Jüdische Sekte*. Plans were made for Marcus to translate the published volume while Professor Ginzberg's colleague at the Seminary, Dr. H. L. Ginsberg, would translate the unpublished segment, and for the whole then to become available to the English-speaking world. Marcus completed most of his assignment before he died in 1956. But it is only now, after many delays, that the book is nearing publication.

The relationship between Professor Ginzberg and the Goldin family, all four of them, is clearly revealed in the several letters that follow.

January 28, 1947

Dear Dr. Goldin:

Because of poor health I was unable to acknowledge your kind letter sooner, and the off-print of your article "Hillel the Elder." I don't want, however, to wait too long as I don't wish to have my long silence interpreted wrongly.

I read your article with great interest and found it very excellent both in form and content. My only objection is that you did not deal fairly with Hillel's brother, as there can be no doubt that the Talmud, far from censuring him, rather bestows praise upon him. By the way, I am not at all convinced that the talmudic tradition about Hillel's descent of Davidic ancestry is a pure invention of later generations. I, myself, can trace back my ancestry to 1460, and I don't see why a Babylonian, where the Jews were very particular to keep family records, should not have had well-authenticated tradition about his descent.

It is true in the Palestinian Talmud it is said that Hillel was on his maternal side of Davidic descent, while according to the

Babylonian Talmud, he was a descendant of David's son, Shaphatiah. But these two statements are really not at all contradictory. It is quite possible that what the Babylonian Talmud meant to say is that Shephatiah was his maternal ancestor.

Will you kindly tell Mrs. Goldin that I greatly enjoyed her letter. As soon as I feel a little stronger, I shall not fail to write to her and also to David for the stars he sent me. I am still waiting for Robin's letter.

Sophie and Bernie are here for a short visit. Their report about the twins is a glowing one. Michael is, of course, also here. It is a good thing that his grandfather had in his earlier years occupied himself with legends, otherwise he would be greatly embarrassed. Michael insists to be told every night before retiring a new story. Last night I reached Jonah and the whale, which according to his view is the most interesting of all the stories I have ever told him.

December 8, 1947

Dear Young and Younger Friends:

I know that you with your fine sense of the English language will find the form of my addressing you rather queer, yet that is the best I could do. Robin and David, my young friends, could not be overlooked, and on the other hand, how could I describe their parents as old?

To all of you my sincerest thanks for the beautiful tie you sent me for my birthday, and still more so, for your friendship which prompted the sending.

I am happy to inform you that I am gradually pulling out from my state of weakness in which I found myself for almost two months. Yesterday I gave the first lecture of this academic year at the Seminary, and as far as I can judge, it had no bad effect on me, and I hope the same may be said of its effect upon my listeners.

October 12, 1949

Dear Gracie:

It was very kind of you to instruct the editor of the *Commentary* to forward to me the October issue which contained your article. If not for your kind thought, I would surely have missed the pleasure I derived from reading your article "The Service of the Temple."

The editor requested me to comment upon your article which, of course, I cannot do well. A great Jewish sage once said, "Only he is my true friend who discovers my faults," and in view of the fact that I cannot find any fault with your article, people would say that I am not your friend. Consequently, there remains nothing for me but to remain silent.

How are Doctor Goldin and the children? I hope that they will in the course of the winter find some time to visit New York. It might sound paradoxical, but it is nevertheless true in my case that the older I get, the more need I have for the company of young people, and I wish the Goldins were a little closer to New York than they are right now.

Maine was delightful this summer. Dry, sunny, and cool, but that was far from ideal. I suffered and still suffer excruciating pain from a neuralgia that developed as an aftermath of my shingles. The physicians assure me that it will disappear, and as one who was brought up on the traditional Prayer Book, I say, "and though he tarry, I still wait daily for his coming," patiently waiting for the time when, according to medical opinion, my pain will disappear.

January 8, 1952

Dear Iowan Friends,

There is no need for "conclusive evidence," nor for any evidence at all to prove that my Iowan friends have not forgotten their old Knickerbocker friend. At the same time, I greatly appreciate your kindness in sending me Nabokov's *Conclusive Evidence*. Mrs. Ginzberg often complains of a husband who has a library of about ten thousand volumes and not a book to read in it. Now she will have to modify her complaint—women never entirely change—but in a way that would make it quite difficult for her. She could not well say "My husband has ten thousand books and only one to read"—that would sound more like nagging than complaining.

Speaking of complaining, I cannot help complaining against my friends Robin and David, who very likely were too busy with Hanukkah celebrations to drop me a line. Tell them that I am a strong believer in the truth of the saying "Better late than never."

I read, dear Doctor Goldin, with great pleasure, the copy of the letter which you sent to the "Superman" of Yale University. Of course, I don't wish to say that I enjoyed the troubles you had with him; I only meant that I greatly admired the way in which you indicated to him between the lines, "You know, you are not a gentleman but I am not going to say it."

Professor Wolfson of Harvard, who visited me yesterday, remarked to me, "You and I ought to be happy that we both are no longer members of the editorial board of the Yale publications, otherwise we might have been accused of participating in the machinations of the editor-in-chief." Of course, I did not show him your letter, but I did mention the fact that you, as well as Professor Gandz, had had your very unpleasant experiences with the gentleman from Connecticut.

January 29, 1952

My dear Goldins,

Very likely my letter will no longer reach the head of the Goldin quartet—pardon an old man for the use of an archaic phrase; I know that in American society the leader is double-headed (husband and wife)—he will be either in New York or on his way to it.

I shall, however, not fail to tell you in a few lines how happy I was to hear the good news of your coming to New York. If I were to consult a psychoanalyst, he surely would tell me that it is pure selfishness on my part to rejoice in your coming to New York. In view of the expected rise in taxes, a poor professor cannot afford to consult a psychoanalyst. I understand that it is a fixed rule with these modern pupils of Hippocrates not to treat a patient without being well paid. Of course, I could consult my nephew Sol, but he knows his uncle too well to analyze him. There is nothing left for me but to analyze myself and the result of that analysis is that while there is a great deal of selfishness in wishing to have you in New York, I think that a part of my happiness is because of you, or to be more accurate, because of Robin and David. I am thoroughly convinced that bringing up young children in a small Jewish community is a hard task and rarely successful. All my good wishes to all of you on your removal to New York.

Over the years, Professor Ginzberg maintained close relations with a group of scholars interested in Bible, Talmud, and Rabbinics, although the two closest of his Christian friends lived outside of New York—George Foote Moore of Harvard and Charles Torrey of Yale. The bonds between Ginzberg and Moore were of long standing: the third volume of Moore's classic *Judaism* has a great many notes that carry in brackets the initials L. G. It was Moore who took the initiative to have my father invited to open the Summer Session at the Harvard Divinity School in 1920. At that time, he delivered an address on "The Religion of the Jews at the Time of Jesus," which was later reprinted in his volume of essays, *Students, Scholars and Saints*. And it is a reasonable guess that the invitation to participate in the Harvard Tercentenary was in part a result of the awareness of the Cambridge community of the very considerable help that my father had extended to Moore over many years.

But on one point Ginzberg was non-responsive. Moore on several occasions encouraged him to write a book on St. Paul, the effective founder of Christianity. But Ginzberg, who considered St. Paul a master organizer, did not find him congenial, and he believed that no man was entitled to undertake an analysis of a religion or a religious leader without great sympathy.

Apparently, the Harvard circle hoped that if my father would not write about St. Paul, he might at least be enticed to deal with a key institution of the new religion, baptism, from the vantage point of its Jewish origins. The following letter from Moore's successor, Professor Arthur Nock, is to the point as is the "Reverend Professor." Harvard takes its degrees, even its honorary degrees, seriously!

November 16, 1936

The Reverend Professor Louis Ginzberg
3080 Broadway
New York, New York

Dear Professor Ginzberg:

Thank you very much indeed for the most useful offprint which I have found extremely instructive. I write in haste, but may I remind you that we are hoping for an article from you on Jewish Baptism for the *Harvard Theological Review?* It would have greatly pleased George Foote Moore to have it appear in the journal which he remade.

The ties between Ginzberg and Moore and Torrey go back to the first years of Ginzberg's relocation to the United States, but his files contained only letters to Torrey from the 1940's. It is hard to say what happened to the others. One reasonable assumption is that up to that point Ginzberg wrote by hand. Here is a brief letter dated October 1942:

Many thanks for your kindness in letting me have your very interesting review of Brooke's *The Old Testament in Greek.*

As a true sage who, according to the rabbis, is more than a Prophet, you underline with red pencil just that part of your review which interests me most. I fully agree with you that some of the Greek "additions" to Esther go back to an Aramaic original. By the way, did it ever strike you that the Targum of Esther is more paraphrastic than the Targum of any other biblical book? Of course, our Targum of Esther is comparatively of late origin, but there can be no doubt that the popular Book of Esther must have had an Aramaic paraphrase at a very early date.

I have extracted key paragraphs from a letter written two years later.

I must confess that some points in your letter of January 1 are not quite clear to me. At the very beginning, you remark that after the calamity of the year 70, the Jews turned away from secular literature. Such books as Jubilees, and the Apocalypses of Ezra and Baruch were no longer written. But, does not, for instance, the Book of Jubilees, a Midrash on Genesis, in parts have any literary correspondence to the Haggadah in Midrashim? Do you call the Midrashic literature a secular one? And, if so, how could one maintain that the Jews turned away for the time being from secular literature if that period saw the Midrashim flourish? And further, if the Apocalypses of Ezra and Baruch belong to secular literature, then they are the very best proof that the Jews did not turn away from these works and similar ones, as, for instance, the Ascension of Moses, pseudo-Philo, which are products of the Yabneh period.

As to the main problems, I am fairly convinced that there was no "resolute policy," or any other policy to suppress secular literature. As a matter of fact, the only truly secular product of literature, a treatise on Mathematics, was composed about the middle of the second century.

If there were any resolute policy to write nothing, it applied just to matters dealing directly with scriptures or law. The tradition that Halakhud must not be written down is undoubtedly a very old one. The references found in talmudic-midrashic literature concerning Books, are to such of a Haggadic nature which covers also what you might call secular literature.

As the opening of my letter begins with a confession, so shall its ending. This confession refers to a wrong interpretation of a passage in your kind congratulatory letter you sent me on the occasion of my seventieth birthday. The reference to yourself as an octogenarian I understood to mean that you are now entering your eightieth year. I have, however, found out that you have passed your eightieth year. Conforming to the rule, "Better late than never," I wish to extend to you my heartiest congratulations and sincerest wishes for a very, very long life of good health and spiritual vigor. . . .

The letter records that the respect and admiration which each had for the other's work did not inhibit them from dealing forthrightly with issues on which they disagreed. This is also indicated by the following excerpt:

I am just preparing a lengthy article on the importance of the Genizah for the study of the talmudic-geonic literature. This brought me back again to the Hebrew Fragments of Ben Sira, and I must confess that I am as puzzled by them as ever.

Though I am fairly convinced that the numerous quotations in the talmudic-midrashic literature are taken from a book and not based on old tradition, I am rather reluctant to assume that the text used was that represented by our Fragments. On the other hand, I don't find in these Fragments any sure proof of their being a translation from the Aramaic. As a matter of fact, I very much doubt whether in talmudic times there did exist a Judeo-Aramaic translation of this apocryphal book. I have, of course, read what you have to say in your admirable introduction to "The Apocryphal Literature," but I cannot accept your conclusions. There are Hebrew phrases and expressions in the Fragments which, to my knowledge, do not occur in the later rabbinic writings. On the other hand, there is a good deal of rabbinic Hebrew in them, and all that I can say is, I am still greatly puzzled as to the origin of these Fragments.

The correspondence also revealed a modesty about what was known and an acknowledgment that much remained obscure. One could speculate about the unknown, but there was no certainty about many matters.

I do not know any Jewish source, old or new, which designates the Second Book of Samuel as the Book of David. Of course, you know the rabbinic tradition Baba Batra, pages 14b bottom to 15a, according to which the Prophets Gad and Nathan completed the Book of Samuel. If I understand the passage correctly, it means to say that these two Prophets are the authors of I Samuel, 28.3 up to the end of II Samuel. One may well assume that the basis for this rabbinic statement is I Chronicles, 29.29. Is there any likelihood that in the Greek text which you discuss, the name of the Prophet Gad is corrupted to Dad?

And now a word about my state of health to explain the brevity of my letter. My doctors are quite satisfied with my general condition. They seem to be quite modest people, but I am far from being a humble man and grumble a good deal about my painful neuritis, which did not stop for a second in the past three and one-half years.

The letter of March, 1952 which follows brings me to an end of the Ginzberg-Torrey correspondence. By way of background, I should report that while still a graduate student, I had written a brief essay on "The Decline of Antiquity" to the consternation of my teacher, Professor William L. Westermann. It was later published. Somehow it had come to Professor Torrey's attention and he wrote me a postcard saying that I had "hit the nail on the head"—a generous compliment!

It was a great pleasure to hear from you and to know that you are basking in the warm sun instead of freezing in the cold, as we do in the North. Mrs. Ginzberg tried for some time to persuade me to go south for the winter. My physician did not permit me to fly southwest, and, on the other hand, I did not care to go southeast, with the result that I remained where I was. On the whole, we had an extremely mild winter in New York, but, of course, only relatively speaking, as for many days I am unable to leave the house because of the weather.

There is a talmudic saying which reads: "One may become envious of anybody except his son or his pupil." I was, therefore, very glad to know that the library in San Diego possesses some of Eli's writings and none of mine. Of course, if I were a materialist historian, I could explain the policy of the library in a way not unfavorable to me. It is not the merit of Eli's writing but that of his publishers who know how to sell him, while my publishers are poor business people.

In rabbinic sources, there is frequently found a play on the word *koresh* and the word *kasher*. Do you think it possible that in Isaiah, 45.1 *"koresh"* is misread for *"kasher"*?

Mrs. Ginzberg and Eli join me in all good wishes to you.

Even in his old age, Torrey retained a brilliance that made him very dear to my father, who never lost his admiration for the aristocrats of scholarship.

Despite the fact that the Seminary was only a stone's throw from both the Union Theological Seminary and Columbia University, my father knew few of the faculty of either. He knew and greatly admired the famous Sanskrit scholar, A. V. W. Jackson, who for many years was one of

Columbia's great luminaries. And he was acquainted with many in the Semitics and auxiliary departments. But except for Salo Baron, whom he had known before he joined the Columbia faculty; and Meyer Schapiro, who used to visit and talk with him about medieval legends; and an occasional lunch with Professor Westermann, whom I think I first brought to my parents' home, the contacts were sporadic. Now and then, Professor Ginzberg was asked to participate in a doctoral examination, but for the most part Columbia could have been not five blocks but five thousand miles away. There was one major exception: Professor Isaac Kandel, who for many years was Professor of Comparative Education at Teachers College, was a good friend, and there was much visiting between the Ginzberg and Kandel families.

Although there were no close ties between Professor Ginzberg and the two neighboring institutions, Columbia and Union Theological, he maintained a connection with General Theological Seminary in lower Manhattan and other institutions. Dr. Frank Gavin was a frequent visitor. A great number of scholars from institutions, academic and theological, from Catholic University in Washington to the Seventh Day Adventists in Los Angeles, kept in contact with my father in person and in writing over a good many years because of shared interests. In every instance that I know of, they came seeking help—which my father offered without regard to his time or work. He had a simple view: if he were a rich man, it would be incumbent upon him to share his material goods with those in need. Since he was a scholar, it was incumbent upon him to help any other scholar who sought his aid.

One of the most unusual, and at the same time productive friendships, was that between Louis Ginzberg and Stephen S. Wise. On the surface it might be hard to understand what bound these two men together since they held diametrically opposite views about the role of law and tradition in contemporary Jewish life. But both were big men with big hearts and minds, and the values that they held in common far exceeded those about which they differed. There are twenty-eight letters from Wise to Ginzberg in the latter's files. In the 1920's my father attempted to elicit Wise's assistance in collecting funds for Dr. Lewin to prepare a critical edition of the Responsa from the Geonic period. From then until the last months of Wise's life, the two were in contact and ever more intimate contact.

In 1932, Wise in his capacity as President of the Jewish Institute of Religion informs Professor Ginzberg that the faculty and Board have voted to confer an honorary degree on him. Here are the key paragraphs of Professor Ginzberg's reply:

You were gracious to add to your official communication a few words of a personal touch. May I comment on them? I never considered humility a virtue—it is a demand of common sense. The part one contributes to his own making, bodily or spiritually, is infinitesimal. The greater part of what we are is due to heredity and to the atmosphere of the time and place into which we are born. If I have rendered any service to Jewish learning, there is no reason whatsoever for me to be proud. A descendant of a long line of Jewish intellectuals, brought up in Lithuanian *Yeshivot* and educated at German universities, could not help contributing something to Jewish learning. There is however something of which I am proud, and this is my relations with Jewish scholars. I may well say that there is no institution of higher Jewish learning with the members of whose faculty I am not bound by the ties of close friendship. I have good reason to suspect that you and your colleagues on the Faculty, in recommending me to such an honor, were prompted rather by the feeling of friendship towards me than by a cool judgment of my merits. But what a pleasure to see the counsel of a friend biased by friendship.

The next day Wise wrote to their mutual friend, George Kohut, as follows:

Did you ever see a more charming and delightful note than this of Professor Ginzberg? What right has a man, in addition to being unique in Jewish learning, to be able to write a letter such as this? It simply means that a man who is as great in scholarship, is great in a particular field because he is great in himself. A man who is not great in himself cannot be great in any aspect of life. What a privilege it will be to confer the degree upon him! You and I will arrange that it be done in the finest possible way.

Several years later, Ginzberg is seeking Wise's assistance in drafting the proposal for the support of unemployed Jewish scholars and students. Wise replies that "I shall be delighted to discuss with you any matter which you consider of importance."

Shortly thereafter, Wise begins to send Professor Ginzberg cigars on various occasions which in turn lead to many thank you notes. A characteristic one follows:

Dear Friend:

Your birthday presents always put me into a state of ambivalence. I greatly enjoyed the cigars you sent me and more so, the friendship that prompted their sending. I feel rather depressed because of my inability to reciprocate.

Don't you think you are now at a spiritual age—I mean the age when the physicians advise us to take some spirits? For more than a quarter of a century, I did not touch any spirits, until recently I was converted by my physician to Hasidism, which preaches the encouragement of the spirit by spirits. I wonder whether the Gaon of Vilna, the pride of our family, would have changed his policy towards Hasidism if he had not been a teetotaler.

On the occasion of his seventieth birthday, the Seminary faculty tendered Dr. Wise a luncheon. Louis Ginzberg spoke on that occasion and what he said led Wise to write, "Nothing in all my birthday celebrations gave me more joy than your words at the Seminary luncheon. It moved my heart and I was proud and happy to have you speak as you did."

There follows Louis Ginzberg's "Tribute by Anecdote" which was printed in *Opinion:*

The following anecdote used to be very popular in the *Yeshivot* of my native country Lithuania, where I studied more than one-half a century ago.

A great rabbi who had received a call from a prominent congregation was greatly embarrassed as to what to do about his inaugural sermon. He was truly a great rabbi by the standards of greatness then and there prevailing which were scholarship, juridical wisdom, and saintliness—oratory was not his métier. He therefore appealed to a famous preacher for guidance, from whom he received these three rules for an effective sermon: brevity, originality, and timeliness. By timeliness, the preacher explained, he meant the construction of the sermon around the text taken from the Sidra: the biblical lesson of the week. For, it would not be well, for instance, to speak about the destruction of Sodom and Gomorrah on the Sabbath on which the biblical story of Adam and Eve dwelling in Paradise was read.

When the eventful day arrived and a large congregation had assembled to listen for the first time to the great rabbi, he ascended the pulpit for a few seconds and delivered his sermon consisting of seven words. "Friends, I have forgotten this week's Sidra." To his astonished friends, he explained that he tried his best to preach in accordance with the rules laid down for him by the expert. He was brief, original—what rabbi does not know the week's Sidra?—and used the Sidra for his text.

I am telling this story firstly for the benefit of Dr. Wise—if I have told it to him before, he will be good enough not to remember it—who has an exquisite sense of humor and greatly appreciates the Jewish brand thereof.

Secondly, I was reminded of the story by the situation in which I find myself at present, which is not unlike that of the great rabbi though I am not a rabbi, either great or small. Dr. Wise, a great leader of American Israel, a valiant warrior for democracy and a famous orator, should, and I hope will, be appraised by his compeers and not by one who is spending his life within the four walls of his study. Like the rabbi in the story told, I can only say "Friends, I do not know what aspect of the dynamic personality of Dr. Wise I am to write about." Ties of close friendship, lasting now for over four decades, bind us together, and I could, of course, speak of my friend, Wise. But it is impossible for me to draw out my innermost feeling of friendship for my own inspection, still less for the inspection of others. For under inspection, the stamp of inwardness is apt to tarnish. I hope and pray it may be granted to him and to me to enjoy our friendship for many, many years to come.

But on one occasion, some years earlier when the Free Synagogue was celebrating its Thirtieth Anniversary, Louis Ginzberg found himself on the spot. His reply to the Chairman's invitation to serve on the Committee follows:

It is, of course, a genuine pleasure to me to be able to give public expression to my great admiration for Doctor Wise, with whom I am bound by strong ties of friendship extending almost four decades. May I, however, ask you to consider whether my participation in this celebration might not cause great astonishment and even strong objection among some members of the Free Synagogue. They may ask the pertinent question, "What has a fervent adherent of Conservative Judaism to do with the celebration arranged by the Institute, standing for an entirely different concept of Judaism?"

Stephen Wise was born on St. Patrick's Day, and that provided Louis Ginzberg with some scope in sending him birthday greetings—

According to the almost unanimous opinion of the Jews—of course, complete unanimity does not exist—Moses was born in Adar, exactly three weeks and a few thousand years before you. There is, however, quite a divergency in the celebration of this memorable day in a leap year. Some observe it in the first Adar, while others in the second.

I am now confronted by a similar problem as to the date of your birth. Am I now a week too late or three weeks ahead of time? At all events, as a man of the "middle way" I have decided to write to you today and extend to you, on behalf of Mrs. Ginzberg and myself, our heartiest congratulations on your birthday. Many happy returns of the day in bodily vigor and spiritual strength.

There were sad occasions too, and the friends then wrote notes of consolation to each other. The passing of Rabbi Louis M. Epstein prompted Wise to write and evoked an equally warm response:

Dear Good Friend:

Wretched as I am, I have been thinking a great deal of you in these days. Of course I know how great must be your sorrow over the passing of that rarely fine man and scholar and very good friend and disciple, Louis Epstein, for whom, I, too, had deep respect and affection. I wish I were well enough to come and take you by the hand and convey to you my sense of deepest sympathy upon his passing; but I am far from well. Still I hope I may soon see you.

Dear Friend Wise:

I deeply appreciate your kindness that prompted your letter of condolence on the occasion of the departure for a better world of my dear friend, Doctor Epstein.

He was to Mrs. Ginzberg and myself like a devoted son and to my children like a loving brother. The loss we all suffered is irreparable, but there is some consolation in thinking of the saying of the Rabbis, "Shared sorrow is half consolation." Dr. Epstein was such an unusual type of a man that I know for sure that he must have left scores of friends who share with us our great loss.

Friendship is its own gratification and provides its own reward, but the long friendship between Louis Ginzberg and Stephen S. Wise was doubly blessed. Wise repeatedly sought Louis Ginzberg's advice and counsel about appointments to the faculty of the Institute. And Professor Ginzberg felt free to recommend scholars to Wise for his consideration. It was rumored at the time that Ginzberg was exercising a very great influence on the Institute. There is no question but that the rumor was correct.

In mentioning dear friends of my father, special note must be taken of his close relationship with Harry G. Friedman, a relationship that began when Friedman came to New York in the early 1900's to enter upon a business career, although he had recently graduated from the Hebrew Union College. Although he turned his back on a rabbinical career, Friedman soon found himself in the Seminary circle, intimate with Schechter, Marx, Davidson and Ginzberg. He married, relatively late, Adele Oppenheimer, who came from a leading German-Jewish family but one that no longer had close ties to tradition. They had one son, Francis Lee, who became a leading physicist, a member of the faculty at M.I.T., and the key person in the revision of the physics curriculum for high schools, and who died prematurely in the prime of life, deeply mourned by all who knew him.

Harry George Friedman had a highly successful career as an investment banker but his heart lay elsewhere. He collected Jewish ceremonial objects for a great many years and his gifts to the Jewish Museum in New York City represent one of the cornerstones of the institution. There was much to decipher and explain on the *objets religieux* that Friedman collected, and he and my father spent many happy hours together in determining the history and use of the various items. Friedman was an anti-Zionist, but he took care never to let his deeply held views, largely founded on his conviction that Palestine was unsuitable both politically and economically as a haven for Jews, to mar his relationship with Professor Ginzberg.

The Friedmans were always at the Ginzbergs on the first night of *seder;* the Ginzberg family spent many a happy Sunday at the Friedman's country home in Westchester, and from the time my father first began to put aside some savings, Friedman took the responsibility for investing them. Their friendship was important to me too, since Friedman had a pronounced influence on my maturing economic views. His great experience and equally great skepticism were wonderful antidotes to an excessively academic approach.

Less long-standing but still intimate was Louis Ginzberg's relationship with Dr. I. S. Wechsler, the distinguished neurologist, who had an intense Zionist orientation and who devoted many years of his life to broadening and deepening support for the Hebrew University in Jerusalem. While not religious, Wechsler was very Jewish in all of his feelings and attitudes, and on a great many points the friends saw matters in much the same light. This friendship, too, was important to me, and I did my best to help Wechsler, in the early post-World War II period, build up a strong American Friends of the Hebrew University. It never became as powerful or as affluent an organization as Wechsler dreamed and hoped it would become, but it was made much stronger by his selfless efforts.

There were always a large number of physicians in and out of the Ginzberg household, not because our family was frequently sick, but because my father's favorite nephew, Dr. Sol W. Ginsburg, had introduced a large number of his friends to his aunt and uncle, especially in the years before he himself married. In addition, the Seminary synagogue, whose services were under my father's general supervision from the time of Dr. Schechter's death in 1915, presented my family with two members of the medical profession who became close friends—Dr. Abram Abeloff and Dr. Irwin Sobel. The Abeloff family were long-time parishioners of the Seminary; when Dr. Abeloff married relatively late in life, my father stood up with him as the oldest adopted member of the family. Mrs. Sobel, senior, had been a leading Hadassah speaker and I had been very friendly with her son, Irwin, and his first wife, Rita, while we were all at Heidelberg.

Since my sister lived in Boston, my parents spent considerable time in the Bay State, especially after World War II, when Sophie had three young boys to take care of. Some of my sister's friends became good friends of my parents. The following letter was written after a visit to Boston.

Dear Dr. Sidel:

Home again, I naturally think back on the pleasant days spent in Brookline and, of course, that reminds me of you and yours.

I do not need to tell you how deeply I appreciate the many tokens of friendship you and Mrs. Sidel showed to Mrs. Ginzberg and me during our stay with Sophie. Above all, I want to thank you for the great pleasure you gave me in bringing your children to see me—whom I consider as if they were my own grandchildren. May they grow up to be the delight of their parents and the joy of their friends.

Of my famous ancestor, the Gaon of Vilna, it is told that he gave up the study of medicine because he thought that it would interfere with his Jewish studies, in view of the fact that as a practicing physician it would be his duty to attend anyone who was in need of his aid. It is only from such a humanitarian viewpoint that, busy as you are, you came to see me on the morning of the day we left, and I may assure you that I greatly appreciate not only your medical advice but no less so, your friendship.

Of quite a different order and yet of great meaning to him was my father's relationship to Sir Philip Hartog after their meeting and working together in Palestine in the winter of 1933. The correspondence between them after they returned to their respective homes was frequent and intimate. Since Sir Philip wrote by hand, my father probably considered it only proper for him to do likewise, so that there are no carbons of letters from Louis Ginzberg to Sir Philip. There are, however, copies of letters written to Lady Hartog after Sir Philip's death in 1947. From one of these one can catch a glimpse of Louis Ginzberg's deep affection for the friend of his late years:

On my return to New York after an absence of three months, I found your book *Philip Hartog*, as well as your letter of September 4th, and I hasten to acknowledge both these two welcome New Year's gifts.

I do not think that you expect me to comment upon your book.

Sir Philip's contributions to the development of education in England and its colonies are too well-known to anybody who is interested in modern education. Great, however, as his contributions were, still greater was the man. I saw in him the embodiment of the sage and of the good man. In my long lifetime I was fortunate to meet many a great man, yet Sir Philip always remained to me the rare combination of a great soul and a keen intellect. You inscribed the book "To Philip Hartog's Friends," which really means to all who know Philip Hartog—to know him means to love and revere him.

Hartog's letters to my father deal with important matters affecting the Hebrew University, refugee scholars, and later, issues of war and peace, but they also have a lighter side. In one of them, he outlined for my father's pleasure an argument in which I was involved in his home with two wealthy Indian girls who were advocating an early revolution to solve the sub-continent's problems. According to Sir Philip's report, I had no faith in the therapeutic value of revolution, at least not for India. Over the years, my father introduced friends of his and mine to Sir Philip, knowing that Sir Philip would be happy to help them if he could. Since I had the good fortune to meet and spend some time with the Hartogs, I can appreciate the depth of my father's feeling for them. They were rare people.

For a quarter of a century, with the lapse of only an occasional year, my parents spent the summer in Maine. They made many acquaintances during these sojourns on the Belgrade Lakes, but it was a warm friendship that my father and I both developed with the Fassett family, with Frederick and Julie and eventually with their daughter, Ellen. Fred was just shifting from a career in journalism to M.I.T., where he has been Professor of English, editor of the *Technology Review* and now Dean of Students.

In the introduction to his *A Commentary on the Palestinian Talmud,* my father acknowledged the help that Fred

Fassett gave him in strengthening the English introduction. Fred's letter acknowledging a copy of the Introduction follows:

My dear friend,

Your gift reached me a day or so ago. And, as I read the introductory section of the first volume, it was for all the world as though we were sitting in the shade in Maine and you were talking—so characteristic of you in the very shading, intonation, rhythm, is that section. Truly, that pleasure of vicarious meeting was a keen one.

I do not need, I know, to tell you how proud you make me by this present. Your own respect for scholarship, and estimate of scholarship, are such that you understand what this gift of his work by a scholar means to a younger man. This source of my gratefulness to you is a more austere, a more remote one, yet a very strong one. It is to be exceeded only by the personal feeling which I have for you.

Something of the quality of this very special friendship is suggested by my father's letter of January, 1949:

Dear Friend:

It is always a great pleasure to receive from you a communication in prose, a still greater pleasure to receive one in poetry. The greatest pleasure, however, is to have a prose and a poetical one. Many and sincere thanks for your kindness.

I wonder whether you know how deep my ignorance of geology is—surely deeper than the Snow Pond. At the same time, I flatter myself that I have some understanding of poetry and I have to admit that I greatly enjoyed your poem, not only for the pleasant memories it brought back, but, also, for its intrinsic qualities. As a proud father, I was particularly pleased to find in your poem a reference to Eli. On reaching old age, one lives his life in the lives of his children, and any praise bestowed upon them is taken by the fond parent to be paid to him, though in truth he could claim, at most, fifty percent for himself.

As to cingulum, it seems that the words of Scriptures (Jeremiah 13.11) are fulfilled on me and the cingulum-"girdle cleaveth on my loins" as ever before. The pain is continuous and of a nagging nature with the result that I am hardly able to do any work which requires concentration.

Mrs. Ginzberg, who is at present in Boston on a visit to her children and grandchildren, maintains that I am old enough to stop working, without, however, suggesting anything that I might take up instead of work. I am too old to learn dancing or visiting night-clubs so that my desire for work is really nothing else than what the psychoanalysts—I think, of course, of my son primarily —would describe as escape from oneself.

And how are the ladies? Especially, how is my particular friend, Miss Fassett? I wonder whether I would recognize her after the many years I have not seen her. Do you not think it would be a good idea to send her on a visit to New York for some time so that we may renew our old acquaintance, which goes back to the time she was an infant in her mother's arms.

As a philologian, I cannot help but add one paragraph of a philological nature. Did it occur to you that the German or, rather to be accurate, the South German "Schatzi" can be used as the diminutive, as well as a caritative? Am I a precious treasure or a small treasure?

With all good wishes to you, Mrs. Fassett, and Ellen.

Each liked to play with words:

Amicissimus:

The first language I was taught was Hebrew and as you well know, the Semitic languages do not permit any septem-pedalian forms of a noun. The best I could do to match your caritativissimus is a quintopedalian. I assure you, however, that this shorter form wishes to express the same feeling for which you used a longer form.

My father would have allowed himself to engage in the kind of badinage which he enjoys in the following only with someone to whom he felt close:

My dear friend:

Being a poor man, I can only afford part-payment. Let me, therefore, first thank you for your kind letter of January 16th. I was delighted to know that Father Knickerbocker's town exerts a powerful attraction upon you. Being partially brought up in Holland, and having spent half a century in New York, you will understand my partiality for this old Dutch settlement. I sincerely hope that some time you will be able to break loose from the stuffy air of Washington to breathe the fresh air of New York.

I started to read your manuscript but because of a severe case of neuralgia, I was unable to cover much ground. I hope, however, that I shall be able to do it in the near future, and then pass it on to Eli, provided I can get hold of him. He and Ruth returned last Wednesday from London where he tried to put the British Empire in good shape. I have my doubts, however, that he succeeded. Churchill's Manifesto and the rejoinder to it by the Labor Party rather show, in the opinion of the leading English statesmen, that there is still room for improvement. Do not, however, accuse Eli of not being efficient. You must not forget that he has also to run the United States.

A day after his arrival, he had to rush down to Washington and yesterday he went to Boston where, I understand, he is to address a big gathering today. He certainly has the energy of his mother, who for the last forty years has been trying to make up for the inertia of her husband.

How is my young friend Ellen? How is her work at college going? I wish she would find time to drop me a line and tell me something about her activities and scholastic work.

As with all people, so with Louis Ginzberg, time played a big role in the making and cementing of friendships. But there was more to a friendship than time. My father knew Sholem Asch for many years and he acknowledged a specially inscribed copy of his new book:

Dear Mr. Asch:

Accept my sincerest thanks for forwarding to me your work *Moses*. I appreciate not only the splendid gift with which you presented me, but still more the inscription. Being an introvert by nature, I am ordinarily not quickly moved either by praise or by blame. I am, however, human enough to know that to be admired by a great master is a source of deep satisfaction and pleasure.

In accordance with the polite rule "Ladies First," Mrs. Ginzberg was first to read your book, but she told me this morning that she had almost completed her reading. I anticipate great pleasure and instruction, which I surely shall derive from your work.

He wrote to General Bliss under whom I had served during the second part of the War, and whom my parents had met at my wedding.

Dear General Bliss:

The French have a favorite saying, "The friends of our friends are our friends." I would like to modify it to make it read, "The friends of our children are our friends."

For several years you have shown such friendship to my son, Eli, and I consider you as a friend of the old Ginzbergs too. I hasten, therefore, to extend to you, in behalf of Mrs. Ginzberg and myself, the friendliest wishes and sincere congratulations on the occasion of your appointment as Surgeon General of the United States Army.

This great honor conferred upon you does not come as a surprise to anybody who knows of the splendid services you have rendered to the Army and the nation during your connections with the Surgeon General's office. One, however, is happy to see the man honored to whom honor belongs.

Scholars and administrators, novelists and generals—all had to make room finally for the ladies to whom my father was specially inclined.

There were a series of young ladies of whom Ellen Fassett was one, with whom my father had particularly deep bonds of affection. The earliest of these special ties that I recall was with the youngest of the Friedlaender girls, Joy.

Dearest Joy,

I do hope that you young people will sometimes make up your minds to see what a nice place New York is.

There is very little to report from here. Mrs. Ginzberg, thank God, is well and active as ever. Eli is now the father of a young lady aged six months, who bears the royal name, Abigail. Of course, you know that the lady Abigail in the Bible was not only a queen, but according to Jewish legend, also a prophetess. Democracy spreading more and more in our days, there is little hope that her namesake, my granddaughter, will ever be a queen, and of course, there are no longer prophets or prophetesses.

Affectionately, your old Schatzi

With one young lady, Lassie West, who lived in a neighboring apartment in the early 1930's, my father developed the closest of ties. She was a girl of extraordinary beauty. She apparently found it particularly enjoyable to have an old gentleman so clearly pleased to spend time telling her stories and listening to hers in return.

The christening of Lassie's firstborn was to take place one Saturday afternoon at the Riverside Church. Whatever scruples my father may have had about participating in a church ceremonial on the Sabbath, he apparently was able to put them aside; accompanied by his daughter-in-law, he acceded to Lassie's warm promptings to be present.

He continued a correspondence with this youngest friend as she moved with her physician husband from one city to another and became the mother of a constantly expanding family.

Dear Lassie:

It has been said "Ask, and it shall be given you," but now I see that it has to be amended to read "Ask, and it shall be given to you more than what you asked for." I asked for a letter and you sent me the lovely picture of Pamela. Mrs. Ginzberg and I, and as a matter of fact, everybody who saw the picture, were charmed with it.

My compliments to the photographer. Of course, there is no need to tell you that you have a beautiful child. How could she be otherwise, looking so much like her mother, in addition to some features of her father. How would it be, if you would let us have yours and your husband's photographs, so that we would be able to settle the dispute between Mrs. Ginzberg and myself. She maintains that Pamela looks more like her father, while to me she looks more like you.

Again many thanks for the picture. But don't forget that my request for a letter has not yet been fulfilled.

With all good wishes, to you, your dear husband and Pamela, in which Mrs. Ginzberg joins me,

Affectionately yours,

Dear Lassie:

Next to the pleasure of receiving a letter from you is writing to you. I surely would have availed myself of the opportunity your letter gave me to write to you sooner; unfortunately, however, the shingles—or, in good Anglo-Saxon, the "girdle"—is still tied around my loins. Yet, there is no reason to worry about it as my general condition is better than the physicians would expect and at old age one must have acquired patience if he did not walk through life blindfolded.

And how is mother Lassie and the baby Lassies? I hope that you and they, as well as your dear husband, are enjoying good health and are in good spirits.

Mrs. Ginzberg returned last week from Boston with glowing reports of the beauty and cleverness of her grandchildren. I suppose all grandmothers are more or less alike and grandfathers are not much different.

With love to you, the babies, and kindest regards to your husband.

Affectionately yours,

Dearest Lassie:

Let me first extend to you and your dear husband my heartiest congratulations on the arrival of Peter Alexander. May he grow up to be a source of great joy and pride to his parents and to their friends.

We, of course, enjoyed receiving from you your kind Yuletide greetings which shows that you did not forget us. I wish, however, you would have found a few minutes to spare to drop us a few lines, and let us know how mother Lassie and the baby Lassies are. Of course, I understand that taking care of four children is a hard task. Yet, at the same time, I am sure that the pleasure you derive from this is compensating you for your work.

We have not seen our Best friends—Best, of course, is a slip for West, and as the wife of a psychiatrist, you know how just a slip will creep in—since they left for the Oranges. Many times we wish to visit them, but because of my poor state of health, which makes any locomotion painful, we never are able to carry out our wishes. Mrs. Ginzberg, however, a few days ago, had quite a long telephone conversation with your dear mother. You know, of course, what a chance I have when Mrs. Ginzberg is on the phone!

With all good wishes.

Affectionately yours
Schatzi

Old age was not a time of joy and happiness for Louis Ginzberg, but his burdens were easier for him to bear because of his never failing interest in the joys and happiness of his young friends.

CHAPTER XIII

THE GENTLE SKEPTIC

LOUIS GINZBERG reached his seventieth birthday two years after the publication of his magnum opus—the first three volumes of his *A Commentary on the Palestinian Talmud*. He lived another decade, during which he attempted to prepare two additional volumes for publication. But he was unable to do this, partly because of the neuritis which plagued him ever after his attack of shingles in 1948, partly because he no longer had the physical and emotional powers required for concentrated scientific work. At the time of his death, a small part of what eventually became Volume IV of the Commentary had been set up in galleys, but Rabbi David Weiss, who later undertook the task of preparing this volume for press, found the manuscript far from polished.

There is no doubt that my father played a game with himself and others in the last years of his life about the state of the manuscript, which when completed, he hoped, would demonstrate *in extenso* his approach to the study of the Jerusalem Talmud. As early as the middle and certainly the late 1940's, his correspondence contains frequent references to his nearing the end of his task and his hope of releasing for press Volumes IV and V in the near future. But it was clear to me at that time and much clearer now in retrospect that he hid from himself and others the true facts. He simply could not admit that his effective working days, especially for such an ambitious undertaking, were over. He had always worked the hard way. He relied exclusively on his phenomenal memory; as Professor Lieberman pointed out to me, he did not ever use a talmudic dictionary. He kept few notes, and he had never used an assistant. He was truly a lone worker in his research and when his strength failed, he could work no more.

The following letter indicates the unhappiness which his failing health and inability to work caused:

Dear Reverend Lewis:

Because of ill health I was unable to reply sooner to your letter of September 26th, in which you asked me about the Excurses II, referred to in my fifth volume of *The Legends of the Jews*. It is a source of real disappointment to me that the eighth volume of my work, which was to contain six lengthy Excursus, has not yet been published, though the material is ready for the press. You may perhaps be interested in knowing that I have a complete translation into Hebrew based on the Ethiopic text. Considering my advanced age and poor health, I have some doubts as to whether the Excursus will be published in the near future.

But his faculties remained unimpaired, and during the last decade of his life he commented on many developments, old or new, with acuity and humor. The letters written in his last years tell us his attitudes about a great many matters that concerned him deeply such as the future of Judaism and the Jews, as well as other matters such as the field of psychiatry, in which he had only a peripheral interest. These last years also gave him an opportunity to look back on his long and interesting life and to confirm, revise, or deny his earlier judgments and actions.

Long before he became a septuagenarian he was unable to

respond sympathetically to all that he had known and experienced earlier. I recall going with him to a Hasidic synagogue on Simchas Torah in Antwerp in 1928 as he had regularly done in his youth, since on that holiday the Hasidim dance with special fervor with and around the Torah. But the unruliness of the services made him uneasy, and we left before they concluded. To the best of my knowledge, this was the last time that he prayed in the company of Hasidim.

My father had rather clear views about Hasidism. He understood and was sympathetic to the forces that led to its emergence and spread, but he was certain that his distinguished ancestor, the Vilna Gaon, had done yeoman service in stemming its further advance. He understood the hold of Hasidism over many in Eastern Europe, but he ridiculed certain Western European literati who sought to popularize it. And he was astounded by the success of some of these authors in the Christian world. It was further proof to him of the public's lack of understanding of or sensitivity for the authentic.

My father was always pleased when distinguished rabbis from Eastern Europe paid him a visit. He told with special pleasure of the occasion when one of these visitors hesitated at the door until he was repeatedly urged to come in: this Polish rabbi was not sure whether my father was still carrying on the "family feud" against the Hasidim.

I am indebted to Professor Heschel for the following story. One of the old-time rabbis who paid my father a visit asked his permission to explain an obscure text, which he did at great length and with great ingenuity. When he had finished, my father suggested that if the several lines which had been misplaced in the transmission of the manuscript were replaced in their original position, the text would be clear. The old rabbi looked at my father and said: "Then where would be the *Chochmah?*"

My father also obtained much pleasure in his later years

from the large number of dissertations, mostly from German universities, that were built up from his notes in Volumes V and VI of the *Legends of the Jews*. Some students had developed their dissertations, even before the appearance of the Index Volume in 1938, by reading through the two volumes; and after the Index was published, many more used the *Legends* for dissertation purposes. One young man whose plagiarism was conspicuous did not hesitate to write to my father and to invite his attention specifically to the theory advanced in the dissertation. My father replied that he was pleased to have the book; that he had read it with interest; and he thought that the author might like to know that he had reconsidered his earlier views—on which the dissertation had been based—and was now convinced that they were erroneous!

He even altered his views about the "higher criticism of the Bible." For a man who had lost his first job in the United States because he was too radical in his approach to the Bible, he became in his late years very circumspect indeed about the theories of the "higher criticism." One clue to his altered views comes from the denigration of German scholarship. Writing in a very critical vein to a former student in 1935, Professor Ginzberg comments, *inter alia*, as follows: "The introduction to your paper pained me greatly. Your remarks on the lack of historical sense of the biblical writers, even if true, are out of place as they have nothing to do with the subject you deal with. They left in my mouth the unpleasant taste one feels after reading 'Arian theology of the Bible.' Have you read Moore, *Die Eigenart der Hebräischen Geschichtshreibung* or Schaeder, *Esra der Schreiber* or Weiser, *Glaube und Geschichte* in A.T. Those scholars—the two last mentioned have recently confirmed their conversion to Nazism!—would have taught you that the Hebrews and the Greeks are the only two people in antiquity who wrote history; and in a certain sense the Hebrews excelled over the

Greeks as only they conceived for the first time a philosophy of history."

Many years later, in acknowledging the receipt of Schauss' book *The Lifetime of A Jew,* Professor Ginzberg wrote: "I found Mr. Schauss' book quite interesting and useful though I, as a skeptic whose skepticism increases with age, am rather skeptical about many of the theories of 'higher criticism' in which Mr. Schauss believes faithfully."

In a letter in 1950 to Dr. Julian Morgenstern, then President of the Hebrew Union College, Ginzberg wrote:

I have not yet read your article "Two Prophecies," but hope to do so soon. You know that my attitude towards biblical criticisms is an extremely skeptical one. At the same time, I enjoy reading what competitive biblical scholars have to say and I have no doubt that I shall greatly enjoy your article whether agreeing or disagreeing with you.

At about the same time, the editor of the Jewish Publication Society, his former student and friend, Dr. Solomon Grayzel, wrote to Professor Ginzberg in connection with the plans that were afoot for a new translation of the Bible. Here are excerpts from Professor Ginzberg's reply.

In my wildest dreams I never thought of myself as a biblical scholar nor an authority on English. Your letter of May 6th, in which you asked me to communicate to you those passages and English translations of the Jewish Publication Society which can and should be improved came, therefore, as a great surprise to me. I shall, however, not fail to make the following two suggestions, that you might not be accused of the prohibition of the rabbis "Not to approach one for a gift who has nothing to give."
1) Micah 1.11:
"O Beth-ezel, the wailing will take its procession with you." The prophets want to say that the inhabitants of the city mansions will be the first ones over whom the public wailing will start.
2) Psalms 90.5 ought to be rendered:

"Thou carriest man away as with a flood, He becomes like moss."

The less one knows of a subject the more one can write and talk about it, but it is one of my foibles only to deal with things I believe to know, and hence do not be afraid that I shall send you too long a letter.

In a letter in 1947 to Professor A. Guttmann of the Hebrew Union College acknowledging his reprint on "The Significance of Miracles for Talmudic Judaism," Professor Ginzberg wrote:

If I were to characterize the view of the rabbis concerning the Miracles, I would say: "They believed in the omnipotence of God and hence also in Miracles." How different from the statement of St. Augustine who said: "The Miracles make me believe in God."

The preceding year the Rabbinical Assembly had published a prayer book under the editorship of Rabbi Morris Silverman. On receiving a copy, Professor Ginzberg replied:

I deeply appreciate your inscription in which you thanked me for my counsel and assistance. I wish, however, my counsel would have been more effective, then the prayer book would have had less omissions and commissions of which I cannot approve.

In six pages of handwritten notes on the prayerbook sent from Oakland, Maine to Rabbi Silverman in the summer of 1941, one finds the following comment of Professor Ginzberg:

I am not particularly fond of *making* prayers—they ought to flow from the heart of inspired poets!

Nevertheless, the exigency of war led him shortly thereafter to compose "A Prayer for Divine Aid."

Our God and God of our Fathers.
We invoke Thy blessing upon our Country, on the government of this Republic, the President of these United States and all who exercise just and rightful authority. Do thou instruct them out of

Thy Law, that they may administer all affairs of state in justice and equity, that peace and security, happiness and prosperity, right and freedom, may forever abide in our midst.

O God, Our Father, In Thy hand is the soul of all life and the spirit of all flesh. In these times of distress, we come before Thee in prayer.

When nations roar, sovereignties totter, and the earth crumbles, we bring before Thee our humble supplications in behalf of all who expose their lives on the fields of battle in defense of our beloved country. Do Thou unto them as Thou has promised saying, "When thou passest thru the waters I will be with thee, and thru the rivers they shall not overflow thee; When thou walkest thru the fire thou shalt not be burned, neither shall the flame kindle upon thee." Send Thy power from on high; may Thy right hand be their salvation. Return them to their land, to their homes, and to their loved ones, rejoicing in the knowledge that tyranny is destroyed, and that doers of evil are no more.

May it also be Thy will to protect our armies from all manner of pestilence and disease.

We pray for those who have been wounded in performance of their duty. Do Thou, O Lord, support them on their bed of illness that they may rise with greater strength and with a stronger Faith in Thee, for Thou art a true and merciful Healer.

Have compassion, O Lord, on our heroic dead, who have valiantly made the supreme sacrifice. May they rest under the wings of Thy glory and their souls be bound in the bond of life.

May this land under Thy Providence be an influence for good throughout the world, uniting men in peace and freedom and helping to fulfill the vision of Thine inspired Seers. "Nation shall not lift up sword against nation, neither shall men learn war any more." Amen.

Starting in 1947, Professor Ginzberg's files contain interesting evidence of the impact of psychoanalysis on the interpretation of Jewish law, ceremonials, and legends. He replied to an inquiry of a Joseph Berger of Pittsburgh:

I fully share your interest in the Jewish version of the "Oedipus Legend" but not in your enthusiasm for psychoanalysis. You see,

I have a nephew who is a brilliant practitioner of psychoanalysis, my son dabbles in it, my daughter reads about it, my wife speaks of it, and I am amused by it. To be serious, when I consider that in my own lifetime, or to be accurate, in that period of it that elapsed from my student days to now, only extending over slightly more than half of a century, no less than a half dozen theories have been established and thrown over in explaining myth and legend, I cannot but be extremely skeptical about the latest of these theories, the psychoanalytical one. Not being a physician, it would be not only presumptuous on my part, but what is still worse, foolish, to express an opinion on the great importance of psychoanalysis for psychology and psychiatry. What I object to is the complete disregard for historical facts and literary forms, in which setting myth and legend came down to us, on the part of many of the ardent disciples of Freud. One must be particularly careful to consider the historical facts in dealing with Jewish legends. The people of the book remained bookish even in their fancies, and I could find no better illustration for this than the cycle of legends connected with Joshua.

Shortly thereafter, he wrote to another correspondent:

Dear Dr. Zimmerman:
    I appreciate your kind thought in sending me your essay on Ecclesiastes XII. Not being a psychoanalyst, however, I must admit that psychoanalytic attempts in the field of literature, especially of classic literature, remind me of the Hasidic interpretations of talmudic texts. Unsophisticated as I am, I cannot conceive that a man of great ability, as the author of Ecclesiastes undoubtedly was, should have used seven verses in heaping symbols upon symbols to describe a natural act which he surely was able to describe in a much simpler way.
    On *Tahan,* as a euphemism for sexual intercourse, see *Legends of the Jews,* VI, 208 top, and *ibid,* 404, note 45. I would like, however, to know how you explain the plural. If the author of Ecclesiastes intended to use *Tahan* in a symbolic sense, he surely would have used the singular and not the plural. The traditional explanation, according to which the "grinders" refers to the molars, seems to me to be the only possible one.
    In post-biblical literature, the finger is often a phallic symbol,

but never arms. After all, Sigmund Freud thought and spoke in German and not in Hebrew. What may be in one language a symbol might sound in another language quite meaningless.

In the following year, he sent a warm but challenging note to his niece Ethel Ginsburg, who had recently published a book *Public Health Is People:*

I read your book very carefully and enjoyed it, though not being a psychologist or a psychoanalyst, I doubt whether I did not miss some subtle point which you made. At times, I have the impression as if the difference between the old and the new in approaching psychological problems is only a matter of terminology. I remember, for instance, a statement by an Arabic author of the ninth century, who writes "The child needs as much the heart of his mother as her breast"—too much of the breast will have a bad effect upon his gastric organs, and too much of the heart, on his emotions. It seems to me as if the modern psychologists came to the very same conclusion, though they put it in words quite different from those quoted.

As a philologian, it is difficult for me to subscribe to the theory that the older child develops at a very early stage feelings of envy against his younger sisters and brothers. The most endearing name for one's love in the Hebrew language as well as in several other Semitic languages is "my sister." This would rather indicate that the older children develop a deep feeling of love and attachment for the younger ones. You undoubtedly know that among many races, the older brother of the mother takes the place of the father in caring and bringing up of her children. Such an institution can hardly be explained if we assume with the modern psychologists that a strong antagonism is firm between the older and the younger children.

These few remarks will show you first that I read your book and second, that I do not know anything about psychology.

A few months later, he wrote to his nephew:

Dear Sol:

I should have acknowledged sooner the receipt of your article "Values And The Psychiatrist," but I thought I should first digest the contents of your paper, and then write you. It seems, however, as if my digestive organs do not function properly, and were I to discuss, in detail, all the points in your article which are obscure to one who is not trained in psychoanalysis, I am afraid the writing of such an epistle would take up too much of your valuable time. To quote your own words, "I always said you are a masochist, and you asked for it." I love you, however, too much to inflict too much pain upon you. I shall, therefore, try to be brief.

1. You begin your essay with a quotation from the prophet Micah, and I have not the slightest objection to it, but I strongly object to the use of "Judaeo-Christian tradition." I know this phrase is very popular today, not so much with Christians but with the Jews. The truth of the matter is, however, that western civilization is the product of Judaeo-Greek culture and not of a Judaeo-Christian one. Christianity—I use it in its dogmatic sense disregarding Liberal Christianity which is as little Christian as the Council of Judaism is Jewish—is anti-cultural from its very beginning, and its historical importance lies therein that it had absorbed a large number of Jewish as well as of Greek elements.

2. As far as I can recollect, Aristotle never used the term "values" which would be entirely out of place in his system of ethics, which is utilitarian, and hence he prefers expressions like cause or benefit.

3. If the definition of values given by Robin Williams is the only one psychoanalysis has to give us, I don't think that we are at all entitled to speak of values instead of causes. My interest in the problem of values centers mainly around cultural values. By this I mean that man today repeats actions and rites of primitive and savage society, but he has changed their values. In the study-ing of cultural values, one has to start with a standard of values, and as far as I can see there is nothing in your paper that would be of any benefit to me.

Of course, you will say that my three remarks contain nothing of value to you. Now we are square. I started with a quotation from your handwritten note attached to your paper, and if you feel like acknowledging this letter, you might start with a quota-tion from my last remark and say, "there is nothing in your paper that will be of value to me."

Professor Ginzberg took another opportunity to set forth his views on psychoanalysis at length when he "talked for the record" to his daughter-in-law: "The basic concept of the psychiatrists cannot be proved. They draw a parallel between the infant and primitive man—the group (human groups in primitive development). They say that religion reflects the father complex of the group; the father is the authoritative body. This concept does not appeal to me. I can understand the infant's relation to his father, but the group doesn't see God. I would consider it ridiculous to pass judgment on psychoanalysts as therapists as I am not a medical man, but I can assess their generalizations about culture and religious ritual. The psychoanalyst simply does not have the proper historical background.

"I was especially interested in their dealings with ritual. There is no religion without ritual. Aristotle had a theory that might be described as monotheistic. It was very close to the Jewish concept of God. However, that was not a religion. It was pure philosophy with a purely intellectual approach. Religion must have an every day bearing on morals, ethics and attitudes toward life. When I read the psychoanalytic literature about ritual, I am astounded.

"For instance, Reik wrote on the *shofar* and phylacteries. Now, of course, one cannot write on these rituals without knowing their history. He didn't. He wrote about the development of the phylacteries as amulets used by a primitive society, whereas the Jews had already developed a great culture.

"To show how ridiculous it is to deal with any subject without knowing its history, suppose I go to Sol and say I am suffering from insomnia. He will say, 'Oh, yes, and since when have you had it?' I say, 'Since I was an adolescent.' He will say, 'Were you ever disappointed in love?' Answer, 'Yes. At sixteen, I was in love with my cousin and I was very unhappy. Then at twenty-one I made a very unfortunate marriage and had to be divorced. Then I married again and I was never able to forget my first wife.' Now, if I tell such a *bobe-meise*, he will try to treat me accordingly; similarly, if a man tries to write on rituals and judges from what little he knows, he will come out with an equally ridiculous answer. Psychiatrists can treat a patient only if they discover the essential facts.

"So if one deals with a far more complicated problem—a development of four thousand years—he cannot make a theory on the basis of the latest developments which he may know unless he knows how those developments came about. I was so annoyed to read that the *shofar* has to do with sex. The *shofar* was the earliest form of musical instrument. It was used in time of war. Today it is used on New Year's Day, which is a day of commemoration, but in the Temple the *shofar* was used every day as a form of music. The old celebration of New Year's Day was transferred from the Temple to the synagogue and from the synagogue to the home. All of this the historian should know.

"I have very much respect for serious study, and Freud was undoubtedly a great genius. Psychiatry is undoubtedly a very important step in modern medicine."

Despite his deep skepticism about psychoanalysis as a method of historical interpretation, Professor Ginzberg was willing, albeit reluctantly, to follow the recommendation of his nephew Sol and consult a distinguished psychiatrist, Dr. Gustav Bychowski, since all other medical assistance had failed to relieve him of his acute pains. He saw Dr. Bychowski a number of times and though he did not take his visits too seriously, he enjoyed them. Regrettably, psychiatry was no more effective than the other medical specialties in relieving him of his symptoms.

While his aging and his neuritis made it impossible for him to proceed with his *A Commentary on the Palestinian Talmud*, it did not stop him completely from continuing to study and to write. In 1948, he wrote to his cousin, Rabbi Louis Rabinowitz in Johannesburg, South Africa:

There is very little to write about myself. Wine may gain in strength with age, but not men. . . . My advanced age does not permit me to work as much as I would like. At present, I am preparing for the future (sicl) volumes four and five of my *Commentary on the Palestinian Talmud.*

The following letter to Professor Gandz, with whom he felt deep bonds of friendship, especially because Gandz, who combined work in Judaica and mathematics, helped to bring my father back to his early love of mathematics, conveys something of his work pattern in his late years:

Dear Professor Gandz:

In preparing my paper on Sa'adia's *Siddur,* I became interested again in the problems of his controversy with Ben-Meir about the calendar. The results of my investigation are for the present merely negative. By this, I mean that I am now convinced that Bornstein's interpretation is absolutely untenable. So far, however, I have not yet succeeded in establishing a sound basis for the controversy. Whether I shall succeed in doing so is very doubtful, especially as I have not enough time for this kind of study.

I had completely forgotten that I ever wrote on Rabbi Meir of Rothenburg, and only looked up my article in the encyclopedia after you called my attention to it. I find it to be a rather fair biographical sketch of this great saint and scholar, but I certainly would not describe it as a classic, and I am afraid that you, carried away by your friendship for me, exaggerate its value. I only glanced at Agus's book and I do not know whether it is a real contribution to the history of the life and work of the great rabbi.

I am very interested in what you have to say about the enigmatic passage in Yerushalmi Sanhedrin I, 2. Send it by all means to the Academy for publication in the *Proceedings.*

He continued to maintain a lively correspondence with scholars, old and new, professionals and amateurs. Any serious question was answered, although frequently briefly:

Dear Mr. Gross:

I received your letter of November 24th, in which you ask me whether there is anything in talmudic law similar to the common law according to which a woman who does a wrong in the presence of her husband is presumed to be acting under his influence and not responsible therefore. The answer to this question is "no," and for the simple reason that according to Jewish law, a person is responsible for his actions even if it could be proved that he acted under the influence of somebody else.

We see that his research and correspondence was not limited to matters Hebraic:

September 18, 1950

Dear Doctor Evans:

On returning home last Wednesday from my vacation in Maine, where we spent more than two months, I found your very interesting letter. For the last half century, I have neglected my Egyptological studies. I believe, however, that I still have retained enough of Egyptology, which I studied as a young man under the greatest Egyptologists of Europe.

The etymology of pyramid is still a moot question, but to my mind, there can be no doubt that it is of Egyptian origin, very likely connected with *pyr-em us*, the slanting edge of the pyramid. I am still more sure that there is no connection whatsoever between raamses and the Hebrew *raam*, as the Egyptian origin of this name is quite obvious.

Many years earlier, Louis Ginzberg had pursued research into calendar reform in connection with the proposals being sponsored by the League of Nations to establish a fixed calendar. It gave him an opportunity to put his mathematical training to use in his historical researches. The opposition of the Catholic Church to a fixed Easter brought an end to the League's effort, but problems connected with the calendar continued to interest many scholars.

November 24, 1952

Dear Dr. Froom:

I am in receipt of your letter of November 7 in re the fixed calendar introduced by the Jews.

You are quite right in assuming that it took place some time in the second half of the fourth century. Whether the later tradition ascribing it to the Patriarch Hillel II is based on fact, I have my doubts. The tendency toward fixation of the calendar was noticed in several centuries before the time of Hillel. Nor is it quite correct to say that the final fixation was established in the fourth century. You undoubtedly know the controversy that arose among the Rabbanite Jews in the tenth century, which almost led to a split between Palestinian and Babylonian Jewry. One might, however, state with some certainty that the persecution of the Jews by the Roman Emperors was a factor which brought about the great calendar reform.

There is a good deal of literature on the history of the Jewish calendar, but almost exclusively in Hebrew. You may, however, find some material that would interest you in the book on the Jewish Calendar by Adolph Schwartz, the title of which is *Der Jüdische Kalender*, Breslau, 1872. If I recollect my previous letter to you, I mentioned to you the name of Dr. Solomon Gandz, professor at Dropsie College, whom I consider the best authority on the Jewish calendar.

Age did not increase Professor Ginzberg's certainty about many matters, even those subjects which he had studied intensely over many decades.

Dear Mr. Guttmann:

Many and sincere thanks for forwarding to me your article on the Testament of Moses, which I read with pleasure and profit. The problem of the dependence of the art of the church on the art of the synagogue is still very puzzling to me, notwithstanding the latest discoveries at Dura and at some centers in Palestine, which show only that at some times and at certain places the second commandment of the Decalog was not taken too strictly. There can, however, be no doubt that a good deal of early Christian art is based not only on the Hebrew Bible but also upon the later embellishments of Jewish folklore. At the same time, many of the so-called Jewish illustrated manuscripts produced in the late Middle Ages and during the Renaissance are works of Christian artists or at least copies of works by Jewish artists. I hope that we shall soon have your thesis on this subject published which will undoubtedly spread some light on this very intricate question.

In the late 1940's and early 1950's, Professor Ginzberg enjoyed a relationship with Julius and Hildegard Lewy whose scholarly researches criss-crossed his own. The Lewys, emigrés from Hitler's Germany, settled in Cincinnati where Julius Lewy became Professor.

Dear Mrs. Lewy:
        I deeply appreciate your kindness in forwarding to me your Marginal Notes. To receive one of your publications is a double pleasure; the pleasure of enriching one's knowledge by it, and the pleasure of knowing that you sometimes think of your New York friends. Many sincere thanks for this double pleasure. . . .
        Here is one short note of a philological nature. As an old pupil of Noeldeke, I cannot accept the suggested identity of Akkadian *epesu* with the West Semitic h-x/s-b: too many irregularities in one word. I would rather connect *epesu* with the West Semitic root, h-p/s-s, which means "search"—a very appropriate description for "calculate."

In May of 1950, Professor Ginzberg wrote to acknowledge another piece by Dr. Hildegard Lewy:

"Old love never vanishes" is an old German saying and hence my great interest in "legend," along which line I have often done work for the last sixty years.
        Consequently, I cannot write you before having carefully read your paper on the Kay Kaus Legend. Now, after having finally done it, I wish to thank you very sincerely for the pleasure and instruction I derived from its perusal.
        For a long time, it was fashionable to derive anything good or beautiful among the Semites from Arian sources. I was, therefore,

particularly pleased to learn from your paper that the Semites were not always the borrower, but also sometimes the lender. . . .

In June 1952, he wrote a letter to Professor Julius Lewy:

Many and sincere thanks to you for forwarding to me your paper on "Tabor, Tibar, Atybymos," which I read with great pleasure and profit.

I have, of course, nothing to add to your very learned essay, especially since it is in a field in which you are the acknowledged master and I an ignorant student. It is about sixty years ago since I studied Assyriology under Schrader and Winkler at the University of Berlin. Unfortunately, however, even the little I have learned from these great masters I have forgotten in the course of the years.

Perhaps it might interest you to know that in later Jewish sources, which often contain a great deal of older material, Naamah plays quite an important part. She is said to be a co-worker of her brother, Tubal-Cain, in "cutting instruments of brass and iron." In some respects, she even surpasses her brother, since she is the woman, who by her beauty seduced the angels and caused their fall.

The concerns of young scholars were always a concern of his own. He wrote the following brief letter to Rabbi Braude of Providence who had earlier consulted him:

Lately I had opportunity to busy myself with some projects of Midrash Tehillim and it occurred to me that you might be interested in the following two remarks.

1. CXIX, p. 490, ed. Buber. The word which the editor had difficulty to explain is nothing but the Greek *protos* and the passage to be translated, "the distinguished generations." It is a play on the word *Elef* which is taken to mean as much as "Class A." (cf. Breshit R., XXVIII).

2. I wonder whether you noticed the remark made by Albeck in his Hebrew translation of Zunz, *Gottesdiens, Vort.*, pp. 408-09 where he strongly argues against Mann's theory about the two versions of Midrash Tehillim.

He pondered about the information and interpretations

which he advanced long after. Dr. Judah Goldin told me that my father asked him to delete a footnote from his galleys, for after reflecting on a point for several months, he was no longer convinced of the validity of an earlier theory which he had advanced. Professor Ginzberg's skepticism cut deep—it applied to his own theories as well as to those of others.

The State of Israel was established in 1948, just five years before my father died. Deeply concerned throughout his life about the future of Jews and Judaism, the establishment of the State, particularly after the Hitler holocaust, brought great and deep satisfaction to him. And yet he had a great many qualms about the future.

First of all, he was not certain that the Zionist leadership should accept the principle of partition. I had had an opportunity of playing a small role in bringing the possibility of partition once again to the fore in the summer of 1946 after my return from Europe, where I had represented the United States in the Five Power Conference on Non-Repatriable Refugees. In connection with this Conference, I had occasion to discuss the Palestine problem with Hector McNeil, Under Secretary of State for Foreign Affairs for the Parliamentary. As a result of our discussion, it seemed increasingly clear that Britain would soon pull out of Palestine and unless a plan were developed in advance for the establishment of two independent states, the problem would be thrown into the United Nations which would give Russia an opportunity to play a leading role in the Middle East. I reported this to Dean Acheson, the Acting Secretary of State, who in turn reported to the President. During my involvement in these activities, I came to see a considerable amount of Eliahu Elath (Epstein), the representative of the Jewish Agency in Washington. On an earlier occasion, I had brought Epstein to my parents' home in New York, and in the following years he frequently visited with my father.

Throughout, my father retained a great deal of skepticism about the wisdom of what came to be the accepted Zionist position in favor of partition. Apparently, he could not agree to any deliberate action which would cancel the claim of Jewry to any integral part of the Holy Land. He felt that no Jew had the right to renounce any part of a claim that had been pending for about 2,000 years. This withholding attitude was reinforced by his skepticism about whether any reasonable compromise offered by the Jews would settle anything in that troubled area. Since my father-in-law, Robert Szold, was likewise unhappy about partition and for much the same reasons, I began to question my own role in resurrecting the proposal. But my doubts were quickly dispelled. I could see no tenable alternative.

The discussions between Professor Ginzberg and Epstein did not concern the political strategy which would be involved in securing the independence of Jewish Palestine, but was concentrated on the role of Jewish law in the new State of Israel. As I sat in on these conversations, I was amazed to see how far my father was willing to go to reduce the difficulties and the conflicts that were inherent in the emerging situation. He developed the position that a tolerable solution would be one in which the new state would respect the Sabbath, *Kashrut,* and would leave to the rabbinate jurisdiction over marriage and divorce. He argued for a basic respect on the part of the organs of the State for religion and tradition and the avoidance of state action that would violate basic tenets. He did not want to see the power of the state used to force conformity from individuals who no longer recognized the authority of the law. He foresaw the doctrinal difficulties and knew that most of the leaders of Orthodoxy would find his stance unacceptable. But he believed that time would prove him right. More state insistence on conformity could not be expected, and less would jeopardize the ties between Israel and the Diaspora.

His greatest fears centered around the involvement of religion and politics. He had lived too long in Germany to ignore the dangers of a political clericalism and he saw only harm in the maneuverings of the religious groups to get and keep a place in the political arena. He felt that this mixture could only redound to the weakening of religion and to the corruption of politics. But he knew that nothing he could say or do would affect the outcome. He shared his thoughts with Epstein and let it go at that.

In 1947, he wrote to a young lady acquaintance who was a member of Kvutzath Yavneh:

. . . . What you said about the lack of religious life and feeling in most of the *Kevuzot* is, of course, disheartening and to my great regret I must say, not even new to me. That is just the impression I gained in Palestine during my stay there in 1928-29 and later in '33-'34. However, you must have hope not only in the Jews, but also in Judaism . . .

A few years earlier, he had written to Dr. Israel Goldstein, then President of the Zionist Organization of America:

It would be more than presumptuous on my part to describe myself as an active Zionist. My participation in Zionist work is limited to a "Plea for Zionism" published almost half a century ago in a Dutch weekly, and to my representing in 1905, the Zionist Organization of America as a delegate to the Zionist Convention in Basle.

A clever lawyer, however, might plead my case and claim my life work has been entirely devoted to Zionism. Whatever the merits of my teaching by spoken or written word might be—of course, I know that they are fantastically exaggerated by my friends—it is based on the firm conviction of historical Judaism which tells us that Jewish nationalism without Jewish religion would be a tree without fruit, and that Jewish religion without Jewish nationalism would be a tree without roots. I fervently hope and pray that American Zionists under your guidance will develop into a deeply rooted tree bearing delicious fruit.

A decade earlier, when David Druck had prepared his biographical sketch, Professor Ginzberg had outlined his views about the respective roles of religion and nationalism in the destiny of the Jews.

If Judaism were to be based entirely on nationalism, with religion completely absent, this would be equivalent to accepting the proposition that the Jewish community in the Diaspora has no right to exist. If the Jewish state were to be founded on the basis of pure nationalism, it would result that the Jews of the land of Israel would be Jews and those of the Diaspora would, of necessity, be regarded as non-Jews. Let us imagine a situation in the future when there would be two million Jews in the Jewish state and fourteen million in the Diaspora. The large majority of the Jewish people would be stateless. There were more Irish in America than there were in Ireland, but they have disappeared as an entity. The same has happened to the twenty million Germans in America. Does one want the millions of Jews in the Diaspora to disappear, as well?

Jews certainly need their own country where they can develop their language, institutions, and their own civilization and culture. However, one cannot sacrifice all the other millions of Jews who cannot belong to the Jewish national state. It goes without saying that individuals within a Jewish state can afford themselves the luxury of being personally atheists, but, were the entire community to become atheistic, Judaism as a whole would cease to exist. Nationalism is not an abstraction; it is a very definite thing, the characteristic of a specific group, with its own particular historical background and experience. Jewish nationalism expresses itself in religion. Subtract religion and there is no Jewish people. One can tolerate the individual who can abandon religion and yet remain a Jew. It is, however, impossible to devise a Judaism for the corporate community, which breaks with the past and makes of the Jews a people of national atheists.

Conversely, one cannot base Judaism on religion alone, without nationalism. This would be an historical absurdity. The entire religious element of Judaism is essentially national. All Jewish holidays would be empty if they were denuded of the national aspect. Passover, Shavuot, Sukkot, Hanukkah, and all the fast days contain national content, even though they are rooted in religion. Without its national background each of the Jewish holidays is inconceivable. Nationalism is our air, and no human being can live without air. Nationalism is not a part of our being; it is rather to be conceived, like the air, as the indispensable element without which we cannot survive.

Judaism must, therefore, be given the content of religious nationalism, or of a national religion. These two forces cannot be separated one from the other. The whole of Jewish history abounds with phenomena where both forces, religion and nationalism, always went together. Those who speak and act contrary to this conception do not understand the whole direction of our history. In the time of great crises the Jewish national state was repeatedly saved by a handful of believing, religious Jews. They were motivated by religious faith, but what they achieved was to save not only our religion but also the Jewish people. Such a synthesis must now be recreated, as we endeavor to build the Jewish state and rebuild the Jewish people. The sundering of both these forces can bring only danger to Jewry.

The uneasiness with which Professor Ginzberg contemplated the future of Jewish scholarship and of Judaism is sharply delineated in a letter to his young colleague, Robert Gordis.

To be candid and rather pessimistic, I doubt whether we can expect a revival of Jewish learning in the near future. The two great centers of Jewry, America and Israel, do not appear to be very promising.

In America, where the laity is extremely ignorant—Jewishly speaking—and the clergy's interest is centered in speech making, sociology and politics, one would have to be more than an optimist to expect a new sprouting up of Jewish learning. In Israel, where the new state offers too many attractions to youth, one doubts whether many of the younger generation would take up Jewish studies. In the course of time, Israel will very likely produce men devoted to the study of biblical archeology, the Hebrew language and perhaps also the Bible, but by that time the knowledge of post-biblical literature and history will be so limited that very few will take up its study. I shudder at the thought that there may come a time when the Jews will depend upon Christian scholars in matters pertaining to rabbinic literature. All this sounds very pessimistic, but what can you expect from an old disappointed man.

Professor Ginzberg appreciated the warmth and sympathy with which American Jews had responded to the needs of their suffering brethren in Europe, the Middle East, and elsewhere. He considered these philanthropic efforts as one evidence of a long tradition. But he feared that the spirit might be neglected while the needs of the body were cared for. He wrote to Herbert Lehman in 1948:

I am very happy to see that men like you and your associates are taking an active part in the guidance of the affairs of the Seminary. May it be granted to you to see the Seminary grow and flourish as the institution of higher Jewish learning for which purpose it was founded.

The great calamity of recent years that came over millions of Jews also resulted in the destruction of almost all the great institutions of learning in Europe. Let us hope that American Israel, that came so generously to the aid of the Jews, will also do its duty in making America take the place of the seat of learning.

On his 70th birthday, when he had been elected an honorary member of the Council of the Jewish Historical Society of England, he wrote to Cecil Roth:

I know I have done nothing in the field of history of the Jews in England. But Jewish scholarship is a unit, and it is this sentiment of unity that you very likely had in mind when you thought me worthy of becoming a member of your Society. I know that my contributions to Jewish scholarship are very meager. But, in all my strivings, I never lost sight of the unity of Jewish history.

The Nazis and World War II had destroyed most of the European centers of Jewish scholarship. No single event was more traumatic to Professor Ginzberg than the destruction of Lithuanian Jewry and its great centers of learning. He did not believe that these centers could be re-established either in Israel or in other countries, no matter how valiantly the survivors went about their tasks. When the heads of his old *Yeshiva* in Telsh asked him to help them to relocate in Israel he refused, for great as the contributions of the Lithuanian *Yeshivot* had been, he did not believe that they could or should take root in Israel. He mourned deeply not only for the millions who had been martyred, but for the learning that was extinguished.

When the Jewish Lithuanian Cultural Society "Lite" asked him to write an Introduction to a commemorative volume, he agreed. The short introduction reproduced below was written by my father apparently in English and translated for publication into Yiddish.

With the catastrophe of Lithuanian Jewry during the last war a development that continued for almost 3,000 years came to an end—a development which we call Talmudic Judaism which is not identical with Biblical Judaism.

Both are so closely related one to another that we may well describe Rabbinic Judaism as a straight line development of Biblical Judaism.

One will understand the close kinship between these two by contrasting them with Alexandrian Judaism or as it is usually called Hellenistic Judaism.

Egyptian Jewry as well as Palestine-Babylonian Jewry recognize the authority of the Bible as a guide of life and a code of law. And yet how great is the difference between Philo and the great Palestine-Babylonian Tannaim and Amoraim, for instance, Rabbi Akiba and Rab.

While the first mentioned one attempted to Hellenize Judaism, the Babylonian as well as the Palestinian leaders of the Jewry strove to Judaize Hellenism.

We are, therefore, safe in stating that the development of Judaism in Palestine and Babylonia was in a straight line with the development of Biblical Judaism, while Alexandrian Judaism, though based upon the Bible, bears the imprint of foreign influences.

These two developments of Judaism have their parallels in post-talmudic times.

The rediscovery of Greek science and philosophy in the eighth and ninth centuries in Arabic-speaking countries did not fail to leave an imprint upon the Jews who lived in these countries.

The golden period of Spanish Jewry is not entirely free from Greco-Arabic influence. Jehuda Halevi and Maimonides, the outstanding figures of Sephardi Jewry, deeply Jewish as they were, cannot be entirely understood without understanding the non-Jewish elements in their backgrounds. Neither the philosophy of Maimonides nor the poetry of Jehuda Halevi are in the straight line of development of the biblical-talmudic thought and literature.

It is only in the works of Franco-German Jews, where we meet with a straight line of continuation of Talmudic Rabbinism. And this continuation was taken over by their descendants in Eastern Europe.

Rabbinism that originated in Palestine about 500 years before the Common Era continued to develop for almost a millennium in Palestine and Babylonia and then it was carried on by the Ashkenazim, first in Franco-German countries and then by their descendants in Bohemia, Poland and Lithuania.

If we would characterize the nature of these developments, we would say that it consisted intellectually in dialectics applied to the study of Rabbinic Laws and emotionally in a simple piety concentrated upon the three cardinal concepts.

The culmination of these developments we see best in the Jewry of Lithuania during the centuries that followed upon the Chmielnicki persecutions in 1648.

In the two personalities of the Gaon of Vilna and Rabbi Israel Salanter, we see the old rabbinic ideal of the saintly scholars and scholarly saints beautifully combined.

Lithuanian Jewry was destroyed by the Nazis, but as long as there will be Jews they will remember with pride the holy men and the great scholars that Lithuania produced.

The last years of his life drew him repeatedly back to his beginnings. In writing to Dr. Sachar, the President of Brandeis University, after having received an honorary doctorate at one of its early graduation ceremonies, Louis Ginzberg commented on his own development: "I lately read an English book—I mean a book published in England—with the title *The History of Science,* a popular, but rather well written symposium by the leading English scientists. In the two chapters on Darwin, the point is made that he was 'a third-generation scientist and hence grew up in the scientific atmosphere.' Your praise of my acumen and devotion to learning, even if it were to be taken literally, would be nothing extraordinary, in view of the fact that I belong to a family who for the last five centuries have furnished German, Italian, Polish, and Lithuanian Jewry with outstanding intellectuals and saints. One must never forget the great part heredity and environment play in our makeup. When I think of the phenomenal achievements of the Gaon of Vilna, one of my ancestors, my own achievements look to me rather picayune. At the same time, one is not to forget that he was not only a great intellect, but also a great saint, and nobody would classify me as such."

The pull to the past is strikingly revealed by the dedications of the three volumes of his *A Commentary on the Palestinian Talmud.* I recall vividly having lunch in my parents' house in the early 1940's, when my father asked my mother and me to guess to whom the first volume was dedicated. I gave my mother ample time to make a series of guesses, but I never doubted for a moment that my guess was the right one—and so it was.

To the glory of our family and the glory of the whole House of Israel, our Rabbi Eliahu of Vilna . . . who enabled my eyes to rejoice in our Torah.

The dedication to Volume Two was in the same vein:

To the memory of my father, teacher and rabbi, our teacher Rabbi Isaac, son of our teacher Rabbi Asher . . . who busied himself all his life with Torah, work, and good deeds and who was sent with a good name to the life of the next world, where the Lord is the father of compassion to all who enter.

And the dedication of the third volume:

To the memory of a wise and great man, our teacher Rabbi Solomon Zalman Abel. . . . who opened for me the gates of learning of the Land of Israel.

About his ties to the past, Louis Ginzberg had no questions. He was less sure about the present and the future, which he viewed with an admixture of humor and skepticism.

However, a grandson bearing the name of Ginzberg—the only great grandson of Rabbi Isaac with the name of Ginzberg—did not bring forth skepticism. Our son Jeremy was born on October 26, 1952.

Eight days later, after the baby had been circumcised in the French Hospital in New York in the presence of a few relatives, Louis Ginzberg went upstairs to visit with his daughter-in-law. They closed the door in order not to disturb the supervising nun who had been passing back and forth, and between them they finished the larger part of a fifth of Scotch. Louis Ginzberg had been granted his dearest wish. The family line was now assured. He lived another year, and then his days of travail came to an end.

Acknowledgments

My mother, Adele Ginzberg, took the initiative in arranging to have my father's correspondence and papers sorted and catalogued and participated in this work. Dr. Menahem Schmelczer, Associate Librarian, Jewish Theological Seminary, supervised the organization of the files. He greatly facilitated my use of these materials.

The long search for my father's letters to Henrietta Szold ended successfully because of the generous assistance of the following: my mother-in-law, Zip Falk Szold, Mrs. Alexandra Lee Levin, Professor Jacob Marcus, Dr. Louis Kaplan, Dr. Isaac Fein, Dr. Alex Bein, and Mr. M. Jastrow Levin. Mr. Levin, on behalf of the family, graciously granted permission for their use.

Professor Saul Lieberman read aloud to me the biographical pieces on my father which David Druck had written in Yiddish. (As he read, he illuminated many obscure points with his own comments.) He also reviewed the draft manuscript.

Professor Shalom Spiegel also read the manuscript in its entirety and gave me the benefit of his advice and counsel on a great many points.

Miss Charlotte Perlberg carried through the onerous task

of checking the manuscript for accuracy. In this, she sought and secured assistance from, among others, Rabbi Jules Harlow and Miss Anna Kleban.

Many others related incidents which I have included and interpreted points which were unclear: my cousin, Arthur Lagawier; Professors Moshe Davis, Louis Finkelstein, Abraham Heschel, Abraham Neuman, Gershom Scholem, David Weiss.

Others who contributed to the manuscript were members of the Rabbinical Assembly who responded to my request for help, in particular, Rabbi Judah Nadich, who culled from his notebooks a large amount of relevant materials.

Rabbi Arthur Hertzberg translated the material from Druck's article which set forth my father's views on the duality between the religious and the nationalistic elements in Judaism.

Dr. Rosemary Park, President of Barnard College, made time in her busy schedule to translate two German letters: from Miss Szold to Frl. Katzenstein and from Professor Noeldeke to Professor Ginzberg.

My sister, Sophie G. Gould, and my cousin, Ethel L. Ginsburg, searched their files for letters and pictures.

My wife, Ruth Szold Ginzberg, succeeded in eliciting from my father a great many opinions and stories about episodes in his life, as well as a great many of his views and reactions to people and events, and wrote them down while they were fresh. She also took particular pains in editing this manuscript.

Professors Meyer Schapiro and Harry A. Wolfson read the page proof and made a series of helpful suggestions.

Mrs. Evelyn Weiman prepared the index.

Sources and Bibliography

Autobiographical Fragment: As related by Louis Ginzberg to his daughter-in-law, Ruth S. Ginzberg: A copy in Library, Jewish Theological Seminary, New York, N.Y.

Correspondence of Louis Ginzberg, Library, Jewish Theological Seminary.

Letters of Louis Ginzberg to Henrietta Szold, Zionist Archives, Jerusalem; print of microfilm in Library, Jewish Theological Seminary.

Letters of Henrietta Szold to Louis Ginzberg, Library, Jewish Theological Seminary.

Unpublished manuscripts of Louis Ginzberg, Library, Jewish Theological Seminary.

Letters about Louis Ginzberg from members of the Rabbinical Assembly in response to a request by Eli Ginzberg, Library, Jewish Theological Seminary.

Louis Ginzberg, by David Druck, New York, 1933: Hebrew translation of serial in Yiddish which appeared in *Jewish Morning Journal and Jewish Daily News* every Monday from Dec. 4, 1933 to March 5, 1934, New York.

Students, Scholars and Saints, by Louis Ginzberg, Jewish Publication Society, Philadelphia 1928.

"Bibliography of Writings of Professor Louis Ginzberg," by Boaz Cohen; *Louis Ginzberg Jubilee Volume,* American Academy for Jewish Research, New York, 1945.

"Dr. Louis Ginzberg: Scholar, Sage and Thinker," by Dr. Louis M. Epstein, *United Synagogue Recorder,* Vol. VII, No. 1, Jan. 1927.

"The Sixteenth Anniversary of Professor Louis Ginzberg" (in Hebrew) by Saul Lieberman, *Haaretz,* Dec. 8, 1933, Jerusalem.

"Louis Ginzberg: An Appreciation," by George Alexander Kohut, *Opinion*, Vol. IV, No. 3, Jan. 1934, New York.

"The Portrait of a Teacher," by Solomon Goldman, *Louis Ginzberg Jubilee Volume.*

Louis Ginzberg, by Louis Finkelstein, *Proceedings of the American Academy for Jewish Research*, Vol. XXIII, 1954; and *American Jewish Yearbook*, Vol. 56, 1955, American Jewish Committee and Jewish Publication Society.

Introduction by Shalom Spiegel to *The Legends of the Bible*, by Louis Ginzberg, Simon and Schuster, New York, 1956.

"What Price Conservatism? Louis Ginzberg at the Hebrew Union College," by Harry H. Mayer, *American Jewish Archives*, Vol. X, No. 2, Oct. 1958, Cincinnati, Ohio.

"Address in Honor of Professor Louis Ginzberg," by Eli Ginzberg, *Proceedings of the Rabbinical Assembly*, 1964, Vol. XXVIII.

"Louis Ginzberg—The Proponent of the Halakhah," in *Architects of Conservative Judaism*, by Herbert Parzen, Jonathan David, New York, 1964.

"Trial and Transfiguration," Part Two of *Woman of Valor: The Story of Henrietta Szold*, by Irving Fineman, Simon and Schuster, 1961.

The Jewish Theological Seminary of America, New York City
Preliminary Announcement, 1902
Documents, Charter and By-Laws, 1903
Circular of Information, 1903-1904
Biennial Report, 1902-1904

Afterword

My father died on November 11, 1953. This year marks the forty-third anniversary of his death. Because this memoir has been out of print for many years, the Jewish Publication Society, the book's publisher, suggested that if I were willing to write an afterword, the Society would reissue the work. In preparing this afterword, I had the benefit of support from Drs. D. Walter Cohen, Michael Monson, Ellen Frankel, and Chaim Potok.

What follows is divided into three parts. In the first, I have added some of stories about my father that had not been known to me earlier or that I had inadvertently omitted, stories that add insights into his personality and work.

Next, because Louis Ginzberg was first and foremost a creative scholar, attention should be called, at least briefly, to his scholarly works published or republished after his death, ending with a brief outline of a volume of his Responsa (legal opinions), which were collected and edited by Dr. David Golinkin of the Seminary of Judaic Studies in Jerusalem and will be published by the Jewish Theological Seminary in New York City.

Finally, I offer some cautious speculations about my father's likely reactions to major events, Jewish and general, that took place after his death. I have taken special care to constrain my interpretations and have dealt with only a limited number of themes that we discussed repeatedly and in depth during his later years.

Because I have injected myself into my father's story, let me call attention to other related linkages: In 1989, I published *My Brother's Keeper* (Transaction Press), which is my "Jewish autobiography" and which contains considerable material about my father's views on a wide range of Jewish and world affairs. In 1993, I published a much longer autobiography about my involvement in academic and public affairs. The second chapter of that work, *The Eye of Illusion* (Transaction Press), is entitled "An Unusual Family" and provides additional insights into my father's value system.

First, then, the new stories. Professor Moshe Davis of the Hebrew University in Jerusalem told me of the following incident after the publication of *Keeper of the Law*. Professor Davis had been my father's student at the Jewish Theological Seminary during the early 1940s, when my father was approaching his seventieth year. During a lecture, my father started to quote a verse from the Bible, and his memory failed him. He became acutely agitated, began to cry, stopped his lecture, and walked out of class saying that he would never teach again, so deep was his chagrin at his lapse of memory. Several students caught up with him as he walked home from the seminary and convinced him that his inability to remember a verse in Job was no reason to stop teaching. Most scholars in their prime are unable to quote the entire Bible by heart, and that he had been unable to recall a single verse was of no significance. My father's students convinced him to reconsider, and he continued to lecture for another decade until a few days before his death, a fortnight or so short of his eightieth birthday.

I am indebted to my friend Louis Linn, M.D., for the following stories, which he heard from my brother-in-law, Bernard Gould, professor of biology at Massachusetts Institute of Technology. Some time after my father's first visit to Albert Einstein at Princeton in 1933 to discuss a trip to Jerusalem that my father was about to undertake together with the two British members of the Survey Commission, to assess academic administrative issues at the Hebrew University, Einstein ran into Cyrus Adler, the president of the Jewish Theological Seminary. Einstein inquired how it happened that the seminary had a professor of mathematics on its faculty. Adler was stumped by Einstein's question until further conversation revealed that Einstein was referring to my father (see page 209).

On one of his frequent visits to New York, my brother-in-law, Bernie, while marking his examination papers, was moaning about how little his students knew about the history of science. My father asked him to elaborate, and Bernie indicated that the student whose paper he was reading could not identify Roentgen. At that point, my father reeled off the successive stages of Roentgen's life and achievements with dates included. When Bernie inquired how he knew so much about Roentgen, my father replied that he recalled verbatim Roentgen's obituary in a Berlin newspaper. Roentgen had died in 1923, but the recall incident occurred more than two decades later.

I owe a related story to Louis Finkelstein, who told it to me during my last visit with him shortly before his death in his mid-1990s. Finkelstein reported that, on the same day in 1940 that my father returned page proof of his three volumes of *A Commentary on the Jerusalem Talmud* to the printer, my father stopped by Finkelstein's office and started a conversation that went as follows: Had my father made a mistake in his career choice? He had always loved mathematics and had a real aptitude for the subject. True, he had not stayed in mathematics long enough to know whether he could have become a major contributor, but on reflection he believed that he could have been.

Finkelstein reported that it was clear to him at the time that my father was searching for reassurance that his life-long commitment to Jewish scholarship had been a sound career decision. Finkelstein went on to point out that, even if my father had become a world-renowned mathematician, his influence and impact would not have equaled his achievements in Judaica, in which he had made such wide-ranging contributions to both Jewish legend and Jewish law.

I neglected to include the next three stories in my original memoir. I was reminded of them after I reread the text before preparing this afterword. The first story relates to my looking over a new book that my father had handed me on one of my routine late afternoon visits to my parents' home, which was located just across the street from Columbia University. The book was a history of the Ginzberg family and its many branches covering five centuries. As I turned the pages, I came across an ancestor of Karl Marx, his grandmother or great-grandmother, with the name of Ginzberg. As a budding economist, I was clearly interested and intrigued by the reference and asked my father whether he had previously been aware of this relationship. He replied that of course he knew of it. I then asked why he had never mentioned it to me. His reply: I never discuss the "black sheep" in the family. My father had no use for Marx because of his anti-Semitic writings, in which Marx turned all Jews into capitalists and as such saw them as the enemies of the common man, exploiters and oppressors.

Just as my father had long been silent about the linkages between the Ginzberg and Marx families, he referred only once or twice to the fact that a cousin of his, a young woman of great beauty, had caught the eye of Count Witte, became his wife, and joined the Russian Orthodox Church. My father hardly approved of such behavior. Realizing his distaste for discussing apostates, I never explored the subject. I suspect that relatively few families, Jewish or other, are related to both the leading revolutionary thinker of the nineteenth century and one of the last and most trusted prime ministers of Czar Nicholas II.

The last story is one that I was recently able to verify during a recent meeting held in Oxford of the Academic Advisory Council to the World ORT Union, which I chair. Isaiah Berlin confirmed that he had visited my parents' home for dinner in 1941. We had sat down to dinner around seven o'clock, and almost immediately Berlin and my father had started to exchange Jewish stories. Each was reminded of a new story even before the last story had been completed. In those years, Berlin spoke at a rapid clip, and as the evening progressed, he accelerated. The storytelling continued almost without interruption until shortly before midnight and would have continued even longer had my mother not interrupted to say that it was long after her Shatzie's retiring time. Here were two raconteurs who had taken each other's measure, neither of whom had any intention of being the first to end the friendly joust.

We turn next to the posthumous publications of Louis Ginzberg, a scholar who had been prodigiously productive at least until his seventieth year. During the last decade of his life, his deteriorating health and diminished energies kept him from additional scholarly output, except for an occasional minor piece.

The first posthumous publication, *On Jewish Law and Lore*, originally published by the Jewish Publication Society in 1955, had been planned to coincide with my father's eightieth birthday. He had been consulted about its contents, which consisted of three of his major contributions to the Jewish Encyclopedia in the early 1900s on "The Allegorical Interpretation of Scripture," "The Codification of Jewish Law," and "The Cabala," together with three more recent efforts: "An Introduction to the Palestinian Talmud," "Jewish Folklore: East and West," and "The Significance of the Halacha for Jewish History."

My Preface notes that the volume came into being largely because of the promptings of my father's close friend, Professor Harry A. Wolfson of Harvard University, who believed that the long pieces from the *Jewish Encyclopedia* should be made accessible to present-day students and scholars, an opinion with which my father concurred. A difficulty arose, however. My father was reluctant to see "The Codification of Jewish Law" reprinted because he had made use of Wellhausen's theories in that article, but a half-century later and in the face of many advances in Palestinian archeology, he had developed serious doubts about Wellhausen's reconstruction of the biblical texts.

Because my father had agreed that I should serve as his alter ego in seeing the volume through the press, it was my task to persuade him that no scholar was committed to views that he had developed a half-century earlier and the best way out of the dilemma was for me to take note of his misgivings in the Preface. He agreed, but reluctantly.

I was more directly involved in the decision of Simon and Schuster to bring out a one-volume condensation of *The Legends of the Jews* under the title *Legends of the Bible*, with an Introduction by Shalom Spiegel, my father's friend and colleague. I had become acquainted with Joseph Barnes, a senior editor of Simon and Schuster (who was bringing out a volume of mine)ˉwho took the initiative with respect to the *Legends of the Bible*. The back of the title page of the first printing in 1956 carries the following notation:

This book is a shorter version of *The Legends of the Jews* by Louis Ginzberg, originally published in seven volumes. A special introduction has been written for the edition by one of the author's colleagues, Professor Shalom Spiegel of the Jewish Theological Seminary in New York. Among the translators who first worked on the author's German manuscript, which he had started writing shortly after arrival in this country from Germany, was Henrietta Szold, founder of Hadassah, and one of the most venerated figures in the history of Israel, and Paul Radin, distinguished American anthropologist.

It had long been my father's view that the title *The Legends of the Jews* had been an error in that it had discouraged Christians from becoming acquainted with his work, but the new title, *Legends of the Bible* proved to have a serious shortcoming. Practicing Christians apparently found the juxtaposition of the terms "Bible" and "legends" jarring, if not distasteful. Difficulties with titles notwithstanding, the *Legends*, in one version or the other, has remained over the decades one of the best sellers on the Jewish Publication Society's list.

In 1961, the Jewish Theological Seminary published Volume IV of *A Commentary on the Palestinian Talmud*, arranged and edited by David Halivni. As I noted in my brief Preface to that volume, my father's intention had been to publish two additional volumes, to provide a rounded view of his approach to studying the Palestinian Talmud, but his deteriorating health prevented him from carrying out his plan.

The following paragraph from the Preface is worth quoting. All of us who have been directly involved—Dr. Finkelstein, Professor Lieberman, Professor Halivni, and I—have been unsure whether we should assume responsibility for publishing materials that my father had been unwilling to release. In the absence of explicit instructions from him to the contrary, however, we decided that, on balance, the publication of his unfinished and unpublished manuscript would add to the contribution made in the first three volumes.

In 1976, the Jewish Theological Seminary published, as Volume I in the *Moreshet* series—Studies in Jewish History, Literature and Thought—Louis Ginzberg's *An Unknown Jewish Sect*. The dust jacket included the following:

Now, for the first time, one of the seminal works of post-Biblical literature, Louis Ginzberg's *Eine Unbekannte Judische Sekte* is published in its entirety in English. In addition to the seven chapters originally published in German, the present work includes three hitherto unpublished chapters in which Ginzberg undertakes a critical review of the many theories that scholars advanced to explain the Zadokite Fragments. The work shows Ginzberg at the full flood of his powers, controlling all the material—philology, theology, history, law, sociology—that he needed to reconstruct from two score fragments a sect about whom history was ignorant, a reconstruction that was proved by the Dead Sea Scrolls to have been uncannily correct.

My lengthy Foreword sets out as best as I was able to piece together the reasons that led my father to lose interest in the "unknown Jewish sect" after the publication of his original articles in the *Monatsschrift für Geschichte und Wissenschaft des Judentums* (Vols. LV to LVIII, (1911 to 1914). The Foreword also provides a condensed account of the twenty years of stalling on my father's part to go through with his promise to George Kohut to let the Kohut Foundation publish the unpublished chapters. I also present in the Foreword a synopsis of the complex and elongated process required to translate the entire volume into English after my father's death and to do so in a manner that would not be totally out of accord with the progress of scholarship over the intervening six decades. I acknowledged the assistance of sixteen persons in Chicago, New York, Philadelphia, and Jerusalem who played a role in helping to prepare the manuscript for publication.

The book ends with the following summary paragraphs:

If, however, our sect actually possessed a temple, enjoying autonomy, then the historical situation fits only the conditions which prevailed during the first half (85-63) of the first century B.C.E. when Damascus enjoyed the liberal role of the Nabateans, granting autonomy and religious freedom.

Neither the Halakah nor the Aggadah, neither theological doctrine nor historical references in our document find their satisfactory explanation if we consider these sectarian fragments as spurious. We have amply demonstrated that they are the genuine literary product of a sectary who flourished during the first century B.C.E. The sect whose history and doctrine are recorded in this document, emerged around 76-67 B.C.E. within the Pharisaic colony of Judeans at Damascus, whither they had fled from Alexander Jannaeus' persecutions. In the beginning the Damascene refugees differed only on political grounds from their fellow Pharisees in Judea. Gradually there evolved, however, also religious and particularly halakic distinctions which set them more and more apart, until a schism and rift consolidated the sect of exiles. The Damascus sect branded both the Pharisees and the Sadducees as backsliding sinners and considered its own sect as the only true Israel.

The study of the Dead Sea Scrolls continues, but to date it appears that Louis Ginzberg's reconstruction has largely stood the test of time.

We come now to the last section of the afterword, in which we explore how my father *might* have reacted to selected events that occurred after his death based on our in-depth and ongoing discussions of the precursors of these events.

To begin with, the American scene: my father would have been surprised and pleased by the explosive growth of Jewish studies at our colleges and universities, particularly because of his own difficulties in securing an academic appointment after his immigration to the United States in 1899 and the modest progress that had been made in the intervening half-century, Harry Wolfson at Harvard and Salo Baron at Columbia being the two outstanding exceptions. I can hear him warn against confusing numbers with quality, however. A large proportion of today's faculty engaged in Judaica are part-timers, offering introductory courses in Hebrew, Bible, or Jewish history. My father would also have pointed out that the faculties of the major rabbinical training institutions—Orthodox, Conservative, Reconstructionist, and Reform—have paid a price now that they must compete both with leading United States universities that have developed major Judaica departments and with the Hebrew University in Jerusalem.

On a related front, Louis Ginzberg would have been surprised and pleased because an ever larger proportion of young American Jews attending elementary and secondary school is exposed to a curriculum that provides a solid introduction to Jewish history, language, texts, and customs. Few markers indicated in 1953 that such a revolution had begun or that the trend would gain strength. Moreover, we know that he saw no future in transplanting Lithuanian yeshivot to the United States (see p. 328). He would have been pleased that a small but significant minority of Orthodox young men—and even some Orthodox young women—who attend-

ed and graduated from a yeshivah relocate for a period of
years to Israel to deepen their knowledge base. Although my
father never believed that the future of Jewry depended on
the actions of the majority, he was too much the historian to
ignore or downgrade questions of scale and scope. He would
have been surprised by the increased numbers of immigrant
and native Orthodox in the United States, but he would have
retained a skeptical view as to their ability to shape the future
of American Jewry.

My father's skepticism would have been reinforced by the
recent startling increases in the numbers of American Jews
who marry non-Jews. The most recent data point to an intermarriage rate currently above 50 percent, in contrast to a 5
percent figure at the time of my father's death in 1953. His
pessimism about the future of American Jewry, always deep
because of its weakening commitment to law and tradition,
would have been reinforced by the data on intermarriage. Nor
would he have found much comfort in the fact that a small
percentage of non-Jews who marry Jews convert or agree that
their children will be reared as Jews, because even when
most Jewish children were being reared by two parents with
direct ties to the Jewish past, he was deeply concerned about
the future of Judaism in the United States. Today, with the
majority of Jews marrying out of the faith, he would have
found the outlook even bleaker.

In considering Louis Ginzberg's views on the future of
American Jewry, we must also take account of several additional developments. The first relates to the ongoing role of
Israel in the evolution of American Jewry; the second is the
much broadened role of women in the life of the synagogue
and the American Jewish community.

My father would surely have found the substantial engagement of many American Jews in the survival and well-being of
Israel a positive force, not only for Israel, but also for
American Jewry. In addition, he would have applauded the
many ties between the American Diaspora and Israeli institu-

tions. Eternal skeptic that he was, however, he would probably have challenged the depth of these ties and whether they
were likely to survive the death of those who knew Hitler and
Ben Gurion and the children of those who had known them.

How my father would have assessed the ongoing support of
American Jews for Israel over the intervening decades is more
problematic. He would have been pleased with the rapid
decline and disappearance of the rabid anti-Zionists, with the
more approving and positive views of the Reform movement
toward Zion and the new state, and with the substantial philanthropic support provided by American Jews year after year.
He would have been uneasy, if not discouraged, however,
about the evolving relations between Israel and the American
Diaspora, because of weaknesses in the ties that really count,
ties that for him had to be based on a shared set of religious
values, knowledge of and respect for halakhah, and a self-
restraint of both the center and the Diaspora to avoid actions
that could weaken the bonds between them.

My father had first-hand knowledge of the equivocal role of
religion in the lives of the early settlers in Palestine, a substantial minority of whom were uninterested in, if not negative toward, religion, without which, in his view, Jewish survival would not have been possible. He surely had no expectation of a strengthening of traditional values among
American Jews. He probably would have kept his pessimism
to himself, but his pessimism would have been deep because
he was aware that halakhah was respected by only a small
minority in Israel and in the United States, and there was little
likelihood of a reversal in the attitudes, behavior, and values
in both the United States and Israel. How long could Jews survive as a people without a commitment to their religious tradition and to Jewish law? Although my father would have felt
that a largely secular state in Israel possibly would survive and
even flourish, he would have considered Jews who were not
steeped in Bible and Talmud as Jews in name only.

This brings us to the last of the more recent developments:

the changing role of women in American Jewish life and institutions. The Jewish Theological Seminary, on whose faculty
Louis Ginzberg served for fifty-one years, did not find it easy
to admit women students to the rabbinical department. I have
every reason to believe that he would have opposed such an
innovation as being against halakhah. In the face of periodic
pressure from my "libber" mother, my father repeatedly
reminded her that Jewish law did not interpose objections to
women's greater participation in religious ceremonial life.
Rather, the law set limits to their *joint* participation with
men.

My father saw little point in accommodating reformers by
weakening the observance of halakhah, fearing to widen
schisms between the orthodox minority who lived by the
halakhah and the others who paid it scant attention.

Let us now look briefly at a few of the major events in the
early decades of the third Jewish Commonwealth and consider how Louis Ginzberg might have responded to them.
Although a man of peace, he surely would have been elated
by the Israeli recapture of Jerusalem after the Six Day War of
1967.

When it comes to speculating about Louis Ginzberg's views
on subsequent Israeli policy relating to the West Bank, however, the outcome is not nearly so clear. From our discussions
about the partition of Palestine in the late 1940s before the
establishment of the state (see p. 323), I knew that my father
was reluctant for me, or any other Jew, to take any initiative
in favor of partition. As he put it, no Jew has the right to cede
any part of the Holy Land. He was quick to add, however, that
if a partition plan were put forward by others in a position of
power, Jews would be free to accept sovereignty over a part,
not the whole, of the Holy Land. He probably would have
favored an arrangement whereby the Arabs in the settled
areas of the West Bank would be placed under Arab self-rule,
subject only to realistic security requirements. There was
nothing to be gained and much to be lost by following the

claims of the ultranationalists who insist that Israel retain control over all the Holy Land. In Louis Ginzberg's view, an Israeli leadership that did not pursue a policy of negotiation and peace would not be a leadership that could claim the inheritance of the prophets who looked on the establishment and maintenance of peace among men as a primary goal.

As the first professor of halakhah at the Hebrew University (1928 to 1929), my father was deeply involved in the welfare and well-being of the nascent university, which had only recently begun to operate on Mt. Scopus. Looking at the Hebrew University in 1996, Louis Ginzberg would have been pleased with its substantial progress and would encourage American and other Diaspora Jews to devote additional time and effort to speeding its continuing growth and development.

Nothing would have given my father more pleasure than to have received every year, as I have, a notification from the administration of the Hebrew University outlining the background of the students who had been awarded the Louis Ginzberg Prize in Talmud. The biography of a recent recipient, Menahem Kister, follows:

> Menahem is in his second year of studies in the Faculty of Humanities working towards his Ph.D. in the Department of Talmud. An only child, he was born in Israel in 1957 to parents who had earlier come from Poland. His father is a university professor and his mother a teacher. He graduated from the University High School in 1975, and thereafter spent four years in the Israel Defense Forces attaining the rank of staff-sergeant. On completion of his army service he enrolled at the University where his subjects were Talmud and Ancient Semitic Languages and Hellenistic Literature. He also studied Syrian, Classic Arabic, Classic Greek, Literature and Semitic Linguistics, and received his B.A. with an excellent average of 97. He received the Epstein and the Rector's Prizes. Menahem's good marks enabled him to enter the Direct Doctoral Program where he wrote a seminar paper on "Geniza Fragments to Babli Tractate Hagigah," in which he was supervised by Prof. I. Zisman. In 1986 he began working on his doctoral thesis which he entitled "Aboth de Rabbi Nathan—Studies in Text, Redaction and Inter-

pretation," again under the supervision of Prof. Zisman. He received a scholarship from the Institute of Jewish Studies, the Golda Meir Prize and the Rosenthal Prize. His work experience has been research assistant at the Hebrew University, assistant and tutor.

My father recognized early on (p. 324) that developing accommodations between the newly established state and the deeply committed religious groups in the Jewish population posed political threats to the nation's civility and progress. His greatest fear was focused on those Orthodox rabbinical leaders who were deeply involved in politics. My father was not anticlerical, but he was deeply concerned and pessimistic about the consequences for Israel and its people from the active engagement of the rabbinical leadership in party politics. He saw nothing but danger and degradation from such involvement in which the moral basis of religious action would be weakened and undermined as the Orthodox leaders sought to trade votes for money and power.

We come now to the third arena that can yield further insights about how Louis Ginzberg would have assessed the changing relations of Jews to the principal centers of power in the modern world, including the governments of the United States, Germany, and the former Soviet Union, as well as such international agencies as the United Nations and the Papacy. No one who had devoted his entire life to studying the history of Jews in Palestine and the Diaspora from the time of the Second Commonwealth to the redaction of the Palestine and Babylonian Talmuds and the period immediately following would need to be reminded of the depth of religious, ethnic, and social prejudice and hatred that the several nations directed at Jews. My father knew that some individual Christians and Muslims carried no prejudice against Jews, but he believed that they constituted a small minority. Anti-Semitism had had centuries, in fact, millenia, to become deeply entrenched.

The behavior of the United States government and its allies with respect to the Holocaust gave Louis Ginzberg no reason to be optimistic about what could happen in the years after World War II when the odds pointed to the withdrawal of the United Kingdom from Palestine. Things turned out better than he would have anticipated, however, after President Truman disregarded most of the advice that he was receiving from his staff and decided to support partition and to recognize the new state within a few hours of its establishment. We never discussed the action of the Soviet Union, which also supported partition and early recognized the new State of Israel, but I suspect that my father was surprised because he had no reason to believe that the Soviets had moderated their negativism to all things Jewish inside and outside their borders.

It is worth recalling that Louis Ginzberg had once referred to the Russians as "cannibals" (p. 256) and had identified Stalin as Hitler's teacher, one who had resorted to genocide many years before Hitler came to power. My father gave substantial weight to the influence of Stalin's cruelty on his pupil Hitler. Having spent the first fourteen years of his life in the land of the czars and the next twelve years in Germany, my father never equated Germany with Russia, not even after the full horrors of the Holocaust were revealed.

Although the United States was quick to recognize the State of Israel, diplomatic relations between the United States and Israel in the early years of the new state's existence were tepid, before and after John Foster Dulles became Secretary of State. Louis Ginzberg's distaste for Dulles was revealed in a comment he made on the day before he died, when he expressed his dislike for the "Bible-touting" Secretary of State, a use of language totally out of keeping with his customary measured words.

I have little doubt that Louis Ginzberg would have been more than a little surprised—in fact, he would have been amazed—to see the extent to which the United States entered into a warm and supportive relationship with Israel after the Six Day War in 1967. The occasional differences that have arisen between Washington and Jerusalem would have surprised

Louis Ginzberg less than the economic aid of more than $2 billion a year, as well as other support, that the United States has continued to extend to Israel during the past quarter-century.

That the United Nations General Assembly passed a resolution in 1975 equating Zionism with racism would have come as no surprise to Louis Ginzberg, who never underestimated the breadth and depth of anti-Semitism among the peoples of the West and the East or the vulnerability of Jews in the international political arena where few, if any, nations would act to protect and defend them, no matter how extreme or outlandish the charges and actions against them. The countless years of study that Louis Ginzberg had devoted to deepening his understanding of the fate of the Jews in the Holy Land and in the Diaspora did not leave him with many, if any, illusions about Jews' having to rely to an optimal degree on themselves for their safety and survival because they could count on few, if any, friends.

This deep conviction of the hostility, overt and latent, of most non-Jews toward Jews goes a fair distance to explain my father's restiveness about the early efforts at ecumenism both in the United States and in Europe. In light of these strongly held views, my father would have been startled and amazed by the Second Vatican Council, convened in 1962, which led the Roman Catholic Church to remove, after almost two millenia, the accusation against the Jews of deicide. Yet my father had deep respect for Roman Catholicism with its dogmas, doctrines, and ceremonials, as well as admiration for its organizational structure and its historical record of survival.

Why Louis Ginzberg would have been surprised by the action of the Second Vatican Council when it lifted the charge against the Jews of deicide may not be immediately clear. He saw deicide as a critical tenet of Roman Catholic belief and thought. It represented the eternal conflict between Judaism and Christianity because the Jews had refused to accept Jesus as a prophet, and certainly as the Son of God. Moreover, Louis Ginzberg could not have imagined that, after so many centuries during which Roman Catholicism had stressed the role of the Jews in bringing about the death of Jesus, that the Roman Catholic Church, with its deep commitment to dogma and tradition, would remove a foundation stone of its belief structure. We know that, with important support from Pope John XXIII, that is what the Council did, however. The early efforts at ecumenism that Louis Ginzberg had disparaged and dismissed as doomed to frustration had their greatest success within a few years after his death.

There is little point in elaborating further on the approach taken in this third section of the afterword in which I explored how Louis Ginzberg might have reacted—and the important word to stress again is *might*—to the series of major developments that affected American Jewry, Israel, and Jewish-Christian relations in subsequent decades. I am reasonably comfortable that my interpretations of my father's views and reactions are consistent with his most deeply held values and assessments as they emerged in our ongoing dialogue during the last two decades of his life.

INDEX OF NAMES,

PUBLICATIONS, AND PLACES

Lightning Source UK Ltd.
Milton Keynes UK
UKHW021816100922
408527UK00016B/384